Twenty Years Of Balkan Tangle

Durham M. Edith

Contents

PREFACE 7
CHAPTER ONE
  PICKING UP THE THREADS 9
CHAPTER TWO
  MONTENEGRO AND HER RULERS 14
CHAPTER THREE
  FIRST IMPRESSIONS OF LAND AND PEOPLE 33
CHAPTER FOUR
  SERBIA AND THE WAY THERE 36
CHAPTER FIVE
  WHAT WAS BEHIND IT ALL 49
CHAPTER SIX
  THE GREAT SERBIAN IDEA 56
CHAPTER SEVEN
  1903. AND WHAT HAPPENED 64
CHAPTER EIGHT
  MACEDONIA, 1903-1904 80
CHAPTER NINE
  ALBANIA 87
CHAPTER TEN
  MURDER WILL OUT 95
CHAPTER ELEVEN 1905 100
CHAPTER TWELVE
  BOSNIA AND THE HERZEGOVINA 116
CHAPTER THIRTEEN
  BOSNIA IN 1906. THE PLOT THICKENS 127
CHAPTER FOURTEEN 1907 144
CHAPTER FIFTEEN
  1908. A FATEFUL YEAR 150

CHAPTER SIXTEEN 1909	174
CHAPTER SEVENTEEN 1910	180
CHAPTER EIGHTEEN 1911. AND THE INSURRECTION OF THE CATHOLICS	186
CHAPTER NINETEEN 1912. THE FIRST DROPS OF THE THUNDERSTORM	191
CHAPTER TWENTY 1914	217
CHAPTER TWENTY-ONE THE YEARS OF THE WAR	241
INDEX	249

TWENTY YEARS OF BALKAN TANGLE

BY
Durham M. Edith

TWENTY YEARS OF BALKAN TANGLE
BY
M. EDITH DURHAM.

AUTHOR OF THE BURDEN OF THE BALKANS,
HIGH ALBANIA,
THE STRUGGLE FOR SCUTARI, ETC.

LONDON: GEORGE ALLEN & UNWIN LTD. RUSKIN HOUSE, 40 MUSEUM STREET,
W.C.1

First published 1920

PREFACE

"And let men beware how they neglect and suffer Matter of Trouble to be prepared; for no Man can forbid the Sparke nor tell whence it come." BACON.

MINE is but a tale of small straws; but of small straws carefully collected. And small straws show whence the wind blows. There are currents and cross currents which may make a whirlwind.

For this reason the tale of the plots and counterplots through which I lived in my many years of Balkan travel, seems worth the telling. Events which were incomprehensible at the time have since been illumined by later developments, and I myself am surprised to find how accurately small facts noted in my diaries, fit in with official revelations.

Every detail, every new point of view, may help the future history in calmer days than these, to a just understanding of the world catastrophe. It is with this hope that I record the main facts of the scenes I witnessed and in which I sometimes played a part.

M. E. DURHAM.

CHAPTER ONE
PICKING UP THE THREADS

It was in Cetinje in August, 1900, that I first picked up a thread of the Balkan tangle, little thinking how deeply enmeshed I should later become, and still less how this tangle would ultimately affect the whole world. Chance, or the Fates, took me Near Eastward. Completely exhausted by constant attendance on an invalid relative, the future stretched before me as endless years of grey monotony, and escape seemed hopeless. The doctor who insisted upon my having two months' holiday every year was kinder than he knew. "Take them in quite a new place," he said. "Get right away no matter where, so long as the change is complete."

Along with a friend I boarded an Austrian Lloyd steamer at Trieste, and with high hopes but weakened health, started for the ports of the Eastern Adriatic.

Threading the maze of mauve islets set in that incomparably blue and dazzling sea; touching every day at ancient towns where strange tongues were spoken and yet stranger garments worn, I began to feel that life after all might be worth living and the fascination of the Near East took hold of me.

A British Consul, bound to Asia Minor, leaned over the bulwark and drew a long breath of satisfaction. "We are in the East!" he said. "Can't you smell it? I feel I am going home. You are in the East so soon as you cross Adria." He added tentatively: "People don't understand. When you go back to England they say, 'How glad you must be to get home!' They made me spend most of my leave on a house-boat on the Thames, and of all the infernal things. ...

"I laughed. I did not care if I never saw England again. . . .

"You won't ever go back again now, will you?" he asked whimsically, after learning whence I came. "I must," said I, sadly. "Oh don't," said he; "tell them you can't, and just wander about the East." He transshipped shortly and disappeared, one of many passing travellers with whom one is for a few moments on common ground. Our voyage ended at Cattaro and there every one, Baedeker included, said it was correct to drive up to Cetinje. Then you could drive down next day and be able to say ever afterwards, "I have travelled in Montenegro."

It was in Cetinje that it was borne in on me that I had found the "quite new place" which I sought. Thus Fate led me to the Balkans.

Cetinje then was a mere red-roofed village conspicuous on the mountain-ringed plain. Its cottages were but one storeyed for the most part, and contained some three thousand inhabitants. One big building stood up on the left of the road as the traveller entered.

"No. That is not the palace of the Prince," said the driver. "It is the Austro-Hungarian Legation."

Austria had started the great Legation building competition which occupied the Great Powers for the next few years. Each Power strove to erect a mansion in proportion to the amount of "influence" it sought to obtain in this "sphere." Russia at once followed. Then came Italy, with France hard on her heels. England, it is interesting to note, started last; by way of economizing bought an old house, added, tinkered and finally at great expense rebuilt nearly the whole of it and got it quite done just before the outbreak of the Great War, when it was beginning to be doubtful if Montenegro would ever again require a British Legation. But this is anticipating.

In 1900 most of the Foreign Ministers Plenipotentiary dwelt in cottages or parlour-boarded at the Grand Hotel, the focus of civilization, where they dined together at the Round Table of Cetinje, presided over by Monsieur Piguet, the Swiss tutor of the young Princes; a truly tactful man whom I have observed to calm a heated altercation between two Great Powers by switching off the conversation from such a delicate question as: "Which Legation has the finest flag, France or Italy?" to something of international interest such as: "Which washer-woman in Cetinje gets up shirt fronts best?" For Ministers Plenipotentiary, when not artificially inflated with the importance of the land they represent, are quite like ordinary human beings.

Their number and variety caused me to ask: "But why are so many Powers represented in such a hole of a place?" And the Italian architect who was designing the Russian Legation replied, more truly than he was perhaps aware: "Because Montenegro is the matchbox upon which the next European war will be lighted!"

Cetinje was then extraordinarily picturesque. The Prince did all he could to emphasize nationality. National dress was worn by all. So fine was the Court dress of Montenegro that oddly enough Prince Nikola was about the only ruling Sovereign in Europe who really looked like one. The inroads of Cook's tourists had stopped his former custom of hobnobbing with visitors, and he dodged with dignity and skill the attempts of American snapshotters to corner him and say: "How do, Prince!"

A vivid picture remains in my mind of the Royal Family as it filed out of church on the feast of the Assumption of the Virgin. The Prince, heavy-built, imposing, gorgeous; his hair iron grey, ruddy-faced, hook-nosed, keen-eyed. Danilo, his heir, crimped, oiled and self-conscious, in no respect a chip of the old block, who had married the previous year, Jutta, daughter of the Grand Duke of Mecklenburg Strelitz, who, on her reception into the Orthodox Church, took the name of Militza. Montenegro was still excited about the wedding. She looked dazzlingly fair among her dark "in-laws." Old Princess Milena came, stately and handsome, her hair, still black, crowning her head with a huge plait. Prince Mirko, the second son, was still a slim and good looking youth. Petar, the youngest, a mere child, mounted a little white pony and galloped past in the full dress of an officer, reining up and saluting with a tiny sword as he passed his father. The crowd roared applause. It was all more like a fairy tale than real life. But the black coated Ministers Plenipotentiary were all quite real.

From Cetinje we went to Podgoritza where for the first time I saw Albanians. Podgoritza was full of them, all in national dress, for Montenegro had as yet done little towards suppressing this. Nor in this first visit did I go further inland.

But I had found "the land where I could have a complete change"; had learnt, too, of the Great Serbian Idea; had had the meaning of the Montenegrin cap explained to me; and been told how the reconstruction of the Great Serb Empire of the Middle Ages was what Montenegro lived for. Also that the first step in that direction must be the taking of the Sanjak of Novibazar, which had been formed as a barrier between the two branches of the Serb race by the Powers at the Berlin Congress. To me it sounded then fantastic—operatic. I had yet to learn that the opera bouffe of the Balkans is written in blood and that those who are dead when the curtain falls, never come to life again.

So much for Montenegro. We returned after a run to Trebinje, Serajevo and Mostar, to the Dalmatian coast and Trieste.

First impressions are vivid. There is a certain interest in the fact that I recorded Spalato in my diary as the first Slav town on our way south from Trieste and that my letter thence was dated Spljet, the Slav form of the name.

The one pre-eminently Italian town of Dalmatia is Zara. From Zara south, the language becomes more and more Slav. But the Slav speaking peasants that flock to market are by no means the same in physical type as the South Slavs of the Bosnian Hinterland. It is obvious that they are of other blood. They are known as Morlachs, that is Sea Vlachs, and historically are in all probability descendants of the pre-Slav native population which, together with the Roman colonists, fled coast ward before the inrush of the Slav invaders of the seventh century. Latin culture clung along the coast and was reinforced later by the Venetians. And a Latin dialect was spoken until recent times, dying out on the island of Veglio at the end of the nineteenth century. The Slavizing process which has steadily gone on is due, partly to natural pressure coastward of the Slav masses of the Hinterland and partly to artificial means.

Austria, who ever since the break-up of the Holy Roman Empire, had recognized Italy as a possible danger, had mitigated this by drawing Italy into the Triple Alliance. But she was well aware that fear of France, not love of Austria, made Italy take this step. Therefore to reduce the danger of a strong Italia Irredenta on the east of Adria she encouraged Atavism against Italianism, regarding the ignorant and incoherent Slavs as less dangerous than the industrious and scientific Italians. Similarly, England decided that the half-barbarous Russians were less likely to be commercial rivals than the industrious and scientific Germans, and sided with Russia.

Future historians will judge the wisdom of these decisions.

During the fourteen years in which I went up and down the coast, the Slavizing process in Dalmatia visibly progressed, until the German-Austrians began to realize that they were "warming a viper," and to feel nervous. Almost yearly there were more zones in which no photographs might be taken and more forts were built.

Having picked up the thread of the Balkans the next thing was to learn a Balkan language, for in 1900 scarcely a soul in Montenegro spoke aught but Serb. Nor was any dictionary of the language to be bought at Cetinje. The one bookshop of Montenegro was carefully supervised by the Prince, who saw to it that the people should read nothing likely to disturb their ideas, and the literature obtainable was mainly old national ballads and the poetical works of the Prince and his father, Grand Voy voda Mirko.

In London in 1900 it was nearly impossible to find a teacher of Serb, and a New Testament from the Bible Society was the only book available. Finally a Pole—a political refugee from Russia and a student of all Slav languages—undertook to teach me. English he knew none, and but little German and had been but a few weeks in England.

I asked for his first impressions. His reply was unexpected. What surprised him most was that the English thought Russia a Great Power and were even afraid of her. I explained that Russia was a monster ready to spring on our Indian frontier—that she possessed untold wealth and countless hordes. He laughed scornfully. In halting German he said "Russia is nothing—nothing. The wealth is underground. They have not the sense to get it. Their Army is large, but it is rotten. All Russia is rotten. If there is a war the Russian Army will be—will be—" he stammered for a word—"will be like this!" He snatched up a piece of waste paper, crumpled it and flung it contemptuously into the waste paper basket.

I never forgot the gesture. Later, when folk foretold Japan's certain defeat if she tackled the monster, and in 1914 talked crazily of "the Russian steam-roller" I saw only that crumpled rag of paper flying into the basket. By that time I had seen too much of the Slav to trust him in any capacity. But this is anticipating.

CHAPTER TWO
MONTENEGRO AND HER RULERS

> In days of old the priest was King,
> Obedient to his nod, Man rushed to slay his brother man
> As sacrifice to God.

THE events seen by the casual traveller are meaningless if he knows not what went before. They are mere sentences from the middle of a book he has not read. Before going further we must therefore tell briefly of Montenegro's past. It is indeed a key to many of the Near Eastern problems, for here in little, we see the century-old "pull devil-pull baker" tug between Austria and Russia, Teuton and Slav, for dominion.

In 1900, Montenegro, which was about the size of Yorkshire, consisted of some thirty plemena or tribes. A small core, mainly Cetinaajes, Nyegushi, Rijeka and Kchevo formed old Montenegro. To this was added the Brda group, which joined Montenegro voluntarily in the eighteenth century, in order to fight against the Turks. These are mainly of Albanian blood and were all Roman Catholics at the time of their annexation, but have since been converted to the Orthodox Church and Slavized. It is noteworthy that they are now strenuously resisting annexation by Serbia. Thirdly, came the extensive lands, some of them wholly Albanian, annexed to Montenegro in 1878 under the Treaty of Berlin, much of which, in spite of the efforts of the Montenegrin Government, is by no means Slavized.

Certain other small districts have also from time to time been joined to Montenegro at different times, e.g. Grahovo. Each of the Montenegrin tribes has a distinct tradition of origin from an individual or family. They tell almost invariably of immigration into their present site in the fifteenth or sixteenth century. Thus

Nyegushi in 1905 told me of descent from two brothers Jerak and Raiko, who fled from Nyegushi in the Herzegovina fourteen generations ago. The Royal family, the Petrovitches, traces descent from Jerak. If we take thirty years as a generation this gives us 1485. The Turks had then begun to overrun Bosnia and the Herzegovina.

Ivan Tsrnoievitch, chief of the tribes of the Zeta, was so hard pressed by the oncoming Turks that he burnt his capital of Zhablyak and withdrew to the mountains, where he founded Cetinje in 1484. Tradition thus corresponds closely with historic fact. The strength of Turkish influence is shown by the fact that even to-day the peasant speaks of Ivan as Ivan Beg.

The oft-repeated tale that Montenegro was founded by the refugees from Kosovo is thus we see mythical, as Kosovo was fought a century earlier in 1389. Lineally, the Montenegrins are Bosnians, Herzegovinians and Albanians rather than Serbs of Serbia. Bosnia and the Herzegovina were independent of the old Kingdom of Serbia, which explains much of the reluctance of Montenegro to be to-day incorporated by the Serbs.

Ivan and his refugee tribes successfully resisted the Turkish attacks on their stronghold and were helped by Venice. But conversions to Islam became frequent. One of Ivan's own sons turned Turk and fought against Montenegro. Finally, the last of the Trsnoievitch line, Ivan II, who had married a Venetian wife, decided that the leadership of a band of outlaws in the poverty-stricken mountains was not good enough. He retired to the fleshpots of Venice, trusting the defence of the district to a civil, hereditary leader and charging the Vladika [Bishop] with the duty of preventing ore of his flock going over to Islam, as the Serbs of Bosnia were now doing in great numbers.

It has been inaccurately represented that Montenegro was singular in being ruled by her Bishop. In this respect Montenegro in no way differed from other Christian districts ruled by the Turks who, with a tolerance at that date rare, recognized everywhere the religion of the country and entrusted all the affairs of the Christians to their own ecclesiastics. To the Turks, the Montenegrin tribes and the Albanian tribes of the mountains—who had also their own Bishops —were but insubordinate tribes against whom they sent punitive expeditions when taxes were in arrears and raids became intolerable. The Montenegrins descended from their natural fortress and plundered the fat flocks of the plain lands. They existed mainly by brigandage as their sheep-stealing ballads tell, and the history of raid and punitive expedition is much like that of our Indian frontier.

Till 1696 the Vladikas were chosen according to the usual methods of the Orthodox Church. After that date they were, with one exception, members of the Petrovitch family. This has been vaguely accounted for by saying that to prevent quarrels the Montenegrins decided to make the post hereditary in the Petrovitch family. As the Vladika was celibate, his successor had to be chosen from among members of his family. Later events, however, throw much light on this alleged interference with the rules of the Orthodox Church.

In June, 1696, Danilo Petrovitch, of Nyegushi, who, be it noted, was already in holy orders, was chosen as Vladika. A man of well-known courage such as the country needed, he accepted office, but was not consecrated till 1700. Till then the Vladikas of Montenegro had been consecrated by the Serb Patriarch at Ipek. But in 1680 Arsenius the Patriarch had decided to accept the protection of Austria and emigrated to Karlovatz with most of his flock. The turns of fortune's wheel are odd. The Serbs have more than once owed almost their existence to Austrian intervention. The Turks permitted the appointment of another Serb Patriarch, but Serb influence in the district waned rapidly and the Albanians rapidly resettled the lands from which their forefathers had been evicted. In 1769 the Phanariotes suppressed the Serb Patriarchate altogether, for the Greek was ever greedy of spreading over the whole peninsula, and the Vladika of Montenegro was thus the only head of a Serb Church in the Balkans and gained much in importance.

Danilo was a born ruler. He soon absorbed all the temporal power, and latterly left matters ecclesiastic to his nephew Sava.

The outstanding feature of his rule was his suppression of Mahommedanism. At this time conversions to Islam were increasing. Danilo, when on a visit to the plain of Podgoritza, to consecrate a small church by permission of the Pasha of Scutari, was taken prisoner by the local Moslems, though he had been promised safe conduct, and put up to ransom. He was bought off only by the sacrifice of the church plate of the monastery, and returned home hot with anger.

To avenge the insult and clear the land of Islam he organized the wholesale massacre of the Moslems of Montenegro. On Christmas Eve 1703 an armed band, led by the Martinovitches, rushed from house to house slaughtering all who refused baptism. Next morning the murderers came to the church, says the song: "Their arms were bloody to the shoulders." Danilo, flushed with joy, cried: "Dear God we thank Thee for all things!" A thanksgiving was held and a feast followed. Danilo thus gained extraordinary popularity. Such is the fame of his Christmas Eve that it was enthusiastically quoted to me in the Balkan War of 1912-13 as an example to be followed, and baptisms were enforced with hideous cruelty. The Balkan Christian of to-day is no whit less cruel than the Turk and is more fanatical.

Danilo's prestige after this massacre was so great that the tribes of the Brda formed a defensive alliance with him against the Turks. And his fame flew further, for Russia, now for the first time, appeared in Montenegro. Peter the Great sent his Envoy Miloradovitch to Cetinje in 1711—a date of very great importance, for from it begins modern Balkan policy and the power of the Petrovitches. Peter claimed the Montenegrins as of one blood and one faith with Russia and called on them to fight the Turk and meet him at Constantinople where they would together "glorify the Slav name; destroy the brood of the Agas and build up temples to the true faith."

The Montenegrins rushed to the fray with wild enthusiasm and on the high ground between Rijeka and Podgoritza won the battle called "The Field of the Sultan's Felling," such was the number of Turks who, entangled in the thorn bushes, were slaughtered wholesale, as the Montenegrin driver recounts to this day when he passes the spot.

A great victory—but Russia and Montenegro have not yet met at Constantinople. The Turks sent a strong punitive force and, not for the first time, burnt the monastery at Cetinje, wasted the land and doubtless removed enough gear to pay the haratch [tax] which Danilo had refused.

1715 is noteworthy as the date of Danilo's visit to Petersburg, when he was given the first of the many subsidies which the Tsars have bestowed till recently upon the Petrovitch family.

In a land which is rat-poor, the family which has wealth has power. The Petrovitches had gained power and they kept it. Fighting almost till the last, Danilo died full of years and fame, in 1735, and named his nephew Sava, who had acted for some time as ecclesiastical head, as his successor.

Sava had no ambition to be aught but a Churchman. He built the monastery of

Stanjevitch and retired to it, leaving his nephew Vassili to govern.

Vassili, who was already in holy orders, had much of the quality of Danilo. He organized the defence of the land and defeated more than one attack upon it. Montenegro was now largely fighting against the Moslem Serbs of Bosnia and the Herzegovina. In fact the "Turk" with whom the Balkan Christian waged war was as often as not his compatriot, turned Moslem.

Vassili and Sava further strengthened their alliance with Russia by visiting Petersburg, where the Empress Elizabeth promised them a yearly subsidy of 3,000 roubles and money for schools. Vassili died in Russia in 1766 and Sava was left to manage alone.

He was quite unfit and his post was usurped by a remarkable imposter who appeared suddenly in Montenegro and said he was Peter III of Russia, who had been murdered in 1706. Russia was a name to conjure with. He thrilled the credulous tribesmen with tales of his escape and adventures. In the words of an old ballad: "He is known as Stefan the Little. The nation turns to him as a child to its father. They have dismissed their headmen, their Serdars, Knezhes and Voyvodas. All eyes turn to him and hail him as Tsar." Sava returned to his monastery and the imposter reigned. Even the Patriarch of Ipek who was on the verge of dismissal, cried for the protection of Stefan Mali, who set to work to govern with great energy. Venice, alarmed by his popularity, joined with the Turks and attacked Montenegro, but was repulsed. Russia, seeing her influence waning with the departed Sava, sent an Envoy to denounce the impostor. But "nothing succeeds like success." Stefan Mali had such a hold over the ignorant tribesmen that Russia, seeing Sava was useless, recognized Stefan as ruler. He reigned five more years and was murdered in 1774 by, it was said, an agent of the Pasha of Scutari. He is believed to have been of humble Bosnia origin and was one of the few successful impostors of history.

Sava had perforce to return to the world, and owing to his incapacity the post of Civil Governor of Montenegro now became important. The office, till now held always by a Vukotitch, had meant little save the leadership of tribal Soviets or councils. The Vukotitches exchanged the office with the Radonitches for that of Serdar, and under the title of Gubernator the first Radonitch rose to power.

This is a very important period for now for the first time Austria appears on the scene and the long diplomatic struggle with Russia for power in

Montenegro begins.

In 1779 an appeal to the Emperor of Austria was sent, signed by Ivan Radonitch, Gubernator; Ivan Petrovitch, Serdar; and lastly by Petar Petrovitch, Archimandrite and Deputy-Metropolitan. From which we must conclude that Sava had definitely retired from power. From this date for several years Ivan Radonitch always signed first. He had just returned from a fruitless trip to Russia, and was seeking help from Austria. Sava died in 1783 and was succeeded by Vladika Plamenatz, a fact which, though well known in Montenegro, is rigidly excluded from her official history by the Petrovitches, whose version, the only "authorized" one, is constructed with more regard to the glory of their dynasty than historic truth.

On Sava's death the Radonitch party at once welcomed the first Austrian Mission to Montenegro and accommodated it in Sava's monastery. One of the Envoys has left a vivid picture of Montenegro in those days.

"The nation has no police, no laws. A kind of equality reigns. The headmen have only a certain authority for managing ordinary business and settling blood-feuds. The father of Radonitch was the first to whom the nation gave the title Gubernator in order to gain the respect of the Venetians and Turks. The Gubernator summons the Serdars, Voyvodas and Knezhes. They meet in the open air. The General Assembly takes place at the village of Cetinje. . . . The Vladika, or at least a couple of monks, are present. The Serdars similarly call local meetings of headmen and thus arrange peace between two families or villages. Their power consists only of persuasion. In practice murder is usually avenged by murder. The land has one Metropolitan, the Vladika, in whose eparchy are included Ipek, Kroja and Dalmatia spiritually, for the consecration of priests, he being, since the removal of the Patriarch of Ipek, the next Archbishop. But the foreign priests obey him in no respect save for consecration. His functions consist in the consecration of priests and churches. He visits the parishes but not so much for pastoral duties as for the collection of the so-called Milostina, the alms which form his payment. The monks too collect on their own behalf. The people who are very superstitious, fast rigorously and give willingly to the clergy. Their terror of excommunication makes them regard their Bishops as the highest and most respected in the land. Radonitch's father, first Gubernator, tried to obtain the highest position for himself but failed. His son now tries to, and would succeed, were he cleverer and had more money, for the Metropolitan Plamenatz is little respected and could not do much to prevent him. The Metropolitans have been used to visit Petersburg from time to time and to receive a subsidy for the Church and gifts in money and in the form of costly vestments for themselves. From which gifts, say the people, they receive no benefit. Since 1779 no Russian money has been received. The feelings of the country have consequently grown cold. People here obey only so long as they gain by so doing."

We now come upon the first notice of the development of the Great Serbian Idea, as a definite political plan in Montenegro. The Austrian Envoy writes:

"The following which was told me by a Montenegrin monk is worthy of further consideration. A little while after the Russian war was ended in 1773 a plan was made by the Metropolitan and some monks to reconstruct the old Serbian Kingdom and to include in it besides Bulgaria, Serbia, Upper Albania, Dalmatia and Bosnia, also the Banat of Karlstadt and Slavonia. The Turks in all the provinces were to be fallen upon at a given moment by the Schismatics, and it was also resolved that all foreign officers should be cleared out of all lands within the Imperial frontiers. The late Orthodox Bishop Jaksitch of Karlstadt is said to have agreed and carried on a correspondence with the Metropolitan of Montenegro by means of priests. . . . Though the carrying out of such a plan is very difficult, yet the project should not be left out of consideration."

The Petrovitch ambition to form and rule over Great Serbia was thus, we see, actually elaborated long before Serbia had obtained independence and before the Karageorgevitches had even been heard of. This explains much that has since happened.

Further the Envoy replies to the question: Whether or not Montenegro can be considered independent?—thus:

"From the frontier drawn by the Venetians with the Turks it follows that Montenegro belongs to the Turks. The nation does not deny that it has been twice conquered by the Turks, who, each time, destroyed Cetinje and the Monastery, where some Turks even settled, but were driven out. In 1768 they were forced to pay tribute by the Vezir of Bosnia. The Montenegrins on the plains, in fact, pay tribute. The Katunska and Rijeka nahias alone have paid no tribute since 1768. These facts show Montenegro belongs to the Porte.

"The Montenegrins on the contrary maintain that they have never recognized

Turkish rule, and never paid tribute save when forced by overpowering numbers; that they do not recognize the assigning of their nahias to the Pashas of Spuzh and Scutari; that they have chosen a Gubernator whose title has not been disputed; that they rule themselves without Turkish interference. In truth, however, the apparent independence of the land depends as much on its mountainous character as on the courage of the inhabitants. The difficulties of the land make it more trouble than it is worth."

The country is described as completely lawless. Blood feuds rage between rival families and in seven months a hundred men have been killed in vengeance. Over this wild group of tribes Russia and Austria now struggled for influence. In 1782 Ivan Radonitch went for seven months to Vienna. Montenegro could not (and cannot) possibly exist without foreign aid. And he sought it.

But the Emperor Joseph II decided that to organize Montenegro as an Ally "would, in peace, be costly and in war of insufficient use." He withdrew the Mission but, to retain Montenegro's goodwill, allotted a small annual subsidy of which 500 ducats were to go to Radonitch, and but 150 to Vladika Plamenatz.

Russia, however, would not let Montenegro slip from her grasp. In May, 1788, a Russian Envoy arrived and began countermining Austria. Austria retorted by sending another Envoy, who reports complete anarchy and ceaseless inter-tribal fighting:

"Some were with us; some sought to destroy us; some fought the Turks; some were in alliance with them. They have a Bishop, Governor and Serdar, but these are mere names. People obey only if they can gain by so doing. We even heard a common man say to the Bishop's face: 'Holy Bishop, you lie like a hound! I will cut out your heart on the point of my knife.' Except that they keep the fasts they have no religion. They rob, steal, and have many wives. Some sell women and girls to the Turks and commit other crimes as one hears daily. All is done with the animal impulse of desire, or hatred, or selfishness. The inhabitants are used to raid neighbourlands for cattle, etc., and are even led by their priests on these expeditions which they think heroic."

This vivid account will be recognized as the truth by all who have lived in native huts and listened to local tradition. It describes the life of the Balkan Christian up till recent days. My Montenegrin guide used to lament the good old times when a second wife could be taken and no fuss made; and when as many as fifteen men were shot in a feud; and his great uncle had commanded a pirate ship which plied between the Adriatic and the Aegean.

There is nothing new under the sun. In 1788, as in the twentieth century, we find the rival Powers trying to buy partisans. "We never could satisfy them," says the Austrian Envoy. "When we thought we had won him with one gift, we found next day he had joined the opposition party or demanded a new gift as if he had not had one. Even the Bishop, though he tried by all means to win our favour, could not hide from us his false intriguing heart."

The struggle was brief. Russia was victorious. Vladika Plamenatz disappeared suddenly, and the Petrovitches came again to the fore. Vladika Petar's name headed all official documents, the Gubernator fell to second rank, and the blood-feud between the Plamenatzes and the Petrovitches compelled some of the former to seek shelter with the Turks. Russia has never permitted a pro-Austrian to rule long in Slav lands. Witness the fate of the Obrenovitches, in Serbia. Vladika Petar was a strong man, which is probably why he obtained Russian support. He drove his unruly team with much success and won its respect.

Russia and Austria came to one of their many "understandings" and in 1788 declared war together on the Turk with the expressed intention of ending the Sultan's rule. Both encouraged the Montenegrins to harry the Turkish borders. The Austrian Envoy, however, distrusted the Montenegrins and wrote: "Very much more can we rely on the faith and courage of the Catholic Albanians of the Brda, the very numerous Bijelopavlitchi, Piperi, Kuchi, Vasojevitchi, Klementi, Hoti, etc., who could muster 20,000 very outrageous fighters whom the Sultan fears more than he does the Montenegrins." A passage of great interest, for to-day many of these Albanian tribes, having fallen under Montenegrin rule, have been completely Slavized and have 'joined the Orthodox Church.

Some of these tribes did support Austria, were left in the lurch by her when she made peace in 1791, and were punished by the Turks. Part of the Klementi dared not return home and settled in Hungary, where their descendants still live.

Montenegro was mentioned in the Treaty of Sistova merely as a rebellious Turkish province, but Vladika Petar had gained much power, for the Brda tribes now definitely accepted him as their head and the Tsutsi and Bijelitch tribes emigrated into Montenegro from the Herzegovina and were given land.

The Turks forcibly opposed the union of the Brda with Montenegro, but could not prevent it, and in the fight the Pasha of Scutari was killed. His head, on a stake, for long adorned the tower at Cetinje.

A hard blow was now struck at Montenegro. The Venetians in 1797 ceded the Bocche di Cattaro to Austria. Till then the frontier had been vague. The Vladika was spiritual head of the Bocchese and the Montenegrins considered them as part of themselves. The new frontier caused much wrath. Russia hurried to support the Vladika. Austria strove in vain for influence. Her Envoy wrote in 1798, "The Gubernator sees his authority daily weakening while that of the Vladika increases." He says the frontier must be fixed "so as to force this horde of brigands to remain within the frontiers which they cross only to molest his Majesty's subjects and make them victims of brigandage. The Metropolitan and the Gubernator have given no satisfaction to the complaints daily addressed to them."

No. They did not. For they had a strong backing. Up hurried a special Envoy of the Tsar with rich gifts for the Vladika, who received him with a salute of guns, and further insulted Austria by hoisting the Russian flag over the Monastery. "Devil and Baker" had both pulled. Which won? I leave that to the reader.

Russia was now ruling power in Montenegro. When Napoleon's troops appeared in the Near East the Montenegrins joined the Russian forces and attacked the French at Ragusa where their ferocity horrified even the hardened soldiers of Napoleon. A Ragusan gave me her grandfather's account of the yelling horde of savage mountaineers who rushed into battle with the decapitated heads of their foes dangling from their necks and belts, sparing no one, pillaging and destroying, and enraging the Russian officers by rushing home so soon as they had secured booty worth carrying off. In considering the Near East of to-day it should never be forgotten that but a century ago much of the population was as wild as the Red Indians of the same date.

The French held the Bocche di Cattaro some years during which the Vladika, as Russia's ally, flatly refused to come to terms with them. And in 1813, so soon as Napoleon's defeat became known Vladika Petar and Vuko Radonitch, the new Gubernator, summoned the tribesmen, swooped down on Cattaro, stormed the Trinity fort and captured Budua. A short-lived triumph. Russia, wishing peace with

Austria and having no further use for Montenegro, ordered the Vladika to yield his newly conquered lands and they were formally allotted to Austria by Treaty.

During these years the resurrection of Serbia was taking place. In this Montenegro was unable to take active part, being more than enough occupied with her own affairs. But the Vladika himself sang Karageorge's heroism and tried to send a force to his aid.

Vladika Petar I died in 1830. He left Montenegro larger and stronger than he found it, for he had worked hard to unite the ever-quarrelling tribes by establishing laws to suppress blood-feuds. Inability to cohere is ever the curse of Slav lands. Only a strong autocrat has as yet welded them. Petar earned the fame he bears in the land.

His body is to this day deeply revered by the superstitious mountaineers. Some years after burial it was found to have been miraculously preserved from decay and he was thereupon canonized under the name of St. Petar Cetinski.

When dying he nominated as his successor his nephew Rada, then a lad not yet in holy orders, and made his chiefs swear to support him.

Such an irregular proceeding as appointing a youth of seventeen to an Archbishopric could hardly have been carried out, even in the Balkans, had it not been for the terror of a dead man's curse—a thing still dreaded in the land. And also for the fact that Rada's election had the support too of Vuko Radonitch the Gubernator.

Vuko hoped doubtless to obtain the upper hand over such a young rival. Rada, with no further training, was at once consecrated as Vladika Petar II by the Bishop of Prizren and this strange consecration was confirmed later at Petersburg, whither the young Petrovitch duly went.

Russia has all along consistently furthered her influence and plans in the Balkans by planting suitable Bishops as political agents. Russia was now powerful in Montenegro. A Russian officer led the clans a-raiding into Turkey and returned with so many decapitated heads to adorn Cetinje, that the Tsar thought fit to protest. The tug between Austria and Russia continued. Vuko, the Gubernator, and his party, finding the youthful Archbishop taking the upper hand with Russian aid, entered into negotiations with Austria. The plot was, however, detected. Vuko fled to Austria. His brother was assassinated; the family house at Nyegushi was burnt down and the family exiled. Russia would tolerate no influence but her own and had begun in fact the same policy she afterwards developed in Serbia. From that date—1832—the office of Gubernator was abolished. Imitation is the sincerest flattery. The Petrovitches began to model themselves on their patrons, the Tsars, and strove for absolutism.

Petar II ranks high as author and poet. He further organized the laws against the blood-feuds which were sapping the strength of the nation and ingeniously ordered a murderer to be shot by a party made up of one man from each tribe. As the relatives of the dead man could not possibly avenge themselves on every tribe in the land the murder-sequence had perforce to end. To reconcile public opinion to this form of punishment he permitted the condemned man to run for his life. If the firing party missed him, he was pardoned. The point gained was that the murder became the affair of the central government, not of the local one.

Petar also did much to start education in the land. He died before he was forty of tuberculosis, in 1851, one of the early victims of the disease which shortly afterwards began to ravage Montenegro and has killed many Petrovitches.

He named as his successor his nephew Danilo.

Danilo's accession is a turning point in Montenegrin history. He at once stated that he did not wish to enter holy orders and would accept temporal power only. He was, in fact, about to marry a lady who was an Austrian Slav. For this, the consent of Russia had to be obtained, for till now it was through the Church that Russia had ruled in Montenegro. She had ever—with the sole exception of the usurper Stefan Mali—supported the Vladika against the Gubernator. This office was, however, now abolished. There had been difficulty more than once about transmitting the ruling power from uncle to nephew. Russia decided that she could obtain a yet firmer hold of the land if she established a directly hereditary dynasty. Danilo was proclaimed Prince and ecclesiastical affairs alone were to be administered by the Bishop.

The Sultan who had accepted the rule of the Bishop in Montenegro as in other Christian districts, protested against the recognition of an hereditary Prince and at once attacked Montenegro, which was saved by the diplomatic intervention of both Russia and Austria, neither of whom wished its destruction. Peace was made and Danilo formally recognized. He was never popular. He had received his title from

Russia, but his sympathies leaned towards Austria. And he offended both Russia and his Montenegrins by refusing to take part in the Crimean war, to the wrath of the tribes who saw in it a fine opportunity for harrying their foes of the border. Attempts to enforce law and order provoked hostility among the recently annexed tribes of the Brda who, though they had voluntarily joined Montenegro as opposed to the Turks, refused flatly to pay taxes. Danilo put down this rising with great severity and gained the hatred of the revolted tribes.

But even with enforced taxation Danilo was short of funds. Russia, angry at his failure to aid her, stood aside. Danilo begged of Austria and Austria refused. Montenegro could not and cannot live without foreign support. The French—now so active again in Balkan intrigue—came in and tried to detach Danilo from their then enemy Russia, by offering him a subsidy and certain concessions from the Sultan if he would accept Turkish suzerainty.

There ensued a quarrel between the Russian agent in Cetinje, B. M. Medakovitch, and Danilo over this. Medakovitch was Danilo's private secretary. "I lived in friendship and harmony with Prince Danilo," he says, "until he said to me, 'I know you wish the Montenegrins well and highly value their liberty. But it cannot be as you wish. We must recognize the Turks in order to obtain more money.' We might have remained friends but foreign intrigues crept in. ... Enemies of our faith and name denounced me as the "friend" of Russia. My faith and blood are dear to me. But I have always kept in view the good of the nation and followed the course which ever led to the fortune of Montenegro. ... I would not agree that Montenegro's glory should be denied in accordance with the wishes of the French Consul at Scutari, who in especial is trying to destroy the power of Montenegro." (History repeats itself. The French now, 1920, are aiming at Montenegro's destruction.) "I opposed Turkish rule . . . but the headmen sided with Prince Danilo and favoured the wish of the French Consul. They were ready to accept the Turk as lord. Only I and Prince George Petrovitch opposed them."

The quarrel was heightened by the fact that Tsar Nikola I, when he died in 1855, bequeathed 5,000 ducats to Montenegro, but stipulated they were to be used for charitable purposes under Russian control. Danilo was enraged by this as he wanted the cash himself. Medakovitch refused to give it him. "He regards as his friend him who gives him gold," says a contemporary; "who gives naught is his arch-enemy." Danilo continued negotiating with France, and Medakovitch carried the 5,000 ducats out of the country to the Russian Consul-General at Ragusa.

Danilo formed a crafty plan. He sent two cunning agents to Ragusa to pretend to the Russian that Montenegro was in a state of unrest, and that they could overthrow Danilo and re-establish Russian influence if they could have the 5,000 ducats. To what more laudable end could they be expended? But the Russian was a yet more wily fox and the plan failed.

Danilo then hurried to Paris to discuss matters and while he was absent George Petrovitch led a rising against him, instigated doubtless by Medakovitch. Danilo hastily returned to Montenegro and according to a contemporary account a reign of terror followed. He feared every popular man: "Thus it is that a series of executions without trial or formal accusation has gone on for months without it being possible to see when this terrible state of things will end. Persons who to-day are the Prince's favourites are to-morrow corpses. His commands, his threats and his gold obtain for him false oaths and false documents." A fierce blood-feud which lasted in effect till a few years ago, arose between him and the Gjurashkovitches. Marko Gjurashkovitch, one of the richest and handsomest of the headmen, dared, during the Prince's absence in France, to marry the widow of Pero Petrovitch, whom Danilo had meant to bestow on his favourite Petar Vukotitch. Danilo therefore bribed heavily Gligor Milanovitch the arambasha of a brigand band, who accused Marko Gjurashkovitch and another of a treasonable plot against Danilo's life. The two were at once arrested and executed in spite of their protestations of innocence. The Gjurashkovitches fled into Turkish territory where the two still held official posts under the Turkish Government till 1912.

Danilo found his scheme for accepting Turkish suzerainty now so unpopular that he dropped it and the Turks consequently at once attacked Montenegro. The land was saved by the valour of Danilo's brother, Grand Voyvoda Mirko, whose exploits are still sung by the peasants. A great battle was fought at Grahovo. The retreat of the Turkish army was cut off and the whole was slaughtered or captured. The prisoners, according to Montenegrin custom, were hideously mutilated and the British report of them as they passed Corfu on their return struck horror in Europe. By this victory Montenegro gained more land, but owed it to the valour of Mirko rather than to Danilo.

Danilo's best work was the codification and reformation of the unwritten law of the land. Code Danilo is rude enough, but an advance upon the laws of Vladika Petar. It was printed in Italian as well as Serb. Italian, till the beginning of the present century, was the only foreign tongue that had made any way in Montenegro.

When Danilo had refused the spiritual headship of the land and had chosen marriage, the superstitious foretold that no good would come of this and that no heir of his body would succeed him.

The prophecy came true. He was assassinated in the summer of 1860 on the shore of the Bocche di Cattaro, and left but two daughters. The assassin, a Montenegrin, was arrested and executed and died without giving any explanation of his deed. It has been ascribed both to Austria and Russia—but was far more probably an act of private vengeance.

Danilo was succeeded by Nikola I the present King of Montenegro, son of Voyvoda Mirko.

Two main points stand clear from this brief sketch.

(1) That the history of Montenegro, as that of all the Balkan peoples, is but a part of the gigantic racial struggle of Slav and Teuton for command of the Near East. The Slav ever pressing Southward and Westward, the Teuton standing as a bulwark for West Europe and holding back the advancing hordes. The one non-Slavonic lace in this group, the Albanian (with the exception of a few Catholic tribes) consistently struggles also against the Slav peril and sides with its opponents.

(2) It is also markedly a struggle for the supremacy of the Orthodox Church. For with the exception of Montenegro's fights against the armies of the Pasha of Scutari and his Albanians, the enemy of Montenegro was always the Moslem Serbs of Bosnia and the Herzegovina, people, that is, who racially and linguistically and by custom are identical with the Montenegrins.

Montenegro's history continued on precisely the same lines under Nikola I, until Slavonic and Teutonic rivalry culminated in the colossal struggle which began in August 1914.

Of all the Petrovitches Nikola is one of the most remarkable. The last of the mediaeval chieftains of Europe—a survival from a past age—he is an epitome of the good and bad qualities of his race. In common with that of other half-wild races the Montenegrin mind is credulous and child-like and at the same time crafty and cunning. With a very limited outlook, the Balkan politician is wont to spend infinite ingenuity in outwitting a rival in order to gain some petty advantage, and meanwhile to lose sight entirely of the larger issues. Prince Nikola, better equipped by a western education than any of his forerunners, rapidly gained a strong hold over his ignorant subjects and in the great game of Near Eastern politics was second only to Abdul Hamid at ruse and intrigue.

From the very first he had but one ambition—the reconstruction of the Great Serbian Empire with the Petrovitches as the reigning dynasty. He lived for it and he did all possible to foster it in the minds of his people. He enforced the wearing of the national cap, invented by Vladika Petar II. Each child was taught that his cap's red crown was blood that had to be avenged. For each tribe he wrote a Kolo song to be danced to at festive gatherings, to stimulate nationalism. And for the whole country he wrote that most popular national song:

> Onward, onward, let me see Prizren,
> For it is mine—I shall come to my home!

The throne and the castle of Tsar Dushan at Prizren became a national obsession.

And to ensure the obedience of the Soviet of headmen he appointed his redoubtable father Voyvoda Mirko as President and chose the members himself.

He was but nineteen at the time of his accession and married almost at once, Milena, daughter of Voyvoda Vukotitch of the fighting tribe of Kchevo, to whom he had been affianced in childhood, as was then customary. Their reign began stormily. The Turks thirsting to avenge Grahovo attacked Montenegro on three sides. Voyvoda Mirko led his son's forces and the Montenegrins defended themselves desperately, but were so severely outnumbered that only the intervention of the Powers saved them. So much was Mirko dreaded that the Turks made it one of their peace terms that he must leave the country. This term was, however,' not fulfilled and the sturdy old savage remained in Montenegro till the day of his death, steadily opposing all western and modern ideas, especially the making of a carriage road into the country; and ever composing and singing to the gusle songs of battle and border fray, which, though devoid of literary merit, give an invaluable picture of the savagery of the land in the middle of the nineteenth century.

Old Mirko died of the great cholera epidemic which swept Montenegro, and Prince Nikola was then free to introduce new visages into the land.

Balanced perilously between Austria and Russia he managed to keep on good terms with both, but his sympathies were Russian. To Russia he turned for help to organize an army. Till then each tribe had fought according to its own ideas. Montenegro had no artillery and no equipment save flintlocks and the hand jar, the heavy knife used for decapitation. In Petersburg he was warmly received by Tsar Alexander II, who gave him funds both for schools and the army. A small-arms factory was started at Rijeka and a gun foundry near Cetinje. Weapons were bought from France and preparations made for the next campaign. You cannot talk to King Nikola long without learning that war, successful war, filled all his mind. Conquest and Great Serbia were the stars of his heaven and of that of his people. Border frays enough took place and when, in 1875, the Herzegovinians broke into open revolt the Montenegrins rushed to their aid. Nikola, commanded by the Powers to keep the peace, declared he could not restrain the tribesmen. Local tradition which is possibly correct states that his efforts to do so were not strenuous. In June 1876 Prince Milan of Serbia declared war on Turkey. Prince Nikola, who had already refused to acknowledge Milan as leader of the Serb peoples and regarded him with jealous eyes, thereupon declared war next day.

The Great Serbian Idea was already causing rivalry.

Nikola fought and won his first battle at Vuchidol. Montenegrin arms were successful everywhere—penetrated far into the Herzegovina; took Podgoritza, Nikshitch and Antivari. When the victorious Russians drew up the Treaty of San Stefano at the very gates of Constantinople Prince Nikola, "the Tsar's only friend," received liberal treatment, and Serbia, suspected of Austrian leanings, but scant recognition.

The Treaty of Berlin reversed this. England was especially anti-Russian and, represented by Lord Beaconsfield and Lord Salisbury, insisted on entrusting the bulk of Montenegro's conquests in the Herzegovina to Austrian administration. "The Tsar's only friend" was regarded with suspicion. Montenegro was unfortunately compensated mainly with Albanian territory. It was a great injustice. The Albanians had made just as stubborn a fight for their nationality as had the Montenegrins, and had never lost local autonomy. They resisted violently and prevented Montenegro from occupying either Plava, Gusinje or Tuzi. The Powers tried to make up by an even worse act of injustice. Mr. Gladstone, having little or no personal experience of the Orthodox Church, was possessed of an extraordinary admiration for it, and, filled with the erroneous idea that every Moslem was a Turk, he was in favour of giving Dulcigno, a wholly Albanian town, to Montenegro in place of the other three. It was a peculiarly unjust and cruel decision. Even in the days of the Serb Kings Dulcigno had kept its autonomy and at one time coined its own money. All old travellers state the spoken language was Albanian. The Montenegrins could not take it and had no claim to it. A naval demonstration of the Powers forced it to surrender, perhaps one of the biggest acts of bullying of which the Powers have as yet been guilty.

Albanian Dulcigno was handed over to its hereditary foe. The strength of its purely Albanian nature is shown by the fact that whereas in Nikshitch, Podgoritza, and Spuzh the Moslems, Serbs and Albanians, were stripped of all their property and expelled wholesale to starve as very many did—the Montenegrins did not dare interfere with the large and hostile population of Dulcigno and have in no way succeeded in Slavizing it: The Dulcigniotes still ask for re-union with Albania.

Montenegro was recognized by the Treaty of Berlin for the first time as an independent Principality, and Serbia, in 1880, was raised to a Kingdom. To Prince Nikola and his Montenegrins who had refused to recognize Prince Milan as leader of the Serb nation this was a most bitter pill. Rivalry between the two branches of the Serb race was intensified. Prince Nikola strove by a remarkable series of marriages to unite himself to any and all of the Powers by means of his numerous offspring.

Russia being his "only friend" he aspired to marry one of his elder daughters to the Tsarivitch. But the poor girl who was being educated for the purpose in Russia, died young.

Two other daughters he however successfully married to the Grand Duke Nikola Nikolaievitch and the Grand Duke Peter. With Great Serbia in view, and on bad terms with the Obrenovitches of Serbia, he married his daughter Zorka in 1883 to Petar Karageorgevitch, the exiled claimant to the Serbian throne. Having thus married his elder children to Russian and Serb he then turned to the Triple Alliance and married Helena to the Crown Prince of Italy, thus securing an ally, as he hoped, across the Adriatic; and his heir Prince Danilo to the daughter of the Grand Duke of

Mecklenburg Strelitz. For his daughter Anna he selected Prince Joseph Battenburg. "How do you think this young man will do as Prince of Macedonia?" he once cheerfully asked Mr. Bouchier, to Prince Joseph's embarrassment.

Lastly, in order to have claim on Serbia whichever way the political cat hopped, he married Prince Mirko to Natalie Constantinovitch, cousin to Alexander Obrenovitch of Serbia. All that Prince Nikola could do to conquer Europe by "peaceful penetration" he certainly did.

Two daughters remained: Princesses Xenia and Vera. Popular report had it that one was destined for Bulgaria and the other for Greece, and there was much disappointment when the Princes of those lands made other choice. Nor I fear are either ladies likely now to mount thrones.

One error of judgment which has largely helped to thwart Prince Nikola's hopes is the fact that, alarmed lest foreign luxury should make his sons discontented with their stony fatherland, he would not send them abroad to be educated. They were taught at home by a tutor who was an able man enough, but the future ruler of even a tiny realm needs a wider experience and training. He further made the fatal mistake of bringing them up as Princes apart from the people, whereas he himself had played with village children. As a result they grew up with exaggerated ideas of their own importance, devoid of discipline and ignorant of all things most needful for a successful ruler in a poor land. They had all the vices of Princes and none of their virtues.

It was a tragic error with tragic consequences. Nikola came to the throne as a mediaeval chieftain in a yet mediaeval land. To succeed in his ambitions, and he was then amply justified in believing that he would succeed, it was needful to train up a successor fit to rule in the twentieth century.

The gates of time were of a sudden flung open. In the space of a few years something like five centuries poured over the land. Nikola stood on the rocks with his sons hoping to escape the devastating torrent. But there was no way of escape. They must swim with the stream of time—or drown.

Nor does it now seem likely that one of his immediate descendants will ever rule Great Serbia.

They failed to take the "tide in the affairs of men" and their golden dream has been swept, into the Never-Never Land. It is bitter tragedy to end life as a failure.

CHAPTER THREE
FIRST IMPRESSIONS OF LAND AND PEOPLE

In 1901 I visited Montenegro and went down the lake to Scutari. Scutari captured me at once. It had colour, life, art. Its people were friendly and industrious and did not spend all their time drinking rakia and swaggering up and down the street as at Cetinje. There was something very human about them and of all things I wanted to go into the Albanian mountains. But our Consul there was but just arrived. He consulted his Austrian colleague and as Austria was then keeping the mountains as its own preserve, he replied, emphatically, that the journey was impossible for me.

No particular political crisis was happening, but there were rumours of a certain Kastrioti in Paris who claimed descent from the great Skenderbeg and his possible arrival as Prince of Albania roused a certain excitement in Albanian breasts. Hopes of independence were already spoken of in hushed whispers.

In Montenegro Great Serbia was the talk, and I was shewn crude prints of the heroes of old, on many a cottage wall. And some flashlights on Montenegrin character showed vividly the different mentality of the Balkans.

The new British Vice-Consul for Scutari came up to Cetinje on business, for the British Minister had left owing to ill-health. The Montenegrins did not like the new Vice-Consul and seriously consulted me as to the possibility of having him exchanged for another. I was extremely surprised. "But why do you not like him?" I asked. "Because he does not like us," was the confident reply. "But he has only been here a week," I urged. "How can he know yet whether he likes you or not? In any case what does it matter. It is not necessary to like a Consul."

"But yes!" came the horrified reply. "How is it not necessary? One must either love or hate!"

One must either love or hate. There is no medium. It was Dushan Gregovitch that spoke.

Lazar Mioushkovitch flashed the next beam on the national character. Some tourists arrived and, at the lunch table, talked with Lazar. One was a clergyman. He told how Canon McColl during the Turko-Russian War of 1877 had reported having seen severed heads on poles, and how all England, including Punch, had jeered at him for thinking such a thing possible in Europe in the nineteenth century. Mioushkovitch was sadly puzzled. "But how, I ask you, could he fail to see severed heads in a war? The cutting off of heads in fact—I see nothing remarkable in that!" Then, seeing the expression of the reverend gentleman's face, he added quickly: "But when it comes to teaching the children to stick cigarettes in the mouths—there I agree with you, it is a bit too strong!" (c'est un peu fort ca!) There was a sudden silence. The Near East had, in fact, momentarily undraped itself.

Last came the days when we daily expected to hear that the Queen of Italy had given birth to a son and heir. A gun was made ready to fire twenty-one shots. Candles were prepared to light in every window. The flags waited to be unfurled. We all sat at lunch in the hotel. The door flew open and a perianik (royal guard) entered. He spoke a few words to Monsieur Piguet, the Prince's tutor. Piguet excused himself and left the room.

After some interval he returned, heaved a heavy sigh, and in a voice of deep depression, said to the Diplomatic table: Eh bien Messieurs —nous avons une fille! It was appalling. No one in Montenegro, it would appear, had thought such a catastrophe even possible. To the Montenegrin the birth of a daughter was a misfortune. "You feed your son for yourself. You feed your daughter for another man." Faced with this mediaeval point of view the Diplomatic circle was struck dumb. Till the British Consul said bravely: "I don't care what the etiquette is! I won't condole with him." And the tension was relieved.

No guns were fired, no candles lighted. Cetinje tried to look as though nothing at all had happened.

One member of the Round Table at this time needs mention. Count Louis Voynovitch from Ragusa was staying in Cetinje to draw up a new code of laws. This clever adventurer was looked on with some jealousy by the Montenegrins and much favoured by the Royal Family whom he amused with anecdotes and jokes.

It was said he was to be permanently Minister of Justice, but he left Montenegro rather suddenly over, it was said, a cherchez la femme affair. He then went to Bulgaria as tutor, I believe, to the young Princes, and afterwards held a post in Serbia.

And he returned again to Montenegro and represented Montenegro at the Ambassadors Conference in London during the Balkan War of 1912-13. He was reputed to be deep dipped in every intrigue of the Balkans and in Jugoslavia we may some day hear of him again.

Nothing else now worth recording occurred in my 1901 holiday. Next year was a full one.

CHAPTER FOUR
SERBIA AND THE WAY THERE

"The wicked flee when no man pursueth, but the righteous is bold as a lion."

Twice had I visited Montenegro and had heard much of Great Serbia. Of the past as seen by Serb eyes I read in any number of cheap pink and blue ballad books. As for the present, big Montenegrins in the most decorative national dress in Europe, swaggered up and down the main street of Cetinje, consumed unlimited black coffee and rakia and discussed the glorious days when all Serbs should again be united under Gospodar Nikita. But that they were taking any active steps to create this earthly paradise I had then no idea.

My 1902 holiday was due. I decided to go further afield and see Serbia itself, but to go first to Montenegro where I might obtain information and introductions. No one in England could tell me anything and only one recent book on the subject could be found. This was of no consequence for the real joy of travel begins with the plunge into the unknown and in 1902 it was still possible to find this joy in Europe. From Whittaker's Almanac I learnt that all passports must be visaed at the Serbian Legation and thither I hastened.

I had never travelled without a passport, for accidents may always happen and even so near home as Paris identity papers may be useful. But I had never before sought a special visa.

Light-heartedly, therefore, I rang the Legation bell and cheerfully offered the youth, who admitted me, the passport with a request for a visa. He told me to wait; and wait I did until—though not quite new to the Near East I began to wonder what overwhelming world-politics were detaining the Serbian Minister. Persons peeped at me cautiously through the half-open door and darted back when I looked round. Finally, I was summoned into M. Militchevitch's presence.

Stiffly he asked why I wanted to go to Serbia. My reply, that having visited Montenegro I now proposed seeing other Serb lands, did not please him at all. I made things worse by enlarging on my Montenegrin experiences for I had no idea then of the fact that there is nothing one Slav State hates so much as another Slav State, and truly thought to please him.

He persisted in wanting "definite information." "What do you want to do there?"

"Travel and sketch and photograph and collect curios."

He suggested sternly that there were other lands in Europe where all this could be done.

His attitude was incomprehensible to me, who then knew foreign lands only as places which received tourists with open arms and hotels gaping for guests. He, on the other hand, found me quite as incomprehensible for, like many another Balkan man, he could conceive of no travel without a political object.

And I was quite unaware that the murders upon which Great Serbia was to be built were even then being plotted.

Point-blank, I asked, "Is travelling in Serbia so very dangerous then?"

The shot told. "Not at all!" said he hastily.

"Then why may I not go?"

After more argle-bargle he consented to give me the visa on condition I went straight to the British Consul at Belgrade and did nothing without his advice. He signed, remarking that he took no responsibility. I paid and left triumphant, all unaware of the hornet's nest I was now free to enter.

Of Serb politics I knew at that time little beyond the fact that King Alexander was unpopular owing to an unfortunate marriage and the still more unfortunate attempt of Queen Draga to plant a false heir upon the country by pretending pregnancy; that his father's career had been melodramatic and that the history of Serbia for the whole period of her independence had been one long blood-feud between the rival dynasties of Karageorge and Obrenovitch, neither of which seemed popular in Montenegro. Off I went to Cetinje and told various people my plan for seeing Serbia. Rather to my surprise no one offered me introductions, but having been repeatedly told that the Montenegrins were the cream of the Serb nation, and would lead Serbia to glory I believed that the mere mention of Montenegro and my acquaintance with it would suffice to assure me a welcome.

Near the door of the Monastery of Cetinje is the grave of one of the Karageorgevitches and the priest who showed it me told that the families Petrovitch and Karageorgevitch had been on very friendly terms. Prince Nikola had married his daughter Zorka to Petar Karageorgevitch, the rival claimant to the Serbian throne, in 1883; that the young couple had lived in Cetinje and their three children were born there; but that, after Zorka's death in 1890, father-in-law and son-in-law had fallen out badly about money matters and Petar had been seen no more in Montenegro. The fact that the present Crown Prince Alexander of Serbia was born in Cetinje is of some interest now, when he is attempting to seize his grandfather's throne—but more of this later. In 1902 it was still undreamed of.

Only Count Bollati, then Italian Minister to Montenegro, took any active interest in my plans. Le bon Dieu, he said, "has created you expressly to travel in the Balkans." He loathed Cetinje and explained he had accepted it only as one degree better than Buenos Ayres because nearer to Rome. "Nothing bites you," he continued; "everything bites me. Your method of seeing lands is undoubtedly the best, but I am satisfied with what I see from the windows of the best hotel." Nor, unfortunately, was Count Bollati in any way unique in his tastes a fact which may have affected the politics of Europe.

He had held a diplomatic post in Belgrade and was very curious to know how I should fare. "Sooner you than I!" he laughed, and meanwhile sketched me a route through the chief towns and told me his first experience in the land.

It was at a court ball, given by the gay and dashing King Milan. The salon was awhirl with dancers when-click—something fell to the ground near the Count's feet. A lady's jewel doubtless. He stooped and picked up a revolver cartridge. Laughing, he showed it to an aide-de-camp near him, who saw no joke in the matter and referred it to King Milan, who turned white and looked gravely anxious. And Bollati for the first time realized the Balkans. Before I left Cetinje it was officially announced that the marriage of Prince Mirko (Prince Nikola's second son) with Mademoiselle Natalie Constantinovitch had been fixed for July 12 O.S. (1902), and the faire parts were sent to the Corps Diplomatique.

The bride was cousin to King Alexander Obrenovitch who had no direct heir.

Failing one, she was one of the nearest relations to the Obrenovitch dynasty. The astute Prince Nikola, having married a daughter to the Karageorge claimant to the throne, now strove to make assurance doubly sure by marrying a son to a possible rival candidate. My diary notes though: "It seems there has been a lot of bother about it and that it was nearly 'off' as Papa Constantinovitch required Mirko to put down a considerable amount in florins. And Mirko could not produce them. I suppose he has now borrowed on his expectation of the Serbian throne. Which is, I imagine, his only asset."

I confess that at this time I did not know the Balkans and saw all these doings humorously, as a comic operetta. But the comic operas of the Balkans are written in blood and what was then fun to me was to end in a world tragedy.

My route to Belgrade was by boat to Fiume and thence by rail via Agram. On the boat I picked up a Croatian lady and her daughter, who moped miserably in the hot and stuffy cabin till they ventured to ask my permission to sit with me on deck. "You are English, so the men will not dare annoy us," they said, "if we are with you." Only English women, they declared, could travel as I did. The mere idea of a journey in Serbia terrified them and they assured me it was quite impossible.

And the cheap hotel in Agram, to which they recommended me, was of the same opinion. The company there assured me that King Alexander was drinking himself to death, and were loud in their expression of contempt for land and people. In those days union between Croatia and Serbia was possible only if Croatia swallowed Serbia. And not very long after I was in Agram riots took place in which the Serbs of the town were attacked and plundered.

As the train lumbered over the plains north of the Save, on the way to Belgrade, my fellow travellers, too, thought I was bound on a mad and impossible errand. As is usual in the Near East they all cross-examined me about my private affairs with boring persistency, and their verdict was that not even a British passport would see me through. "You will never see Serbia," they declared. I did though. For, being wholly innocent of any plots, all the efforts of all the multitudinous police of Serbia failed to turn me from my plan. "The wicked flee when no man pursueth, but the righteous is as bold as a lion."

The train thundered over the iron bridge at night and deposited me in Belgrade. I had to give up my passport and my troubles began. I had come to see Serbia, and finally saw the whole of it and have described it in another book. But for obvious reasons I did not then recount all that befell me; I did not even understand it all.

Looking back on that tour I can only wonder at the dogged persistence with which I overcame all the obstacles which the Serb police put in my way. Short of forbidding me to travel they did all they could.

In accordance with my promise to M. Militchevitch, "To do nothing without consulting the British Consul," I went to the consulate, where I found a nice young man, who had but recently arrived and seemed to know nothing whatever about the country. He was playing with a dachsdog and told me cheerfully I could go anywhere I liked "and none of them will dare touch you." But he warned me that it would be very expensive as carriages were two pounds a day. I suggested mildly that the land being a poor one this could not possibly be the regular charge, but that people sometimes had to pay extra for the privilege of being British Consul; which apparently he had never thought of. It proved correct though. Serbia in those days was the cheapest spot in Europe. Never again in all probability will the peasant be so well off.

But before starting up country I meant to see Belgrade, and began by asking at the hotel where the King was to be seen. For a King, in 1902 at any rate, was still an object of interest, and one of the "show sights" of most European countries. The waiter replied "You want to see our King? You won't see him. He dares not come out of the Konak. He is probably drunk." Nor in fact during the time I spent in Belgrade did he ever come out.

In Belgrade the first thing I learnt was that I was "shadowed" by the police. To the uninitiated this is most uncanny. The same man keeps turning up. He does it very badly as a rule. You sit and have coffee on one side of a street and he sits and drinks beer at the restaurant opposite. You wander on and think: "What an ass I was to think he was following me!" and meet him at the next corner. Most disquieting of all perhaps is to come suddenly out of your bedroom and almost tumble over him in the corridor. All these and more were my experiences in the first weeks of my tour. And always I said to myself in triumph: "They can't do anything to me for I have not done anything." I could not even buy a railway ticket for a day's outing without being cross-examined as to my purpose, my father, my uncles and other relatives. The officials in Vain assured me that there was nothing to see in the place

I wished to visit. I played the card which had succeeded with Militchevitch and asked if it were dangerous. I could not enter a village without being at once asked by the local policeman for my passport. Blankly ignorant of what was behind these proceedings I steadily pursued my way, smiling at all questions and supplying at demand long biographies of various members of my family. No; my father had not been in the diplomatic service, nor my uncles, nor brothers, nor cousins. No; none of them were officers.

"I have come to see Serbia," said I, in return to the enquiry of a police officer. "But what do you see?" he asked, gazing wildly round. "I see nothing!"

Every official I think in every village, saw my sketch book, demanded an explanation of why I had selected such things as wells, gravestones, carts and cottages to draw, and remained mystified. For the common objects of Serbia were of no interest to them. I merely looked on all these vagaries as so many peculiar and silly Serbian customs—wondered what the Serbs would do if a hundred or so tourists appeared, for then there would not be enough police to go round—and did not allow myself to be ruffled even when three times in one day I had to show my passport to individuals who pounced down on me in the street.

When I arrived at the' least bad hotel in Nish the hotelier said he did not wish to be mixed up in the affair; gave me the worst room in the house and told me I had better leave by the first train next morning. I said I was going to stay and did. And explored Nish conscious of "guardian angels" at my heels.

But it was here that I realized that there was something sinister in the background, for so suspicious were the hotel people that when, for two days I was seriously unwell, not one of them would come in answer to my bell but an old woman, who flatly refused to bring me anything and never turned up again. I lived on Brand's beef lozenges till I was well enough on the evening of the second day to crawl downstairs and bribe a waiter to fetch me some milk. Once recovered I went to Pirot by rail in spite of pressing requests that I would return to Belgrade. I wanted to see the Pirot carpet factories, but of course no one believed this. They all imagined, as I learnt later, that I was bound for Bulgaria with evil intentions: messages from Montenegro for the undoing of Serbia. I was quite unaware at the time that Prince Ferdinand and Prince Nikola were plotting together. Arrived at Pirot it was obvious that I was considered dangerous. I was stopped in the station by police and military authorities, who had doubtless been warned of my arrival, and told that I was not to go near the Bulgar frontier, much less cross it. Only after some argument did they consent to let me stay two days in the town. Then I was to leave for Belgrade by the early morning train, and to make sure that I could not escape by any other route, they confiscated my passport and said it should be returned to me at the station when I left.

Tension between Serbia and Bulgaria was obviously extreme. By way of warning, I was told that a Bulgar spy had just been caught and was in prison. But I had come to see the carpet making and I saw it. The carpets are very interesting. They are made in no other part of Serbia and are in truth Bulgarian in origin. Pirot before its annexation to Serbia in 1878 was an undoubtedly Bulgar district. Old books of travel call Nish Bulgar. In Pirot a distinctly Bulgar cast of countenance and build is to be seen. And the neighbouring peasants play the bagpipe, the typical Bulgar instrument. The type extends not only into the south of Serbia (of 1902), but in the east spreads over the Timok. The population along the frontier and around Zaitchar I found Bulgar and Roumanian, the flat-faced, heavily built Bulgar with high cheekbones and lank black hair predominating—all being Serbized, of course. Having seen the carpet making at Pirot, I obediently appeared at the railway station at the appointed time as bidden. Suddenly, the whole atmosphere changed. The same officials who had received me so inimically now wanted me to stay! Having first worn my quite respectable supply of patience almost threadbare, the Serbs turned right round and did all they could to efface first impressions. The whole thing seemed to me childish and astonishing. But I profited largely by it and went the rest of my way in comparative comfort.

By this time I had learnt that Serbia was in a state of intense political tension, and that my ingenuous statement that I had come straight from Cetinje had gone badly against me.

Stupid officials asked me so many leading questions that they revealed far more than they had learnt and showed me quite clearly that a plot to put Prince Mirko on the throne of Serbia at no distant date, was believed to exist.

That most wily of Royal stud-grooms, Prince Nikola, had so married his family that he undoubtedly believed that "What he lost on the roundabouts he would gain on the swings," and that his position as Head of Great Serbia was assured.

Having heard so much of the Petrovitches as the natural lords of Great Serbia, this plan did not seem to me so unreasonable. But I soon found it had very little support in Serbia. Only in the extreme south—at Ivanjitza, Studenitza and thereabouts did I find Montenegro at all popular.

Elsewhere it was looked on with jealousy and suspicion. The Montenegrins, folk said, were incurably lazy and very dirty, and their immigration into the country was not desired.

Some Montenegrin students came to the Serbian schools, but were denounced as ungrateful and impossible. A Montenegrin, I was told, was a lout who would sit all day on the doorstep wearing a revolver and doing nothing, and would expect high pay or at least good keep for so doing. In 1898 the Serb Government had actually forbidden the immigration of Montenegrins.

In brief, it was clear Serbia would not accept a Montenegrin Prince at any price, and Mirko's chances were nil.

Montenegro was despised. Bulgaria was hated—was the enemy, always had been and always would be.

But even after I had been accepted by the country strange things still happened.

At Kraljevo there was almost a fight over me between the Nachelnik (Mayor) who ordered me to leave next day, and a man to whom I had been given a letter of introduction. He said I should stay: the other that I was to go, and they shouted at each other till both were scarlet.

When mentioning this later to a company of Serbs they asked "What was the name of the man you had an introduction to?" I gave it. They exchanged glances. "That family was in trouble formerly about the murder of Prince Michel" was all that was said. He was in point of fact a partisan of the Karageorgevitch family. And the Mayor was a pro-Obrenovitch.

At Kragujevatz I fell right into the Karageorgevitch party. That I met them in strength in Kragujevatz is now a matter of interest. At the time I little dreamed that from this straggling big village—it could hardly be called a town—would emanate bombs that would set Europe on fire.

The Royal Arsenal is at Kragujevatz, and when I was there in 1902 the place was certainly a centre of disaffection. It was here that I was told outright that Alexander must either divorce Draga—or go. What was to follow was uncertain. They wished, if possible, to avoid a revolution. I was even begged to work a propaganda in favour of Petar Karageorgevitch in England. Above all to write to The Times, and my informants said they trusted to my honour not to betray their names.

Had I pursued the subject I have now little doubt that I might have learnt much more and even have got in touch with the leaders of the movement—if indeed I had not already fallen into their hands! But it was my first contact with a plot of any kind and I instinctively recoiled from having anything to do with it. It is almost impossible for those who have led a peaceful life to realize that real human blood is going to be shed. The thing sounded more like melodrama than real life. But it was definitely stated that "something was going to happen" and that I should watch the papers and see at no distant date.

My new acquaintances were vexed that I should have$ been so harassed in the early stages of my journey, but oddly enough ascribed it not to the folly of their own officials, but to the fact that the British Consul had not given me letters of introduction! "If your own Consul will not guarantee you, of course it seems suspicious!"

This remark alone is enough to show the abyss that separated Serbia from West Europe. Politics in the Near East are an obsession—a nervous disease which may end in acute dementia and homicidal mania.

Having decided to confide in me, folk then began pouring out disgusting tales about Queen Draga. So disgusting that I soon cut all tales short so soon as her name occurred. Nor is it now necessary to rake up old muck-heaps. One point though is of interest. Among many races all over the world there is a widespread belief that sexual immorality, whether in the form of adultery or incest will inevitably entail most serious consequences not only upon the guilty parties, but upon the community as a whole, and even menace the existence of a whole people. Thebes, for example, suffered blight and pestilence owing to the incest of Oedipus. I found it widely believed in Serbia that before marrying Alexander, Draga had been his father's mistress and was told emphatically that the marriage must bring a curse. Serbia could never flourish while she was on the throne. It is highly probable that though the subsequent murders were arranged and carried out for a definite political purpose by an organized gang, they were acquiesced in by the ignorant mass for the above reason—a genuine belief that there was a curse on the land that would be removed only by Draga's death.

The country, I was told, was in a terrible state. None of the officers had been paid for six months. Draga, it was said, took all the money to buy diamonds. The wretched woman's little collection of jewellery which was sold at Christie's after her death, proved, however, the falsity of this tale. But it doubtless accounted partly for the unbridled ferocity with which the military gang fell upon her.

That there was not enough money to pay them seemed to me not surprising, for the land swarmed with officers. I was told that in proportion to its size there were more officers in Serbia than in Germany and noted in my diary at the time "the whole land seems eaten out of house and home with officers who seem to have nothing on earth to do but play cards. It is a great pity for the country. As soon as the peasants learn a little I expect they will turn Socialist." An army is an expensive luxury and "Satan finds some mischief still for idle hands to do" is a true saying. Serbia has paid dearly for the lot of swankers, clad in most unnecessarily expensive uniforms, whom I saw gambling in the cafes from morning till night.

All these points are noteworthy in the light of the present. One other may yet strongly influence the future of the Serb race. That is their religious fanaticism, which then surprised me. It was not astonishing that the Serbs hated Islam, but that they should fiercely hate every other Christian Church I did not expect.

It is but one more instance of the fact that it was largely to the fanaticism of the Orthodox Church that the Balkan people owed their conquest by the Turks. Evidence enough there is to show that when their fate was in the balance the Orthodox of the Balkans regarded the Turk as a lesser evil than the Pope. Even in 1902, though a few mosques were still permitted to exist, no Catholic Church was tolerated save that attached to one of the Legations over which, of course, the Serb Government had no control. Most of the foreign women I met, who had married Serbs, told me frankly that for the sake of peace they had had to join the Orthodox Church; "you cannot live here unless you do."

The American missionaries who have done so much for Bulgaria and were permitted to work freely under the tolerant Turk, were only allowed to travel through Serbia on condition they held no services.

I was astonished at the intense bitterness with which the ex-Queen Natalie's conversion to Rome was spoken of. As the poor woman had led a wretched life in

Serbia and had left it for ever, her religion could be no concern whatever now of the Serbs. But it seemed to be considered on all sides as an insult to the nation.

Nor was it, so far as I could see, because the people were devout believers—the upper classes certainly did not appear to be—but because the Church was Serbian, and represented a frenzied and intolerant Nationalism. To such an extent was this carried out that a Catholic Albanian, of whom I subsequently saw a good deal, had to add "itch" to the end of his name and conform to the Orthodox Church outwardly in order to obtain leave to open a shop in Belgrade.

That frenzied Nationalism and not religion is at the base of this intolerance is further proved by hatred of the Serb for the Bulgarian Church, which on all points of dogma and doctrine and in its services is precisely the same as that of the Serbs.

And this same frenzied Nationalism, if persisted in, may yet lead to Serbia's undoing.

On looking back I see that my tour in Serbia was a turning point in my Balkan studies. Till then the Balkans had been a happy hunting ground filled by picturesque and amusing people, in which to collect tales, sketch and forget home miseries for a time in a quite new world.

I left Serbia with very mixed feelings. Much of the tour I had enjoyed. After the police difficulties of the beginning I had met with great hospitality and much kindness and it is always a pleasure to penetrate an unknown land, ride through great forests and see the new view open at the top of the pass. When the Belgrade police visaed my passport for the last time they bade me a friendly farewell. But I was severely disillusioned as to Great Serbia. Instead of brethren pining to be united, I had found a mass of dark intrigue—darker than I then knew—envy, hatred and all uncharitableness. No love was lost between Serb and Montenegrin. Alexander was to divorce his wife or go. "Something" would happen soon. And I knew that if Prince Mirko really aspired to the throne of Serbia he would be disappointed—no matter which way the cat hopped.

The Balkans were in future to be to me a Sphinx—an asker of ceaseless riddles each of which led to one yet more complicated; riddles which it took long to solve.

The riddle of my strange reception in Serbia was not explained until four years afterwards. And the tale fits in rightly here.

It was Militchevitch who told me—he who had signed my passport in the spring of 1902. I did not see him again till 1907. "I have been reading your book," he said. "I wondered if you had noticed what happened. I see you did at once."

"Noticed what!" I asked.

"That from the time you left Pirot you were differently treated." He laughed. "Now it is all over long ago you may as well know. You have no idea the excitement you caused. The Serbian Government spent a small fortune in cypher telegrams about you." And he told this astonishing tale: Among the banished members of the Karageorgevitch family was a certain woman who came to England and studied at an English college. She wore her hair short. When therefore I arrived at Belgrade, as ignorant as any babe of the dark undercurrent of politics, the Serbian police at once leapt to the conclusion that I was the lady in question come on a political errand. My passport bothered them as they could find no flaw in it. It was arranged to keep me under supervision and Militchevitch was at once telegraphed to. What did he know about the so-called Englishwoman whose passport he had signed? He could only reply "Nothing." Followed an angry telegram asking what business he had to sign the passports of people of whom he knew nothing, and that in fact he had let one of the Karageorgevitch gang get into the country, who was about to be arrested. Much alarmed, he replied that he was under the impression I was certainly English, and that it would be rash in the highest degree to arrest me without further evidence. They then did all they could to prevent my tour, short of forbidding it. My imperturbable persistence thwarted them. Telegrams flew backwards and forwards. London to Belgrade, Belgrade to London. Militchevitch was ordered to make enquiries about me of the police, who knew nothing at all about me, which surprised him. He ascertained, however, that persons of my name actually lived at the address I had given and were locally of good repute. He implored that my arrest—which was imminent—should be delayed lest international complications ensued. Why the Serb authorities did not impart their doubts to the British Consulate in Belgrade must remain a Balkan mystery. Instead of doing so the Serb police replied, "We are having her followed everywhere. The names of all she speaks to are noted. She goes everywhere. She talks to any one who will talk to her. She draws all kinds of things for what purpose we cannot ascertain. She speaks Serbian very badly, but it is evident she does so on purpose and that she understands everything." My arrest was almost decided on, when some one had a brilliant idea. A photograph of the suspected Serbian lady was somehow obtained in England and Militchevitch was then able to swear that it had no resemblance to the Englishwoman whose passport he had signed. Serbia was saved—that time! I was then in Pirot. Orders at once flew over the country that the treatment should be at once reversed and that the unpleasant impression that had been produced should be, as far as possible, obliterated.

The episode gives a clear idea of the state of nervous tension that existed.

The sublime folly of the Serbian police consisted in thinking that if I were really an agent of Prince Mirko, bringing messages and intending to take them on to Sofia I should have been such a fool as to tell every one I met that I had just come from Cetinje. But perhaps they judged others by themselves. The semi-oriental mind is born to suspicion and can conceive of no straightforward action. In truth "DORA" hails from the Near East. Is not her very name of Greek origin?

To me it was a useful experience for it hardened me to being "shadowed," and I bore it serenely ever afterwards. So much so in fact that when in 1915 at Marseilles I was twice cross-examined by the French Intelligence Officers and three times and very minutely, by the English ones, I thought it funny, which surprised them. They would have been still more surprised had I told them that they reminded me of the police of Belgrade, and asked them why they were called "Intelligence."

Their efforts were as vain as those of their Serb forerunners and for the same reason. I had no plots to reveal.

CHAPTER FIVE
WHAT WAS BEHIND IT ALL

It is a strange Desire to seeke Power and to lose Libertie. . . .
The standing is slippery, and the Regresse is either a Downefall, or
at least an Eclipse. Which is a Melancholy Thing.—BACON.

I went to Serbia as a tourist, but, thanks to the misdirected energy of the Serb police, was made aware for the first time of the unseen forces which were at work in the Balkans. What these forces were we must now consider. Since the end of the seventeenth century Russia and Austria had competed for expansion into the Balkans. Each had gone to war nominally, "to free Christians from the Turkish yoke," but actually in order to annex these populations themselves. Each, by promoting risings in Turkish territory and by financing rival Balkan sovereigns, had silently and ceaselessly worked towards the same goal.

In the great game Montenegro, as we have seen, hall been Russia's pawn since the days when Peter the Great sent his Envoy to Vladika Danilo. Montenegro had become Russia's outpost in the West. Russia was Montenegro's God—and her paymaster. "The dog barks for him that feeds him!" says an Albanian proverb. Montenegro barked, and bit too, at Russia's behest.

Serbia throughout the nineteenth century was rent by the ceaseless blood-feud between the Karageorgevitches and the Obrenovitches, a history bloody as that of the Turkish Sultans, the results of which are not yet over—one that has so largely influenced the fate of yet unborn generations that we must understand its outlines in order to follow modern events.

Serbia, at the end of the eighteenth century, was bitterly oppressed, not so much by the Turkish Government, as by the Jannisaries, the insolent and all powerful military organization which had broken loose from restraint and was now a danger to the Turkish Empire. The Jannisaries actually elected their own chiefs and were semi-independent. And of all the Jannisaries of the Empire none were more opposed to the Sultan than those of Belgrade. Their commanders called themselves Dahis and aimed at complete government of the province.

It is a singular fact, and one which should be emphasized, that the Jannisaries were themselves to a very large extent, of Balkan origin. Their ancestors had been either forcibly converted or had, as was not infrequent, voluntarily adopted Islam. The Moslem Serb was a far greater persecutor of the Christian Serb than was the Turk. We find that the leading Dahis of Belgrade hailed from Focha in the Herzegovina.

Sultan Selim in, terrified of the growing power of these Jannisaries, sided with his Christian subjects, sent troops against them, and forcibly evicted them from Belgrade. A Turkish Pasha, Hadji Mustafa, was appointed as Governor, whose rule was so just and beneficent that the land was soon at peace and the grateful Serbs called him "Srpska Majka"—the Serbian Mother.

But the Jannisaries had retired only as far as Widin which was commanded by the brigand leader Pasvanoglu, whose savage hordes were devastating the country-side in defiance of the Government. Together they attacked the Serbs. Hadji Mustafa, true to his trust, organized the Serbs to resist. The Serbs were now by no means untrained to war, for many had served in the Austrian Army during the late campaigns against the Turks. But the spectacle of a Turkish Pasha inciting Christian rayah against an army of Moslems aroused the wrath of the Faithful throughout the Empire. They demanded the deposition of Hadji Mustafa and the re-admission of the Jannisaries to Belgrade. The Sultan was unable to resist and the Jannisaries returned. Thirsting to avenge the humiliation of their forced retirement they assassinated Hadji Mustafa, seized power, and to prevent a further Serb rising, fell upon the Serb villages and murdered numbers of the headmen. By so doing they precipitated what they wished to prevent.

The Serbs rose in mass and called Karageorge, grandfather of the present King Peter of Serbia, to be their leader. He refused at first, saying that his violent temper would cause him to kill without taking council first. But he was told that the times called for violence. Born of peasant stock about 1765, his upbringing was crudely savage; his ferocity was shown from the first.

In 1787 a panic seized the peasants when an Austrian attack upon the Turks was expected. To save themselves and their flocks from the approaching Turkish army they fled in crowds, hurrying to cross the Save and finding safety in Austria. George's father was very reluctant to go, and on reaching the river would not cross it. George, in a blind fury, refusing either to stay himself and make terms with the Turks, or to leave his father behind, snatched the pistol from his sash and shot the old man down. Then, shouting to a comrade to give his father a death-blow, for he was still writhing, George hurried on, leaving behind him a few cattle to pay for the burial and the funeral feast.

On his return later to Serbia he took to the mountains for some time as a heyduk or brigand.

Such was the man called on to lead the Serbs. Rough and completely uneducated, he yet possessed that strange power of influencing men which constitutes a born leader. His practice as a heyduk and a natural capacity for strategy enabled him for long to wage successful guerrilla warfare, which baffled the Turks. The dense forests and the roadless mountains were natural fortresses of which he made full use.

Alternating with astonishing outbursts of energy and ferocity, were periods of sullen silence during which he sat for days without speaking, gnawing his nails. That there was a strain of insanity in his genius appears certain—an insanity which has reappeared in his great-grandson and namesake who, subject to similar fits of loss of control, used to terrorise the populace by galloping furiously through village streets, and was finally forced to abdicate his right to the throne in March 1909, after the brutal murder of his valet. A case worth the study of students of heredity.

A contemporary of old Karageorge thus describes him:

"His bold forehead bound with a tress of black hair gave him a look rather Asiatic than European.... This man was one of the bold creations of wild countries and troublous times—beings of impetuous courage, iron strength, original talent and doubtful morality."

The might of his personality overcame all obstacles. He appealed to Russia for aid, and a Russian Minister was sent to Serbia along with money and men. He freed and ruled over a large tract of land. But his rule was not much milder than that of the Jannisaries, and his harsh tyranny made him many enemies. When his wrath was once aroused it was unrestrainable, and he struck down and killed many of his own followers. Discontent arose and spread.

The Serbs divided into many parties, each with rival leaders. Russia, who had supported Karageorge, was now herself engaged in a life and death struggle with Napoleon. The Russian regiment which had been quartered at Belgrade, left the country. The turn of the Turks had now come. They attacked the Serbs in force. With no aid from without to be hoped for, the country was in greater danger than ever. But even common danger, as history has again and again shown, does not suffice to cure that fatal Slav weakness—the tendency to split into rival parties led by jealous chieftains. There was no union among the Serb forces now, at the very hour when it was most needed. And for some never explained reason Karageorge failed to appear.

His Voyvodas struggled with the foe and were beaten back and suddenly, in October 1813, Karageorge, the chosen leader of the Serbian people, fled into Austria with a few followers, without even having struck a blow.

This tragic and most fatal failure was due in all probability, to a mental collapse to which his unstable and unbalanced nature would be peculiarly liable.

The Austrians promptly interned both him and his men in fortresses, but released them at the intercession of Russia, and they retired into Bessarabia.

Meanwhile, his place was taken by **Milosh Obrenovitch**, also a peasant, who led the Serb rising of 1815 with such success that he was recognized as ruler, under Turkish suzerainty, of a considerable territory. And as a ruler, moreover, with hereditary rights.

It is said that Russia never forgave the Obrenovitches that they were appointed by the Sultan and not by herself. Scarcely was Milosh well established when Karageorge returned from his long absence.

The break-up of the Turkish Empire had begun. The Greeks were in a ferment. Russia supported them. The Hetairia had been formed and a plan was afoot for a great simultaneous rising of Greeks and Serbs and Roumanians. Karageorge was to be one of its leaders.

But Milosh was in power, id did not mean to relinquish it. And he dreamed already of wide empire. He examined the question with sangfroid and decided that if the Greek revolution succeeded in its hopes, an Empire would be reborn in the East which would regard Serbia as its province and might be more dangerous than the Turk. Did not the Greeks, in the fourteenth century, call the Turks to Europe to fight the "Tsar of Macedonia who loves Christ?" Milosh remained faithful to the Turk, saying "Let us remain in Turkey and profit by her mistakes." He suppressed all pro-Greek action, executed twenty pro-Greek conspirators, and exposed their bodies at the roadside, and—in an evil hour for Serbia—had Karageorge assassinated and sent his head to the Pasha.

From that day onward the feud between the two houses raged with ever increasing fury. Until to-day every ruler of Serbia has been either exiled, murdered, or has had his life attempted.

"Family tradition comes first" says Vladan Georgevitch. "All the families of Serbia have, from the beginning, been followers of either the Karageorgevitches or the Obrenovitches." As time went on, the Obrenovitches became the choice of Austria, while Russia supported the Karageorges, and the puppets jigged as the Great Powers pulled the wires.

Milosh's subjects revolted against his intolerable tyranny and exiled him in 1839. His son Michel succeeded him, a cultivated man who strove to introduce Austrian educational methods. He was evicted in 1842, and the Karageorges again swung into power. Alexander, father of King Petar, was put on the throne, only in his turn to be chased out in 1858. And old Milosh came back and died in 1860 —fortunately for himself perhaps—for he was the same old Milosh, and his renewed tyranny was again provoking wrath.

Serbia had now come to a parting of the ways. There was a Prince of either line, and each had already occupied the throne. Michel Obrenovitch was re-elected. All agree that he was the most enlightened Prince that had as yet occupied the throne, but the blood of old Black George was unavenged, and Michel paid the penalty. He and his cousin, Madame Constantinovitch, and his aide-de-camp were all assassinated on June 10, 1868, in the Park near Belgrade. So set were the murderers on fulfilling their task that they hacked their victim's body with forty wounds. The complicity of Alexander Karageorgevitch and his son Petar—now King —was proved. The plot was engineered by means of Alexander's lawyer, Radovanovitch. The Shkupstina hastily summoned demanded the extradition of the two Karageorgevitches of Austria, whither they had fled, and failing to obtain it outlawed them and all their house for ever and ever, and declared their property forfeit to the State. Fifteen accomplices arrested in Serbia were found guilty and executed with a barbarity which roused European indignation. We can scarcely doubt what would have been the fate of the two principals had they fallen into Serb hands. The grotesque fact remains that it is to Austria that King Petar owes not only his crown, but his life!

It was an odd fate that thirty years afterwards gave me an introduction to a relative of one of the conspirators, and almost caused a fight to take place over me at Kraljevo.

The Karageorgevitches having been exiled by the unanimous vote of the Shkupstina for ever—till next time—Milan, cousin of the murdered Michel, succeeded him on the throne at the age of fourteen. And there was a Regency till 1872.

Milan was a handsome dashing fellow with not too much brain—a typical, boastful, immoral Serb officer.

As a result of the Russo-Turkish War of 1877, in which, however, he displayed little military skill, Serbia was raised from a principality to a Kingdom.

Russia at this time showed little or no interest in Serbia. She was devoting all her energy and diplomacy to the creation of a big Bulgaria, which should ultimately serve her as a land-bridge to the coveted Constantinople. She had no use then for Serbia, and was no friend of the Obrenovitches, and in the Treaty of San Stefano dealt so scurvily by Serbia that Prince Milan opposed the Treaty and said he would defend Nish against Russian troops if necessary.

At the Berlin Congress, Milan called for and obtained a good deal more land than Russia had allotted him—territory which was, in fact, Bulgar and Albanian. He, moreover, made a Convention with Austria by which the frontiers and dynasty of Serbia were guaranteed. One of those many "scraps of paper" which fill the World's Waste Paper Basket.

It was now plain that Milan, if allowed to gain more power, would be an obstacle to Pan-slavism in the Balkans.

The claims of the disinherited and exiled Petar Karageorgevitch began to be talked of. Nikola Pashitch, hereafter to be connected with a long series of crimes, now appears on the scenes. Of Macedonian origin, he soon became one of Russia's tools, and was leader of the so-called Radical party, though "pro-Russian" would be a more descriptive title. It was "radical" only in the sense that it was bent on rooting up any that opposed it. Things began to move. In 1883 Prince Nikola married his daughter to Petar Karageorgevitch, and that same year a revolt in favour of Petar broke out at the garrison town of Zaitshar. Oddly enough it was at Zaitshar in 1902 that I was most pestered by the officers to declare whom I thought should ascend the Serbian throne should Alexander die childless. By that time I was wary and put them off by saying "The Prince of Wales!"

I have often wondered how many of those suspicious and swaggering officers were among those who next year flung the yet palpitating bodies of Alexander and Draga from the Konak windows while the Russian Minister looked on.

The revolt of 1883 was quickly crushed and Pashitch, along with some other conspirators, fled into Bulgaria for protection. Others were arrested in Serbia and executed. The pro-Russian movement was checked for a time.

Pashitch owed his life to Bulgaria, and not on this occasion only. His subsequent conduct to that land has not been marked with gratitude.

CHAPTER SIX
THE GREAT SERBIAN IDEA

"Oh what a tangled web we weave,
When first we practice to deceive."—SCOTT.

The Great Serbian Idea—the scheme for the reconstruction of Tsar Dushan's mediaeval Empire—now began to sprout and germinate. In truth that Empire had been constructed by Dushan by means of mercenary armies, partly German, by aid of which he temporarily subdued Bosnians, Albanians, Bulgars and Greeks. And he paid those armies by means of the silver mines, worked largely by Italians. Great Serbia was an incoherent mass of different and hostile races, and it broke to pieces immediately on his death. But five centuries of Turkish rule in no way modified the hate which one Balkan race bore for another. Each, on gaining freedom, had but one idea—to overthrow and rule the other. Milosh Obrenovitch had already begun to toy with the Great Serbian Idea when he refused to support the Greeks in their struggle for freedom. The success of the wars of 1876-77 raised fresh ambitions.

But now there were two possible heads for Great Serbia—Milan Obrenovitch, who had been raised to kingship, and who owed his position to Austria; and Nikola Petrovitch, recognized as Prince of an independent land, and "the only friend" of the Tsar of All the Russias. The bitter rivalry, not yet extinct, between the two branches of the Serb race—Serbia and Montenegro—now began.

One thing the Serb people have never forgotten and that is that in Dushan's reign Bulgaria was Serbia's vassal. The reconstruction simultaneously of Big Bulgaria and Great Serbia is impossible. And neither race has as yet admitted that a middle course is the safest.

The Zaitshar affair had shown King Milan pretty clearly that the blood of the murdered Karageorge still howled for vengeance. His position was further complicated by the fact that his beautiful Russian wife, Natalie, was an ardent supporter of the plans of her Fatherland.

He made a bold bid for popularity. Filled with exaggerated ideas of his own prowess, and flushed by victories over the Turks, he rushed to begin reconstructing Great Serbia by attacking Bulgaria, which, though newly formed, had already shown signs of consolidating and becoming a stumbling block in Serbia's path to glory. The declaration of war was immensely popular. Had Milan succeeded, the fate of the Obrenovitches might have been very different. But he and his army were so badly beaten that only swift intervention by Austria saved Serbia from destruction.

Pashitch, it should be noted, remained in Bulgaria during this war, and in fact owed his life to that country which he has since done so much to ruin.

The pieces on the Balkan chessboard then stood thus: A Serbia which was the most bitter enemy of Bulgaria and whose King was Austrophile.

A violently pro-Russian Montenegro, filled with contempt for the beaten Serbs, and ruled by a Prince who regarded himself confidently as the God-appointed restorer of Great Serbia, and who was openly supporting his new son-in-law, the rival claimant to the Serb throne.

The throne of Serbia, never too stable, now rocked badly. King Milan declared that Pan-Slavism was the enemy of Serbia and he was certainly right. For in those days it would have simply meant complete domination by Russia—the great predatory power whose maw has never yet been filled.

He pardoned Pashitch, thinking possibly it was better to come to terms with him than to have him plotting in an enemy country, Pashitch returned as head of the Radical party and Serbia became a hot-bed of foul and unscrupulous intrigue into which we need not dig now.

Between the partisans of Russia and Austria, Serbia was nearly torn in half. After incessant quarrels with his Russian wife, Milan in 1888 divorced her—more or less irregularly—and in the following year threw up the game and abdicated in favour of his only legitimate child, the ill-fated Alexander who was then but fourteen.

Torn this way and that by his parents' quarrels, brought up in the notoriously corrupt court of Belgrade and by nature, according to the accounts of those who knew him, of but poor mental calibre, Alexander is, perhaps, to be as much pitied as blamed. His nerves, so Mr. Chedo Miyatovitch told me, never recovered from the shock of a boating accident when young. He was the last and decadent scion of the Obrenovitches and was marked down from his accession.

Vladan Georgevitch, who was Prime Minister of Serbia from 1897 till 1900, in his book The End of a Dynasty, throws much light on the events that led up to the final catastrophe. It is highly significant that after its publication he was sentenced to six months' imprisonment, not for libel or false statements, but "on a charge of having acted injuriously to Serbia by publishing State secrets." His account is therefore in all probability correct. He begins by relating Prince Alexander's visit to Montenegro shortly after the termination of the Regency. Here the astute Prince Nikola tried to persuade him to marry Princess Xenia. Princess Zorka was dead; Prince Nikola had quarrelled rather badly with his son-in-law, Petar Karageorgevitch, and, it would appear, meant to lose no chance of obtaining a matrimonial alliance with any and every possible claimant to the Serbian throne. Alexander would not consent to the match, and stated that his object in visiting Montenegro was to bring about a political alliance between that country and Serbia in order to defend Serb schools and churches in Turkish territory and generally protect Serb interests. This Nikola refused unless the said lands were definitely partitioned into "spheres of interest" and Prizren were included in his own. He was already determined to occupy the throne of Stefan Dushan. The two ministers who accompanied Alexander supported this claim. "I tell you," says Alexander, "these two men when with me at Cetinje acted not as Ministers of mine, but as Ministers of the Prince of Montenegro." He denounced such a division of the territory and the negotiations broke off. The visit to Montenegro was a failure.

Some years afterwards in Montenegro I was told triumphantly that the match would not have been at all suitable for Princess Xenia and that her father had refused it on the grounds that "no King of Serbia has yet died except by murder, or in exile." But the death of Alexander was then already planned—though I of course did not know it—and Alexander's version of the affair is more probably correct.

In 1897 the nets began to close round the wretched youth. Russia made up her long quarrel with Bulgaria and enlisted a new foe to the Obrenovitches—Prince Ferdinand. She had long refused to recognize this astute and capable Prince who was rapidly raising Bulgaria to an important position in the Balkans, and now decided to make use of him. The benefits might be mutual, for without Russian support Ferdinand could not hope to reconstruct the Big Bulgaria of the Middle Ages. Russia cynically used either Bulgaria or Serbia as best suited her purpose at the moment. In August of the same year Russia further strengthened her position by her alliance with France, who at once obediently ranged herself against the Obrenovitches.

In the following October, Alexander appointed Vladan Georgevitch Prime Minister, and bade him form a Government. The merits or demerits of this Government we need not trouble about. What is of interest is that it was at once attacked by the French Press. The Temps accused Vladan of secret understandings with Goluchowsky and Kallay, before forming it. The Courier de Soir thought that "such a policy is the result of the Triple Alliance and is an offence to the balance of Europe." Serbia apparently was to be used as the determining weight on the European scales. La Souverainte went farther and said boldly: "The moment has come when Tsar Nicholas should show the same firmness of character as his father showed to the Battenburg and Coburg in Bulgaria!" The Nova Vremya declared "that the new Government clearly meant to bring Serbia into economic dependence on Austria-Hungary."

And most of the newspapers of Europe announced the fact that the Tsar had granted an audience to Prince Petar Karageorgevitch and had conversed with him on the critical state of Serbia. Vladan then recommended to Alexander the rash plan of inviting General von der Golte to xmdertake the reform of the Serb Army as he had done that of Turkey. The plan pleased von der Goltz, but was dropped in consequence of the violent anti-Serb campaign which it aroused in the French Press. The Serb Minister in Paris, Garashanin, tried to buy some of the French papers, but had to report to his Government that this was impossible so long as Serbia was hostile to Russia.

France was paying the Russian piper—but it was the piper that called the tune. The Russo-French policy of ringing in the Central Powers was already aimed at.

The wretched Alexander, not knowing whom to trust, nor where to turn, then begged his exiled father to return from Austria and take command of the army.

Milan did so and Russia was more than ever furious.

Warnings were now frequently received that Russia was planning the deaths of both Milan and Alexander. One such warning was sent by the Berlin Foreign Office.

In May 1898 Nikola Pashitch, who had been working an anti-Obrenovitch propaganda in Bulgaria, was again in Serbia, and led the Radical party in the general elections. The Government, however, won by a large majority.

His work in Bulgaria seems to have been effective for in June the Serb Minister to Sofia sent in a very important report to his Government:

1. That Russia was determined that Milan should leave Serbia.

2. That Prince Ferdinand was willing to support Russia in this way by any means—even bad ones.

3. That the Princes of Montenegro and Bulgaria were co-operating.

Shortly afterwards Ferdinand of Bulgaria, Nikola of Montenegro, the Russian Minister and the Bulgarian diplomatic agent to Cetinje all met at Abbazia. And Ferdinand is reported to have promised Nikola the support of his army to overthrow the Obrenovitches with a view to finally uniting Montenegro, Serbia, Bosnia and the Herzegovina into one state with Nikola as head. Nikola began to sow the ground by starting a newspaper which attacked Austrian policy in Bosnia severely.

This is a most important turning point in Balkan history, and we shall see many results.

Mr. J. D. Bourchier, whose knowledge of Bulgarian affairs is unrivalled, has further told me that not only did Montenegro and Bulgaria work together for a long while, but Bulgaria also supplied Montenegro with much money—she was, in fact, another of the many States who have put money into Montenegro—and lost it.

Things soon began to move. Prince Nikola got in touch with the Radical party in Serbia and they began to prepare the downfall of the Obrenovitches.

Bulgaria refortified her Serbian frontier. The Narodni Listy of Prague described Prince Nikola as the only true Serb upon a throne.

King Alexander proposed at this time to visit Queen Victoria, but was informed by Lord Salisbury that Her Majesty's health had already obliged her to decline other visits and she was therefore unable to receive him.

The Serb Government then complained that Queen Victoria had conferred a high Order on Prince Nikola, who was but a vassal of Russia, and had given nothing to the King of Serbia. Some papers even declared she had shown preference to Nikola precisely on account of his pro-Russian tendencies.

Russia showed her feelings plainly. The Tsar at a reception spoke sharply to the Serbian Minister and ignored the new Serbian military attache who had come to be presented.

Tension between Serbia and Montenegro was now acute. Large numbers of Montenegrins had been emigrating into Serbia attracted by the better livelihood to be obtained. The Serb Government in October 1898 formally notified Montenegro that this immigration must cease. No more land was available for Montenegrins.

The Magyar Orsyagu went so far as to say "Montenegrin agents wander over Serbia with their propaganda and Serbia has therefore forbidden the further settlement of Montenegrins in Serbia." Pashitch again came to the fore and was sentenced to nine months' imprisonment for publishing an offensive letter to the ex-King Milan. And in November a plot, alleged to be Bulgaro-Montenegrin, against Milan, was discovered.

Russia was furious that Milan, in spite of these warnings, remained in Serbia.

And in July 1899 he was fired at and slightly wounded. Milan insisted on martial law being proclaimed and many arrests were made. The would-be assassin was a young Bosnian—Knezhevitch. The Times spoke of the conspiracy as a Russo-Bulgarian one. It is stated to have been planned in Bucarest by Arsene Karageorgevitch and a Russian agent.

Pashitch, who since 1888 had been in close connection with the Karageorges, was accused of complicity and Milan insisted on his execution. His guilt was by no means proved and he was finally sentenced to five years' imprisonment, but at once pardoned by Alexander. In reply he telegraphed, "I hasten in a moment so happy and so solemn for my family, to lay before your Majesty my sincere and humble gratitude for the very great mercy which you, Sire, have shown me from the height of your throne. I declare to you, Sire, that I will, in future . . . give my whole soul to strengthening that order in the State which your Majesty introduced in 1897, from which, thanks to your distinguished father, King Milan, as commander-in-Chief of the Army, the country has derived so much benefit." He further promised to put the remainder of his life to the exclusive service of King Alexander and his country, and ends with, "Long live the hope of the Serb nation, your Majesty our Lord and King Alexander!" signed, "The most sincere and devoted servant of the House of Obrenovitch and the throne of your Majesty, Nikola Pashitch." This amazing telegram caused consternation in Russia. And well it might. The annals of crime scarcely contain a more gross example of perjury.

We now enter upon the last act of the sordid drama. For several years Alexander had kept a mistress, Madame Draga Maschin, nee Lungevitza, the widow of a Serbian officer. She was a handsome woman, considerably older than Alexander, and possessed such a hold over him that the more credulous of the Serbs—including an ex-Minister to the Court at St. James's—believed that she had bewitched him by means of a spell made by a gypsy woman who had chopped some of Draga's hair fine and made a mixture which she put into Alexander's food. Only by magic, I have been assured, could such results have been obtained. Alexander "was crazy about her."

The Serbs are not particular about morals by any means. But this liaison was a national misfortune Especially to all supporters of the Obrenovitches. Not only under these circumstances could there be no legitimate heir to the throne but a matrimonial alliance with one of the Great Powers was desired by the country. By 1899 the situation had become acute. The spectacle of Alexander waiting in the street till Draga chose to admit him was a national scandal.

He was repeatedly approached on the subject, both by his father and the nation, but Draga held him in a firm grip. Enmeshed as he knew he was in hostile intrigues, surrounded by spies and traitors, and himself a fool at best, maybe the luckless youth regarded her indeed as the one human creature for whom he had any affection or trust. Be that as it may Alexander, under her influence, promised his father and Vladan Georgevitch that he would marry if a suitable match could be arranged. He persuaded them to leave the country to visit a foreign Court with this object, and so soon as they had gone he publicly and formally announced his betrothal to Draga, and informed his father of the fact by letter. Milan, horrified, replied that the dynasty would not survive the blow, and that even a mere lieutenant would scorn such a match.

The Russian Minister Mansurov, however, called at once to offer his congratulations to Alexander, and called also upon Draga. It has even been suggested that Russia arranged the affair, and that Draga was her tool. This is, however, improbable.

It was more likely the achievement of an ambitious and most foolish woman. But that Russia jumped at it as the very best means of compassing Alexander's ruin cannot be doubted, for no less a person than the Tsar accepted the post of Kum (Godfather) at the wedding, thus publicly announcing his approval of the marriage at which he was represented by a proxy, when it was celebrated at Belgrade shortly afterwards. Alexander never saw either of his parents again. Milan resigned the command of the army and retired to Austria and his stormy and variegated career came to an end in the following year. He was only forty-seven at the time of his death, but had compressed into those years an amount of adventure unusual even in the Balkans.

Alexander's marriage, as doubtless foreseen by Russia, soon proved disastrous. Draga, having achieved her ambition and mounted the throne, showed none of the ability of Theodora. Clever enough to captivate the feeble-minded Alexander, she was too stupid to realize that her only chance lay in gaining the popularity of the people who were none too well disposed. With incredible folly, before in any way consolidating her position, she formed a plot worthy only of a second-rate cinematograph, pretended pregnancy and planned to foist a "supposititious child" upon the nation. A plan, foredoomed by its folly to failure, which brought down on her the contempt and ridicule not only of Serbia, but of all Europe. Such was the history of Serbia up to the date when I plunged into it and found it on the verge of a crisis.

CHAPTER SEVEN
1903 AND WHAT HAPPENED

For Leagues within a State are ever pernicious to Monarchic.

Early in 1903 I received an invitation to stay with certain of the partisans of the Karageorgevitches in Serbia. The "something" that was to happen had not yet come to pass. My sister wished to travel with me, and my experiences of last year were not such as to lead me to take her to Serbia. One takes risks without hesitation when alone, into which one cannot drag a comrade. We went to Montenegro. It was hot even at Cetinje. We were resting in one of the back bedrooms of the hotel on the afternoon of June 11, when there came a loud knocking at the door and the voice of Ivan, the waiter, crying "telegramme, telegramme." We jumped up at once, fearing bad news, and Stvane cried excitedly as I opened the door, "The King and Queen of Serbia are both dead!" My brain re-acted instantly. The "something" had happened, the crisis had come. Without pausing a minute to reflect, I said: "Then Petar Karageorgevitch will be King!"

"No, no," cried Ivan; "Every one says it will be our Prince Mirko!" "No," said I decidedly, for I was quite certain, "It will not be Mirko"; and I asked "How did they die?"

"God knows," said he; "some say they quarrelled and one shot the other and then committed suicide. And it will be Mirko, Gospodjitza. There was an article in the paper about it only the other day." He ran off and fetched a paper. I regret now that I took no note what paper it was, but it certainly contained an article naming Mirko as heir to the Serb throne, supposing Alexander to die without issue.

Cetinje was excited as never before. Ordinarily, it lived on one telegram a day from the Correspondenz Bureau. Now the boys ran to and fro the telegraph office and bulletins poured in. One of the earliest stated that the King and Queen had died suddenly, cause of death unknown, but bullet wounds found in the bodies.

Later came full details. According to Belgrade papers a revolution had been planning for three months and there were secret committees all over the country; that the decision to slaughter both King and Queen had been taken by the Corps of Officers at Belgrade, and the work entrusted to the 6th Infantry Regiment; that the band of assassins gained access to the Palace at 11 p.m.; and, as the King refused to open the door of his bedroom, it was blown in by Colonel Naumovitch with a dynamite cartridge the explosion of which killed its user.

What followed was a shambles. The bodies of the victims, still breathing, but riddled with bullets, were pitched from the window. Draga, fortunately for herself, expired at once. But the luckless Alexander lingered till 4 a.m.

According to current report the assassins, drunk with wine and blood, fell on the bodies and defiled them most filthily, even cutting portions of Draga's skin, which they dried and preserved as trophies. An officer later showed a friend of mine a bit which he kept in his pocket book.

Alexander was a degenerate. His removal may have been desirable. But not even in Dahomey could it have been accomplished with more repulsive savagery. And the Russian Minister, whose house was opposite the Konak, calmly watched the events from his window. Having wreaked their fury on the bodies, the assassins rushed to kill also Draga's two brothers, one of whom it was rumoured was to be declared heir to the throne by Alexander. Some seventeen others were murdered that night and many wounded. These details we learned later.

The afternoon of the 11th passed with excitement enough. Evening came and we went in to dinner. Upon each table, in place of the usual programme of the evening's performance at the theatre, lay a black edged sheet of paper informing us that the Serbian travelling company then playing in Cetinje "in consequence of the death of our beloved Sovereign King Alexander" had closed the theatre till further notice. The tourist table was occupied solely by my sister and myself; the diplomatic one solely by Mr. Shipley, who was temporarily representing England, and Count Bollati, the Italian Minister. Dinner passed in complete silence. I was aching to have the opinion of the exalted persons at the other table on the startling news, but dared not broach so delicate a subject. The end came however. The servants withdrew and Count Bollati turned to me and said suddenly:

"Now, Mademoiselle, you know these countries What do you think of the situation?"

"Petar Karageorgevitch will be made King."

"People here all say it will be Mirko," said Mr. Shipley.

Count Bollati maintained it would be a republic. I told them the facts I had learned in Serbia, and said that Petar was practically a certainty. They were both much interested.

"In any case," said Mr. Shipley, "I should advise you to say nothing about it here. They are all for Mirko and you may get yourself into trouble."

"I have never seen them so excited," put in the Count.

"You are too late," said I; "I've told them already, Mirko has not a chance. He had better know the truth. You will see in a few days."

Both gentlemen expressed horror at the crudity of my methods. As a matter of fact a good deal of international misunderstanding could be avoided if the truth were always blurted out at once. The Italian thought I was stark mad. The Englishman, having a sense of humour, laughed and said, as I well recollect: "Your mission in life seems to be to tell home truths to the Balkans. It is very good for them. But I wonder that they put up with it." Both gentlemen commented on the grim matter-of-factness of the telegrams. "Business carried on usual during the alterations," said Bollati. His blood was badly curdled by the fact that when he was in Belgrade he was well acquainted with Colonel Mashin, the ill-fated Draga's brother-in-law, who—according to the telegrams—had finished her off with a hatchet.

"And I have shaken hands with him!" said Bollati, disgustedly. Mr. Shipley suggested that as I had first hand information I had better write an article or two for the English papers; which I did at once. "It is an ill wind that blows nobody any good." I had written my first Balkan book and hawked it unsuccessfully round the publishers, who told me that as nobody in England took the faintest interest in the Balkans, they could not take it, though they kindly added that as travels went it was not so bad. But the assassination of a King appealed at once to the great heart of the British people and I sold that book as an immediate result. This, by the way.

I came down early next morning to post the articles written overnight, and found a whole crowd of officers and intelligentsia (for in no land are these necessarily the same) around the hotel door. Vuko Vuletitch, the hotelier, in his green, red-embroidered coat, was haranguing them from the doorstep with the latest telegram in his hand. Loud and lively discussion filled the air.

Vuko waved his hand as I approached. "Here," he said, "is the Gospodjitza who says Petar Karageorgevitch will be King." I repeated my belief cheerfully: "Your man is elected!" cried Vuko, holding up the telegram. The news had arrived. Mirko's hopes were hopelessly dashed. The accuracy of my information caused a small sensation and I acquired a great reputation for political knowledge. Vuko never failed to ask me in future what I made of the situation.

It was the morning of the 12th when this news came in. Officially, Petar was not elected till the 15th, and then not by a really legal method. The military gang having chosen him, summoned a Parliament which had already been legally dissolved and was therefore non-existent, and caused it to ratify the choice. Whence it has been maintained by many that King Petar never was legally elected.

The 12th, 13th, and 14th passed quietly, though there was a certain air of disappointment. More details came in. Murder is bound to be unlovely. This one was peculiarly so. One fact was prominent. And that was that although many persons expressed horror of the methods and condemned the treachery of officers who had sworn fealty, yet Cetinje as a whole regarded the affair as a blessing. Not only was the populace pleased, but, with childish ignorance of the Western point of view (and at that time West Europe was really very fairly civilized), actually expected Europe to rejoice with them. It was a cleansing of the Temple; a casting out of abominations.

And so ready was every one with a candidate for the throne that it was impossible not to suspect that there had been foreknowledge of the event.

Subsequent enquiry through persons connected with the post office revealed to me the fact that a most unusual amount of cypher telegrams had been buzzing between Belgrade and Cetinje immediately before the bloody climax.

Petar Karageorgevitch, we learnt by telegram, was dwelling in a "modest apartment" in Geneva, and was quite unable to furnish journalists with any information. The Paris Havas found Bozhidar Karageorgevitch more communicative and published an interview in which he pleasantly stated that the event had caused him no surprise as he had foreseen it ever since the marriage with Draga.

On the 14th I drove down to Cattaro with my sister to see her off by steamer. Cattaro, as usual in the summer, lay panting at the water's edge. No more news; any amount of gossip; the Petrovitches were tottering, said some; Prince Mirko had lately fought a duel upon Austrian territory with his brother, Prince Danilo; they would certainly fight for the throne. The Austrian papers were full of "digs" at the Petrovitches. I arrived back at Cetinje on the evening of the 15th to find it beflagged and rows of tallow candles stuck along my bedroom window for the coming illuminations. A telegram had announced the election by the Shkupstina of "our son-in-law" and his accession had already been celebrated by a service at the Monastery Church and a military parade.

"Bogati!" cried Vuko to me, "you are better informed than all the diplomatists." He added that there was to be a gala performance at the theatre. I flew to the Zetski Dom. Not a seat was to be had. "If you don't mind a crowd," said the ever-obliging Vuko, "you can come into my box." And he hurried up dinner that we might all be in time. The diplomatic table complimented me on having "spotted the winner," and on either table lay a festive programme informing us that the Serbian theatrical company, which had abruptly shed its mourning, was giving a gala performance "in honour of the accession of our beloved King Petar."

The theatre was packed from roof to floor. The performance opened with a tableau—a portrait of Petar I, bewreathed and beflagged. A speech was made. There were shouts of "Zhivio!" ("Long life to him!" an eminently suitable remark under the circumstances). The whole house cheered. I felt like an accessory after the act. Up in the Royal Box, the only representatives of the reigning house, sat Prince Mirko and his wife. I watched his stony countenance. But for the devil and Holy Russia, we might have been shouting "Zhivio Kralj Mirko!" I wondered if it hurt badly and felt sorry for him, for I have been ploughed in an exam, myself.

We were a tight fit in our box. Gazivoda, head of the police at Podgoritza and brother-in-law to Vuko, was there. He, too, was assassinated a few years afterwards. And there was a crowd of Vuko's pretty daughters. The eldest, still a pupil at the Russian Girls' School (Russia Institut) was shuddering with horror at the crime. "Poor Queen, poor Queen!" she muttered at intervals, "she was still alive when they threw her from the window. If I had been there I would have wept on her grave." She was but fifteen, and it was her initiation into those Balkan politics in which, as

Madame Rizoff, she was herself later to play a part.

We shouted our last "Zhivio!" The play was over. Petar was King and the Near East had entered upon a new path which led as yet none knew whither.

I noted in my diary, "Will the army, now that it has taken the bit between its teeth, be more than King Petar can manage?" In truth no greater curse can befall a land than to be ruled by its own army. A nation that chooses to be dictated to by its military has sunk low indeed.

Cetinje showed signs of relapsing into dullness. I started on a tour up country. The country I have described elsewhere, and will deal now only with the political situation.

There were no roads then over the mountains and travelling was very severe work. At every halt—for rest in the midday heat, or a cup of black coffee to stimulate me for another two or three hours on horse and on foot—the Serbian murders were the one topic. Boshko, my guide, with the latest news from Podgoritza was in great request and a proud man. Everywhere the crime was approved. The women raged against Draga, even saying "She ought to lie under the accursed stone heap!"—a reminiscence of the fact that stoning to death was actually inflicted in Montenegro in the old days, upon women for sexual immorality. Vuk Vrchevitch records a case as late as 1770. And in quite recent times a husband still, if he thought fit, would cut off the nose of his wife if he suspected her of infidelity. No man, it was explained to me cheerfully, was ever likely to make love to her again after that.

West Europe was, in 1903, quite ignorant of the state of primitive savagery from which the South Slavs were but beginning to rise. Distinguished scientists travelled far afield and recorded the head hunters of New Guinea. But the ballads of Grand Voyvoda Mirko—King Nikola of Montenegro's father—gloating over slaughter, telling of the piles of severed heads, of the triumph with which they were carried home on stakes and set around the village, and the best reserved as an offering to Nikola himself for the adornment of Cetinje; and the stripping and mutilating of the dead foe, give us a vivid picture of life resembling rather that of Dahomey, than Europe in 1860.

In the breast of every human being there is a wolf. It may sleep for several generations. But it wakes at last and howls for blood. In the breast of the South Slav, both Serb and Montenegrin, it has not yet even thought of slumbering. Montenegro approved the crime.

It was to lead to "something"—indefinite, mysterious. Serdar Jovo Martinovitch ruled in Kolashin, a strong man then, who rode the clansmen on a strong curb. He had come up there as governor about four years ago on account of the constant fighting, not only on the border, but between the Montenegrin plemena (tribes). The latter he had put a stop to. Thirty years ago he assured me the clans were in a state of savagery. His own life was very Balkan; many women figured in it; and to escape blood-vengeance he had fled—with one of them—to Bulgaria, where he had served long years in the Bulgarian Army; and had returned to Montenegro only after the affair had blown over. Of the Bulgars he spoke in the highest terms.

At Andrijevitza, to which he passed me on, great excitement reigned. Some great event was expected at no distant date. I was told that it was now impossible for me to go to Gusinje, but that next year all would be different. That they were well informed about the Bulgar rising which was about to take place in Macedonia I cannot, in the light of what followed, doubt. Prince Danilo's birthday was feted magnificently with barbaric dances by firelight, national songs and an ocean of rakija. We drank to the Prince and wished him soon on the throne of Prizren, a wish which at that time every Montenegrin expected to see soon realized. The reign of the Turk, I was told, was all but over. I remarked that this had been said for a hundred years at least and was told that the end must come some time, and that I should see it soon.

Meanwhile, the' authorities of Andrijevitza were extremely anxious to get me to go across the border. Though I was not aware of it at the time, they meant to use me to cover a spy. That the expedition was dangerous I knew. The Ipek district had scarcely been penetrated by a foreigner for fifteen years, and was a forbidden one. The danger I did not mind. My two months' liberty each year were like Judas's fabled visit to the iceberg—but they made the endless vista of grey imprisonment at home the more intolerable. And a bullet would have been a short way out. I made the expedition and gained thereby a reputation for courage which in truth I little deserved.

As I was being used for political purposes, though I did not know it, I was, of course, shown only the Great Serbian view of things. The plan was carefully laid. My guide, who was disguised, spoke Albanian and some Turkish.

At Berani, our first stopping place, just over the Turkish border, I met the first objectors to the murders—the monks at the very ancient Church of Giurgevi Stupovi and a little company consisting of a wild-looking priest clad as a peasant and with a heavy revolver in his sash, and a couple of schoolmasters very heavily depressed. They, too, had evidently expected "something" to happen soon. I gathered, in fact, that an attack on the Turk had been planned, and now with this revolution on their hands the Serbs would be able to do nothing. In the town, however, I met the nephew of Voyvoda Gavro, then Montenegro's Minister for Foreign Affairs—a decadent type of youth on vacation from Constantinople, where he was at college. For the Montenegrins, though always expressing a hatred of all things Turkish, have never missed an opportunity of sending their sons for Education—gratis—to the enemy's capital. His conversation—and he was most anxious to pose as very "modern"—showed that Constantinople is not a very nice place for boys to go to school in. He was furious with me for daring to criticize the Serbian murders. He said no one but an enemy of the Serb people would do so, and threatened to denounce me to his uncle. Leaving Berani I plunged into Albanian territory. This land, fondly called by the Serbs "Stara Srbija," Old Serbia, was in point of fact Serb only for a short period.

The Serbs, or rather their Slav ancestors, poured into the Balkan Peninsula in vast hordes in the sixth and seventh centuries and overwhelmed the original inhabitant, the Albanian. But though they tried hard, they did not succeed in exterminating him. The original inhabitant, we may almost say, never is exterminated. The Albanian was a peculiarly tough customer. He withdrew to the fastnesses of the mountains, fought with his back to the wall, so to speak, and in defiance of efforts to Serbize him, retained his language and remained persistently attached to the Church of Rome. Serbia reached her highest point of glory under Tsar Stefan Dushan. On his death in 1356, leaving no heir capable of ruling the heterogeneous empire he had thrown together in the twenty years of his reign, the rival feudal chieftains of Serbia fought with each other for power and the empire was soon torn to pieces. Albania split off from the mass almost at once, and was a separate principality under the Balsha chiefs. And from that time Albania has never again fallen completely under Serb power. The Turkish conquest crushed the Serbs and the Albanians grew in power. We cannot here detail the history, suffice it to say that in 1679 the Serbs of Kosovo, finding themselves unable to resist the advance of the Albanians and the power of the Turks, evacuated that district. Led by Arsenius, the Serb Patriarch, thousands of families emigrated into Austria, who saved the Serb people. Since then the Albanians had poured down and resettled in the land of their ancestors.

From Berani our route lay through Arnaoutluk. We passed through Rugova; nor did I know till afterwards that this was reputed one of the most dangerous districts in Turkish territory and that no European traveller had been that way for some twenty years. There was a rough wooden mosque by the wayside. We halted. The people were friendly enough and some one gave us coffee. I little thought 'that in a few years time the place would be the scene of a hideous massacre by the Montenegrins modelled on the Moslem-slaying of Vladika Danilo. We reached Ipek after some sixteen hours of very severe travel and knocked at the gates of the Patriarchia long after nightfall—the very place whose Bishop had led the retreating Serb population into Austria over two centuries before.

My arrival was a thunderbolt, both for the Patriarchia and the Turkish authorities, who had forbidden the entry of strangers into the district and closed the main routes to it, but had never imagined any one would be so crazy as to drop in over the Montenegrin frontier by way of Rugova.

The whole district was under military occupation. About thirty thousand Turkish troops were camped in the neighbourhood, and I learnt that a great deal of fighting had recently taken place. Briefly, the position was that for the past two and a half centuries the Albanians had been steadily re-occupying the lands of their Illyrian ancestors and pressing back the small remaining Serb population, and since the time of the Treaty of Berlin had been struggling to wrest autonomy from the Turks and obtain recognition as a nation. The whole of this district had been included in the autonomous Albanian state proposed and mapped out by Lord Goschen and Lord Fitzmaurice in 1880. Ipek, Jakova and Prizren were centres of the Albanian League. The British Government report of August 1880 gives a very large Albanian majority to the whole district.

"The Albanians are numerically far superior to the Serbians, who are not numerous in Kosovopolje and the Sanjak of Novibazar. The Albanian population in the vilayet of Kosovo has lately (1880) been still further increased by the accession of many thousands of refugees from districts now, in virtue of the Treaty of Berlin, in Serbian possession and which prior to the late war were exclusively inhabited by descendants of the twelve Greg tribes, which at a remote period emigrated from Upper Albania."

A fundamental doctrine of the Great Serb Idea is a refusal to recognize that history existed before the creation of the Serb Empire, or even to admit that Balkan lands had owners before the arrival of the Serbs. Nothing infuriates a "Great Serbian" more than to suggest that if he insists on appealing to history another race has a prior claim to the land, and that in any case the Great Serbia of Stefan Dushan lasted but twenty years.

In pursuance of this theory that the greater part of the Balkan Peninsula is the birthright of the Serbs (who only began coming into these lands at the earliest in the fourth century A.D.) the Serbs behaved with hideous brutality to the inhabitants of the lands they annexed in 1878, and swarms of starving and destitute persons were hunted out, a large proportion of whom perished of want and exposure.

The hatred between Serb and Albanian was increased a hundredfold, and the survivors and their descendants struggled continuously to gain complete control over the lands still theirs and to regain, if possible, those that they had lost. The adoption of Lord Fitzmaurice's plan would have spared the Balkans and possibly Europe much bloodshed and suffering.

When I arrived on the scene in the summer of 1903 the Turks had sent a large punitive expedition to enforce the payment of cattle tax and, at the command of Europe, to introduce a new "reform" policy in Kosovo vilayet.

The Albanians were well aware that the so-called reforms meant ultimately the furtherance of Russia's pan-Slav schemes; that so long as even a handful of Serbs lived in a place Russia would claim it as Serb and enforce the claim to the best of her power; that the "reforms" meant, In fact, the introduction of Serb and Russian consulates, the erection of Serb schools and churches under Russian protection, the planting of Serb colonies and ultimate annexation. Russia was actively endeavouring to peg out fresh Serb claims. The Russian Consul at Mitrovitza, M. Shtcherbina, had taken part in a fight against the Albanians and was mortally wounded, it was reported, while he was serving a gun.

Russia, in fact, having already made sure of the removal of the pro-Austrian

Obrenovitches and being in close touch with Montenegro and Bulgaria was planning another coup in the Balkans. Albania was resisting it. The Turks under pressure from the Powers were striving to smooth matters down sufficiently to stave off the final crash that drew ever nearer. They arrested a number of headmen and exacted some punishment for Shtcherbina's death. Though if a consul chooses to take part in a local fight he alone is responsible for results.

I had, in fact, arrived at a critical moment. The Turkish authorities telegraphed all over the country to know what they were to do about me. My Montenegrin guide showed anxiety also and begged me on no account to reveal his origin.

From a little hill belonging to the Patriarchia I saw the widespread Turkish camp on the plain.

The Igumen and the few monks and visitors gave me the Serb point of view. Because some six centuries ago the Sveti Kralj had been crowned in the church they regarded the land as rightfully and inalienably Serb. They looked forward to the arrival of Russian armies that should exterminate all that was not Serb. Shtcherbina to them was a Christ-like man who had died to save them, and they treasured his portrait. Russia, only the year before, had insisted on planting a Consul at Mitrovitza against the wish of the Turkish Government. Serb hopes had been raised. And it was possible that his presence had in fact caused the fight.

They admitted, however, that the Turks were responsible for the state of Albania, for they prohibited the formation of Albanian schools and made progress impossible; an independent Albania would be better.

News of the deaths of Alexander and Draga had reached Ipek, but no details, for Serbian papers could only be smuggled in with great difficulty. I gathered that the murders caused some anxiety, for a great movement against the Turks was planned, and owing to the upheaval in Serbia, perhaps Serbia would not now take part. As I was English they believed that the Turks would be obliged to permit me to travel further if I pleased. But they implored me on no account if I went further afield, to take the train as all the railways were shortly to be blown up.

Meanwhile the Turkish authorities could not decide what to do about me and called me to the Konak about my passport. There I waited hours. The place was crowded with applicants for permission to travel. Half-starved wretches begged leave to go to another district in search of harvest work and were denied. The Turks were in a nervous terror and doubtless knew a crisis was at hand. As I waited in the crowd a youth called to me across the room and said in French: "It is pity you were not here a week or two ago. You could have gone to Uskub and met all the foreign correspondents. Now they have all gone. I was dragoman to The Times correspondent. He has gone too. They think it is all over and it has not yet begun." He laughed. I was terrified lest any one present should know French. The boy declared they did not.

Finally, the Pasha refused me permission to go to Jakova as I had asked. And quite rightly, for fighting was still going on there between the troops and the Albanians. I was allowed only to visit the monastery of Detchani, a few hours' ride distant. Detchani is one of the difficulties in the drawing of a just frontier. Though in a district that is wholly Albanian, it is one of the monuments of the ancient Serb Empire and contains the shrine of the Sveti Kralj, King Stefan Detchanski, who was strangled in 1336 in his castle of Zvechani, it is said, by order of his son who succeeded him as the great Tsar Stefan Dushan, and was in his turn murdered in 1356.

St. Stefan Dechansld is accounted peculiarly holy and yet to work miracles. The Church, a fine one in pink and white marble, was built by an architect from Cattaro, and shows Venetian influence. A rude painting of the strangling of Stefan adorns his shrine. I thought of the sordid details of the death of. Serbia's latest King and the old world and the new seemed very close. Except in the matter of armament, things Balkan had changed but little in over five centuries.

A Turkish officer and some Nizams were quartered at the monastery, but the few monks and students there seemed oddly enough to have more faith in a guard of Moslem Albanians who lived near. They were expecting shortly the arrival of Russian monks from Mount Athos. Russia was, in fact, planting Russian subjects there for the express purpose of making an excuse for intervention. The young Turkish officer was very civil to me and offered to give me a military escort to enable me to return to Montenegro by another route. My disguised Montenegrin guide who was pledged to hand me over safe and sound to Voyvoda Lakitch at Andrijevitza signalled to me in great anxiety. Each day he remained on Turkish territory he risked detection and the loss of his life.

I returned therefore to the Patriarchia, recovered my passport from the Pasha and was given by him a mounted gendarme to ride with me as far as Berani. This fellow, a cheery Moslem Bosniak, loaded his rifle and kept a sharp look out. And a second gendarme accompanied us till we were through the pass. And both vowed that a few months ago they wouldn't have come with less than thirty men; Albanians behind every rock and piff paff, a bullet in your living heart before you knew where you were. They wondered much that I had made the journey with only one old zaptieh. Still more, that I had been allowed to come at all.

Berani received me with enthusiasm. Nor had my cheery Turkish gendarme an idea that my guide was a Montenegrin till he took off his fez at the frontier. Then the gendarme slapped his thigh, roared with laughter and treated it as a good joke.

The said guide's relief on being once more in his own territory showed clearly what the risks had been for him.

Andrijevitza gave us quite an ovation. Countless questions as to the number and position of the Turkish Army were poured out. My guide had fulfilled his task. I was reckoned a hero. What hold the Voyvoda had over the Kaimmakam of Berani I never ascertained. But it was the Voyvoda's letter to the Kaimmakam that got me over the border. All that I gathered was that I had been made use of for political purposes and successfully come through what every one considered a very dangerous enterprise. The same people who had urged me to go now addressed me as "one that could look death in the eyes."

Had I met death, what explanation would they have offered to the questions that must have cropped up over the death of a British subject?

A number of schoolmasters had gathered in Andrijevitza for their holidays. Many of them were educated in Belgrade and these were especially of the opinion that the murder of Alexander and Draga was a splendid thing for Serbia, and when I said it might bring misfortune were not at all pleased. Even persons who at first said the murder was horrible now said since it was done it was well done. The Voyvoda and the Kapetan told me that every country in Europe had accepted King Petar except England and that the Serb Minister had been sent from London. "England," they declared, "has often been our enemy." They hoped that good, however, would result from my journey.

The whole of my return to Cetinje was a sort of triumphal progress. Jovo Martinovitch, the Serdar at Kolashin, was delighted to hear of the Ipek expedition, but admitted frankly that he had not dared propose it himself. Voyvoda Lakitch, he said, was well informed and no doubt knew the moment at which it could be safely attempted. Every place I passed through was of opinion something was about to happen soon. Next year the route to Gusinje would be open. At Podgoritza I was received by the Governor Spiro Popovitch and taken for a drive round the town.

I arrived at Cetinje in time for dinner and appeared in my usual corner. Mr. Shipley and Count Bollati hailed me at once saying that they thought I was about due. Where had I been? "Ipek," said I.

The effect on the diplomatic table was even more startling than upon Montenegro. "But the route is closed!" said every one. I assured them I had nevertheless been through it, and Mr. Shipley said if he had had any idea I was going to attempt such a thing he would have telegraphed all over the place and stopped it. At the same time he admitted, "I rather thought you were up to something," and gave me a piece of excellent advice, which I have always followed, which was "Never consult a British representative if you want to make a risky journey." Really, he was quite pleased about it and crowed over the rest of the diplomatic table, that the British could get to places that nobody else could. I received a note next morning from the Bulgarian diplomatic agent praying for an interview.

He had not been long in Cetinje, but later became one of the best known Balkan politicians. For he was Monsieur Rizoff, who, as Bulgar Minister at Berlin, played a considerable part in the Balkan politics of the great war.

He was a Macedonian Bulgar born at Resna, a typical Bulgar in build and cast of countenance, and a shrewd and clever intriguer. His excitement over my journey was great and he wanted every possible detail as to what were the Turkish forces and where they were situated. I told him that I understood a rising was planned. And he told me quite frankly that all was being prepared and a rising was to break out in Macedonia so soon as the crops were harvested.

I gathered that Rizoff himself was deeply mixed in the plot, an idea which was confirmed later on. For among the papers captured on a Bulgar comitadgi, Doreff, was a letter signed Grasdoff, describing his attempts to import arms through Montenegro, a plan he found impossible owing to the opposition of the Albanians in the territories that must be passed through. He visited Cetinje and reports: "I have spoken with M. Rizoff. With regard to the passage of men and munitions through Montenegro . . . even at the risk of losing his post he is disposed to give his assistance. But owing to the great difficulty the plan would meet in Albania we must renounce it. M. Rizoff hopes to be transferred soon to Belgrade. M. Rizoff having met M. Milakoff (PMilukoff) at Abbazia, has decided to continue the preparations for the organization until public opinion is convinced of the inutility of the (Turkish) reforms or until the term fixed—October 1905." Rizoff, in his talk with me, seemed hopeful of inducing European intervention.

Desultory fighting between Bulgar bands and Turkish troops had been going on in Macedonia throughout the year and many Bulgar peasants had fled from Macedonia into Bulgaria where fresh bands were prepared. A bad fight had taken place near Uskub, the Slav peasants of which were then recognized as Bulgars. But the Serbo-Bulgar struggle for Uskub—which, in truth, was then mainly Albanian—had begun.

Throughout Turkish territory, Greek, Serb and Bulgar pegged out their claims by the appointment of Bishops. Once a Bishop was successfully planted, a school with Serb, Greek or Bulgar masters at once sprang up and under the protection of one Great Power or another a fresh propaganda was started.

Every time a Bishop was moved by one side, it meant "Check to your King!" for the other. English Bishops talked piously of, and even prayed for "our Christian brethren of the Balkans," happily unaware that their Christian brethren were solely engaged in planning massacres or betraying the priests of a rival nationality to the Turks.

Serbia had just triumphantly cried "Check" to Bulgaria. In 1902 the Bishop of Uskub had died. The Serbs had had no Bishop in Turkish territory since the destruction of the Serb Bishopric of Ipek in 1766, which was the work of the Greek Patriarch rather than of the Turk. They now put in a claim. The Russian Vjedomosti published a learned article on the Ipek episcopate. The Porte regarded with dread the increasing power of the Bulgars. So did the Greek Patriarch at Constantinople. He of 1766 had aimed at the destruction of Slavdom. He of 1902 thought Serbia far less dangerous than Bulgaria. Firmilian was duly consecrated in June, 1902—a small straw showing that Russia had begun to blow Serbwards. She began to see she could not afford to have a powerful Bulgaria between herself and Constantinople.

At Cetinje I gathered that my jpurney to Ipek was mysteriously connected with "something" that was going to happen, and was interested to find that though the populace still heartily approved of the murder of Alexander and were filled with anger and dismay at England's rupture of diplomatic relations, the mighty of the land had realized that in public at any rate, it was as well to moderate their transports. King Nikola had been interviewed by several British and other journalists, had looked down his nose, lamented the wickedness of the Serbs and assured his interviewers that the Montenegrins were a far more virtuous people. Montenegro posed as the good boy of the Serb race, and as the gentlemen in question had not been present either at the thanksgiving in the church nor the gala performance at the Zetski Dom, they accepted the statement. Interviewing is, in fact, as yet the most efficient method by which journalism can spread erroneous reports.

I returned to London and read shortly afterwards in The Times that Macedonian troubles had settled down and recollecting that at Ipek I had learnt they had not yet begun I wrote and told The Times so. But it was far too well informed to print this statement. Had it not withdrawn its correspondent? And, as Rizoff had told me, a general Bulgar rising broke out all through Macedonia in August.

CHAPTER EIGHT
MACEDONIA, 1903-1904

THE Macedonian rising of 1903 was a purely Bulgar movement. As is invariably the case with such risings, it was ill-planned; and untrained peasants and irregular forces never in the long run have a chance against regulars. Its history has been told more than once in detail. I need only say that, instead of revolting simultaneously, one village rose after another, and the Turkish forces rode round, burning and pillaging in the usual fashion of punitive expeditions. Thousands of refugees fled into Bulgaria—thus emphasizing their nationality—and within the Bulgarian frontier organized komitadji bands, which carried on a desultory guerrilla war with the Turkish forces for some time. But it was soon obvious that, unless strongly aided by some outside Power, the rising must fail.

The most important point to notice now is that not a single one of these many revolutionaries fled to Serbia, or claimed that they were Serbs. They received arms, munitions and other help from Bulgaria, from Serbia nothing. They were rising to make Big Bulgaria, not Great Serbia. Serbia now claims these people as Serbs. She did not then extend one finger to assist them.

Milosh would not help the Greeks to obtain freedom because he did not want a large Greece. Similarly, Serbia and Greece in 1903 did nothing at all to aid the Macedonian revolutionaries. Most of us who have worked in old days to free the people from the Turkish yoke have now recognized what a farce that tale was. Not one of the Balkan people ever wanted to "free" their "Christian brethren" unless there was a chance of annexing them.

The Bulgar rising died down as winter came on and acute misery reigned in the devastated districts. In December, as one who had some experience of Balkan life, I was asked to go out on relief work under the newly formed Macedonian Relief

Committee. The invitation came to me as an immense surprise and with something like despair.

I had had my allotted two months' holiday. I had never before been asked to take part in any public work, and I wanted to go more than words could express. Circumstances had forced me to refuse so many openings. I was now forty, and this might be my last chance.

The Fates were kind, and I started for Salonika at a few days' notice, travelling almost straight through. Serbia was depressed and anxious, I gathered from my fellow travellers, as we passed through it. Bishop Firmilian, whose election to the see of Uskub the Serbs had with great difficulty obtained in June 1902, had just died. The train was full of ecclesiastics going to his funeral at Uskub. Russia had aided his election very considerably. It had coincided with Russia's support of Petar Karageorgevitch to the throne of Serbia, and all was part of Russia's new Balkan plans in which Serbia was to play a leading role.

Petar was not received by Europe. Firmilian was dead. Serbia was anxious. They buried Firmilian on Christmas Day in the morning, dreading the while lest they were burying the bishopric too, so far as Serbia was concerned—and I reached Salonika that night.

The tale of the relief work I have told elsewhere. I will now touch only on the racial questions.

In Monastir I tried to buy some Serb books, for I was hard at work studying the language, and had a dictionary and grammar with me. Serbian propaganda in Monastir was, however, then only in its infancy, and nothing but very elementary school books were to be got. The Bulgars had a big school and church. If any one had suggested that Monastir was Serb or ever likely to be Serb, folk would have thought him mad—or drunk. The pull was between Greek and Bulgar, there was no question of the Serbs. There was a large "Greek" population, both in town and country, but of these a very large proportion were Vlachs, many were South Albanians, others were Slavs. Few probably were genuine Greeks. But they belonged to the Greek branch of the Orthodox Church, and were reckoned Greek in the census. Those Slavs who called themselves Serbs, and the Serb schoolmasters who had come for propaganda purposes, all went to the Greek churches.

As for the hatred between the Greek and Bulgar Churches—it was so intense that no one from West Europe who has not lived in the land with it, can possibly realize it. The Greeks under Turkish rule had been head of the Orthodox Christians. True to Balkan type, they had dreamed only of the reconstruction of the Big Byzantine Empire, and had succeeded, by hooks and crooks innumerable, in suppressing and replacing the independent Serb and Bulgar Churches.

But Russia, when she began to scheme for Pan-Slavism, had no sympathy with Big Byzantium, and was aware that when you have an ignorant peasantry to deal with, a National Church is one of the best means for producing acute Nationalism. Under pressure from Russia, who was supported by other Powers—some of whom really believed they were aiding the cause of Christianity—the Sultan in 1870 created by firman the Bulgarian Exarchate. Far from "promoting Christianity" the result of this was that the Greek Patriarch excommunicated the Exarch and all his followers, and war was declared between the two Churches. They had no difference of any kind or sort as regards doctrine, dogma, or ceremonial. The difference was, and is, political and racial.

Never have people been more deluded than have been the pious of England about the Balkan Christians. In Montenegro I had heard all the stock tales of the Christian groaning under the Turkish yoke, and had believed them. I learnt in Macedonia the strange truth that, on the contrary, it was the Christian Churches of the Balkans that kept the Turk in power. Greek and Serb were both organizing komitadjis bands and sending them into Macedonia, not to "liberate Christian brethren"—no. That was the last thing they wanted. But to aid the Turk in suppressing "Christian brethren."

I condoled with the Bulgar Bishop of Ochrida on the terrible massacre of his flock by the Turks. He replied calmly that to him it had been a disappointment. He had expected quite half the population to have been killed, and then Europe would have been forced to intervene. Not a quarter had perished, and he expected it would all have to be done over again. "Next time there will be a great slaughter. All the foreign consuls and every foreigner will be killed too. It is their own fault." Big Bulgaria was to be constructed at any price.

I suggested that, had the Bulgars risen in 1897 when the Greek made war on the Turk, the whole land could have been freed. He replied indignantly, "I would rather the land should remain for ever under the Turk than that the Greeks should ever obtain a kilometre."

Later I met his rival, the Greek Bishop. He, too, loudly lamented the suffering of the wretched Christian under the Turkish yoke. To him I suggested that if Greece aided the Bulgar rising the Christian might now be freed. The mere idea horrified him. Sooner than allow those swine of Bulgars to obtain any territory he would prefer that the land should be for ever Turkish.

Such was the Christianity which at that time was being prayed for in English Churches.

Bulgars came to me at night and begged poison with which to kill Greeks. Greeks betrayed Bulgar komitadjis to the Turkish authorities. The Serbs sided with the Greeks. They had not then the smallest desire "to liberate their Slav brethren in Macedonia." No. They were doing all they could to prevent the Bulgars liberating them. Of Serb conduct a vivid picture is given by F. Wilson in a recently published book on the Serbs she looked after as refugees during the late war. She gives details taken down from the lips of a Serbian schoolmaster, who describes how he began Serb propaganda in Macedonia in 1900. "We got the children. We made them realize they were Serbs. We taught them their history. . . . Masters and children, we were like secret conspirators." When the Bulgars resisted this propaganda he describes how a gang of thirty Serbs "met in a darkened room and swore for each Serb killed to kill two Bulgars." Lots were drawn for who should go forth to assassinate. "We broke a loaf in two and each ate a piece. It was our sacrament. Our wine was the blood of the Bulgarians."

A small Serb school had recently been opened in Ochrida, and I was invited there to the Feast of St. Sava. The whole Serb population of Ochrida assembled. We were photographed together. Counting the Greek priest, the schoolmaster and his family, who were from Serbia, and myself, we were a party of some fifty people. Ochrida had a very mixed population. More than half were Moslems, most of them Albanians. Of the Christians the Bulgars formed the largest unit, but there were many Vlachs. These were reckoned as Greeks by the Greeks, but were already showing signs of claiming their own nationality. The Serbs were by far the smallest group, so small in fact as to be then negligible.

The Kaimmakam was an Albanian Moslem, Mehdi Bey, who kept the balance well under very difficult circumstances, and to-day is one of the leading Albanian

Nationalists. He asserted always that Ochrida should, of right, belong to Albania. Albanian it was indeed considered until the rise of the Russo-Bulgar movement. As late as 1860 we find the Lakes of Ochrida and Presba referred to as the Albanian Lakes by English travellers.

Through the winter of 1903-4 trouble simmered, arrests were made, murders occurred. I learnt the ethics of murder, which, in Macedonia, were simply: "When a Moslem kills a Moslem so much the better. When a Christian kills a Christian it is better not talked about, because people at home would not understand it; when a Christian kills a Moslem it is a holy and righteous act. When a Moslem kills a Christian it is an atrocity and should be telegraphed to all the papers."

In February 1904 the Russo-Japanese quarrel, which had been for some time growing hotter, burst into sudden war, and the whole complexion of Balkan affairs changed.

At the beginning the Bulgar leaders took it for granted that Russia was invincible, and anticipated speedy and complete victory for her. They were also supplied with false news, and refused to credit at first any Russian defeat. The Bishop of Ochrida was furious when I reported to him the sinking of the Petropalovski, and fiercely declared that the war was in reality an Anglo-Russian one, and that Japan was merely our tool.

When riding on relief work among the burnt villages it was easy to learn the great part Russia had taken in building up the Bulgar rising in Macedonia. The same tale was told in almost each. Once upon a time, not so very long ago, a rich, noble and generous gentleman had visited the village. He was richer than you could imagine; had paid even a white medjid for a cup of coffee; had called the headmen and the priest together and had asked them if they would like a church of their own in the village. And in due time the church had been built. Followed, a list of silver candlesticks, vestments, etc., presented by this same nobleman—the Russian Consul. The Turks had looted the treasures. Could I cause them to be restored? Sometimes the Consul had had an old church restored. Sometimes he had given money to establish a school. Always he stood for the people as something almost omnipotent.

In August M. Rostovsky, the Russian Consul at Monastir, had been murdered. There was nothing political in the affair. The Russian had imagined the land was already his, and that he was dealing with humble mouzhiks. He carried a heavy riding-whip and used it when he chose. I was told by an eye-witness that on one occasion he so savagely flogged a little boy who had ventured to hang on behind the consular carriage that a Turkish gendarme intervened. One day he lashed an Albanian soldier. The man waited his opportunity and shot Rostovsky dead on the main road near the Consulate. Russia treated the murder as a political one, and demanded and obtained apology and reparation of the Turkish Government. The Consul's remains were transported to the coast with full honours. All this for a Russian Consul in Turkey. Truly one man may steal a horse and another not look over a fence. Russia mobilized when Austria insisted on enquiry into the murder of an Archduke. So well was Rostovsky's funeral engineered that the native Slav peasants looked on him as a martyr to the sacred Slav cause, not as a man who had brought his punishment on himself.

Russia was not, however, the only Power in Monastir. It seethed with consuls. And the most prominent was Krai, the Austrian Consul-General, a very energetic and scheming man who "ran" Austria for all she was worth, and was a thorn in the side of the British Consul, whom he endeavoured to thwart at every turn. He persuaded the American missionaries, who were as innocent as babes about European politics, though they had passed thirty years in the Balkan Peninsula, that he and not the Englishman could best forward their interests, and they foolishly induced the American Government to transfer them and their schools to Austrian protection. And he pushed himself to the front always, declaring that he had far more power to aid the relief work and trying to make the English consult him instead of their own representative. This annoyed me, and I therefore never visited him at all. Up country among the revolted villages it was clear that the luckless people had been induced to rise by the belief that, as in 1877, Russia would come to their rescue! But as time passed, and Russia herself realized that the Japanese were a tough foe, it became more and more apparent that no further rising would take place in the spring. The Balkan Orthodox Lenten fast is so severe that a rising before Easter was always improbable. This Easter would see none.. I remembered with curious clearness the words of the Pole who gave me my first Serbian lessons. "Russia is corrupt right through. If there is a war—Russia will be like that!" and he threw a rag of paper into the basket scornfully. His has been a twice true prophecy. The Bulgarian Bishop of Ochrida still believed firmly in Russia's invincibility. Furious when I refused to have cartridges, etc., hidden in my room—which the Turks never searched—he turned on me and declared that England was not a Christian country and would be wiped out by Holy Russia, who had already taken half Japan and would soon take the rest and all India too.

By the middle of March I was quite certain no rising would take place. The Foreign Office in London still expected one, and notified all relief workers up country to wind up work and return. The others did, but I stayed and managed to ride right through Albania.

CHAPTER NINE
ALBANIA

"Where rougher climes a nobler race displayed."—BYRON.

Study of the Macedonian question had shown me that one of the most important factors of the Near Eastern question was the Albanian, and that the fact that he was always left out of consideration was a constant source of difficulty. The Balkan Committee had recently been formed, and I therefore decided to explore right through Albania, then but little known, in order to be able to acquire first-hand information as to the aspirations and ideas of the Albanians.

Throughout the relief work in Macedonia we had employed Albanians in every post of trust—as interpreters, guides, kavasses and clerks.

The depot of the British and Foreign Bible Society at Monastir was entirely in Albanian hands. The Albanian was invaluable to the Bible Society, and the Bible Society was invaluable to the Albanians.

Albania was suffering very heavily. Every other of the Sultan subject races had its own schools—schools that were, moreover, heavily subsidized from abroad. The Bulgarian schools in particular were surprisingly well equipped. Each school was an active centre of Nationalist propaganda. All the schoolmasters were revolutionary leaders. All were protected by various consulates which insisted on opening new schools and protested when any were interfered with.

Only when it was too late to stop the schools did the Turks perceive their danger. First came the school, then the revolution, then foreign intervention—and another piece of the Turkish' Empire was carved off. This had happened with Serbia, Greece and Bulgaria. The Turks resolved it should not happen in the case of Albania.

Albania was faced by two enemies. Not only the Turk dreaded the uprising of Albania, but Russia had already determined that the Balkan Peninsula was to be Slav and Orthodox. Greece as Orthodox might be tolerated. No one else.

The Turkish Government prohibited the printing and teaching of the Albanian language under most severe penalties. Turkish schools were established for the Moslem Albanians, and every effort made to bring up the children to believe they were Turks. In South Albania, where the Christians belong to the Orthodox Church, the Greeks were encouraged to found schools and work a Greek propaganda. The Turks hoped thus to prevent the rise of a strong national Albanian party. The Greek Patriarch went so far as to threaten with excommunication any Orthodox Albanian who should use the "accursed language" in church or school. In North Albania, where the whole of the Christians are Catholics, the Austrians, who had been charged by Europe with the duty of protecting the Catholics, established religious schools in which the teaching was in Albanian, and with which the Turkish Government was unable to interfere. The Jesuits, under Austrian protection, established a printing press in Scutari for the printing in Albanian of religious books. But this movement, being strictly Catholic, was confined to the North. It was, moreover, initiated with the intent of winning over the Northern Christians to Austria, and was directed rather to dividing the Christians from the Moslems and to weakening rather than strengthening the sense of Albanian nationality. The results of this we will trace later.

None of these efforts on the part of Albania's enemies killed the strong race instinct which has enabled the Albanian to survive the Roman Empire and the fall of Byzantium, outlive the fleeting mediaeval Empires of Bulgar and Serb, and finally emerge from the wreck of the mighty Ottoman Empire, retaining his language, his Customs and his primitive vigour—a rock over which the tides of invasion have washed in vain.

When threatened with loss of much Albanian territory by the terms of the Treaty of Berlin, the Albanians rose in force and demanded the recognition of their rights. There is a popular ballad in Albanian cursing Lord Beaconsfield, who went to Berlin in order to ruin Albania and give her lands to her pitiless enemy the Slav. The Treaty did nothing for Albania, but it caused the formation of the Albanian League and a national uprising by means of which the Albanians retained some of the said lands in spite of the Powers. This induced Abdul Hamid for a short time to relax the ban upon the Albanian language. At once national schools were opened, and books and papers came from Albanian presses. The Sultan, alarmed by the rapid success of the national movement, again prohibited the language. Schoolmasters were condemned to long terms of imprisonment. As much as fifteen years was the sentence that could be, and was, inflicted upon any one found in possession of an Albanian paper, and the Greek priests entered enthusiastically into the persecution. But Albanian was not killed. Leaders of the movement went to Bucarest, to Sofia, to Brussels, to London, and set to work. With much difficulty and at great personal risk books and papers published abroad were smuggled into Albania by Moslem Albanian officials, many of whom suffered exile and confiscation of all their property in consequence.

But there was another means by which printed Albanian was brought into the country. During the short interval when the printing of Albanian had been permitted, a translation of the Bible was made for the British and Foreign Bible Society. This Society had the permission of the Turkish Government to circulate its publications freely. When the interdict on the language was again imposed a nice question arose. Had the Society the right to circulate Albanian Testaments? The Turkish Government had not the least objection to the Gospels—only they must not be in Albanian. A constant war on the subject went on. The director of the Bible Depot in Monastir was an Albanian of high standing both as regards culture and energy. Grasping the fact that by means of these publications an immense national propaganda could be worked, he spared no pains, and by carefully selecting and training Albanian colporteurs, whose business it was to learn in which districts the officials were dangerous, where they were sympathetic, and where there were Nationalists willing themselves to risk receiving and distributing books, succeeded to a remarkable degree.

The Greeks, of course, opposed the work. A Greek Bishop is, in fact, declared to have denounced the dissemination of "the New Testament and other works contrary to the teaching of the Holy and Orthodox Church." Nevertheless it continued. It was with one of the Society's colporteurs that I rode through Albania. I was thus enabled everywhere to meet the Nationalists and to observe how very widely spread was the movement. The journey was extremely interesting, and as exciting in many respects as Borrow's Bible in Spain.

Leaving Monastir in a carriage and driving through much of the devastated Slav area I was greatly struck on descending into the plain land by Lake Malik to see the marked difference in the type of man that swung past on the road. I saw again the lean, strong figure and the easy stride of the Albanian, the man akin to my old friends of Scutari, a wholly different type from the Bulgar peasants among whom I had been working, and I felt at home.

Koritza, the home of Nationalism in the South, was my first halting-place. It was celebrated as being the only southern town in which there was still an Albanian school in spite of Turk and Greek. Like the schools of Scutari, it owed its existence to foreign protection. It was founded by the American Mission. Its plucky teacher, Miss Kyrias (now Mrs. Dako), conducted it with an ability and enthusiasm worthy of the highest praise. And in spite of the fact that attendance at the school meant that parents and children risked persecution by the Turk and excommunication by the Greek priest, yet the school was always full. The girls learned to read and write Albanian and taught their brothers. Many parents told me very earnestly how they longed for a boys' school too. The unfortunate master of the Albanian boys' school, permitted during the short period when the interdiction was removed, was still in prison serving his term of fifteen years. Could not England, I was asked, open a school? Now either a child must learn Greek or not learn to read at all. And the Greek teachers even told children that it was useless to pray in Albanian, for Christ was a Greek, and did not understand any other language.

Everywhere it was the same. Deputations came to me begging for schools. Even Orthodox priests, who were Albanian, ventured to explain that what they wanted was an independent Church. Roumania, Serbia, Greece, even Montenegro, each was free to elect its own clergy and to preach and conduct the service in its own language. At Leskoviki and Premeti folk were particularly urgent both for schools and church.

Not only among the Christians, but among the Moslems too, there was a marked sense of nationality. A very large proportion of the Moslems of the south were by no means, orthodox Moslems, but were members of one of the Dervish sects, the Bektashi, and as such suspect by the powers, at Constantinople. Between the Bektashi and the Christians there appeared to be no friction. Mosques were not very plentiful. I was assured by the Kaimmakam of Leskoviki that many of the Moslem officials were Bekiashifj and attended mosque only as a form without which they could not hold office. He was much puzzled about Christianity and asked me to explain why the Greeks and | Bulgars, who were both Christian, were always killing each other. "They say to Europe," he said, "that they object to Moslem rule. But they would certainly massacre each other if we went away. What good is this Christianity to them?" I told him I could no more understand it than he did.

The Bulgarian rising had had a strong repercussion in Albania. Our relief work was everywhere believed to be a British Government propaganda. Other Powers scattered money for their own purpose in Turkish territory. Why not Great Britain? It was a natural conclusion. Moreover the Bulgars themselves believed the help brought them was from England the Power. And the name Balkan Committee even was misleading. In the Near East a committee is a revolutionary committee, and consists of armed komitadjis. Times innumerable have I assured Balkan people of all races that the Balkan Committee did not run contraband rifles, but they have never believed it.

The Albanians everywhere asked me to assure Lord Lansdowne, then Secretary for Foreign Affairs, that if he would only supply them with as much money and as many arms as he had given the Bulgarians they would undertake to make a really successful rising.

As for our Albanian testaments, Moslems as well as Christians bought them; and the book of Genesis, with the tale of Potiphar's wife, sold like hot cakes.

At Berat, where there was a Greek Consul and a Turkish Kaimmakam, we were stopped by the police at the entrance of the town and all our Albanian books were taken from us. But no objection was made to those in Turkish and Greek. It was the language and not the contents of the book that was forbidden. But there were plenty of Nationalists in the town. It is noteworthy that though our errand was well known everywhere, and people hastened to tell "the Englishwoman" Albania's hopes and fears, not once did any one come to tell me that Albania wanted to be joined to Greece. It was always "Give us our own schools," "Free us from the Greek priest." At Elbasan we found a bale of publications awaiting us, sent from Monastir in anticipation of what would happen at Berat.

Here there was a charming old Albanian Mutasarrif, who did all he could to make my visit pleasant and begged me to send many English visitors. He had been Governor of Tripoli (now taken by Italy), and told me that on returning home to Albania after very many years' foreign service he was horrified to find his native land worse used than any other part of the Turkish Empire with which he was acquainted. He was hot on the school question, and declared his intention of having Albanian taught. As for our books we might sell as many as we pleased, the more the better. The little boys of the Moslem school flocked to buy them, and we sold, too, to several Albanians who wore the uniform of Turkish officers.

The Albanian periodical, published in London by Faik Bey, was known here. A definite effort was being made at Elbasan to break with the Greek Church. An Albanian priest had visited Rome, and there asked leave to establish at Elbasan a Uniate Church. He was the son of a rich man, and having obtained the assent of Rome returned with the intention of building the church himself, and had even bought a piece of land for it. But leave to erect a church had to be first obtained from the Turkish Government. This he was hoping to receive soon. The Turkish Government, aware that this was part of the Nationalist movement, never granted the permit, though characteristically it kept the question open for a long while. The mountains of Spata near Elbasan are inhabited by a mountain folk in many ways resembling the Maltsors of the north, who preserved a sort of semi-independence. They were classed by the Christians as crypto-Christians. I saw neither church nor mosque in the district I visited. As for religion, each had two names. To a Moslem enquirer he said he was Suliman; to a Christian that he was Constantino. When called on to pay tax, as Christians in place of giving military service, the inhabitants declined on the grounds that they all had Moslem names and had no church. When on the other hand they were summoned for military service they protested they were Christians. And the Turks mostly left them alone. But they were Nationalists, and when the proposal for a Uniate Church was mooted, declared they would adhere to Rome. The news of this having spread, upset the Orthodox Powers to such an extent that a Russian Vice-Consul was sent hurriedly to the spot. The Spata men, however, who were vague enough about religious doctrines, were very certain that they did not want anything Russian, and the Russian who had been instructed to buy them with gold if necessary had to depart in a hurry.

It was a district scarcely ever visited by strangers, and my visit gave extraordinary delight.

So through Pekinj, Kavaia, Durazzo Tirana and Croia, the city of Skenderbeg and the stronghold now of Bektashism, I arrived at last at Scutari, and was welcomed by Mr. Summa, himself a descendant of one of the mountain clans, formerly dragoman to the Consulate, and now acting Vice-Consul. He was delighted about my journey, and told me he could pass me up into the mountains wherever I pleased. He explained to me that on my former visit, Mr. Prendergast being new to the country had consulted the Austrian Consulate as to the possibility of my travelling in the interior, and that the Austrians who wished to keep foreigners out of the mountains, though they sent plenty of their own tourists there, had given him such an alarming account of the dangers as had caused him to tell me it was impossible. He arranged at once for me to visit Mirdita.

The Abbot of the Mirdites, Premi Dochl, was a man of remarkable capacity. Exiled from Albania as a young man for participation in the Albanian league and inciting resistance to Turkish rule and the decrees of the Treaty of Berlin, he had passed his years of exile in Newfoundland and India as a priest, and had learned English and read much. He was the inventor of an excellent system of spelling Albanian by which he got rid of all accents and fancy letters and used ordinary Roman type. He had persuaded the Austrian authorities to use it in their schools, and was enthusiastic about the books that he was having prepared. His schemes were wide and included the translation of many standard English books into Albanian. And he had opened a small school hard by his church in the mountains.

His talk was wise. He Was perhaps the most far-seeing of the Albanian Nationalists. We stood on a height and looked over Albania —range behind range like the stony waves of a great sea, sweeping towards the horizon intensely and marvellously blue, and fading finally into the sky in a pale mauve distance. He thrust out his hands towards it with pride and enthusiasm. It was a mistake, he said, now to work against Turkey. The Turk was no longer Albania's worst foe. Albania had suffered woefully from the Turk. But Albania was not dead. Far from it. There was another, and a far worse foe —one that grew ever stronger, and that was the Slav: Russia with her fanatical Church and her savage Serb and Bulgar cohorts ready to destroy Albania and wipe out Catholic and Moslem alike.

He waved his hand in the direction of Ipek. "Over yonder," he said, "is the land the Serbs called Old Serbia. But it is a much older Albania. Now it is peopled with Albanians, many of whom are the victims, or the children of the victims, of the Berlin Treaty: Albanians, who had lived for generations on lands that that Treaty handed over to the Serbs and Montenegrins, who drove them out to starve. Hundreds perished on the mountains. Look at Dulcigno—a purely Albanian town, threatened by the warships of the Great Powers, torn from us by force. How could we resist all Europe? Our people were treated by the invading Serb and Montenegrin with every kind of brutality. And the great Gladstone looked on! Now there is an outcry that the Albanians of Kosovo ill-treat the Slavs. Myself I regret it. But what can they do? What can you expect? They know very well that so long as ten Serbs exist in a place Russia will swear it is a wholly Serb district. And they have sworn to avenge the loss of Dulcigno.

"The spirit of the nation is awake in both Christian and Moslem. People ask why should not we, like the Bulgars and Serbs, rule our own land? But first we must learn, and organize. We must have time. If another war took place now the Slavs would overwhelm us. We must work our propaganda and teach Europe that there are other people to be liberated besides Bulgars and Serbs. The Turk is now our only bulwark against the Slav invader. I say therefore that we must do nothing to weaken the Turk till we are strong enough to stand alone and have European recognition. When the Turkish Empire breaks up, as break it must, we must not fall either into the hands of Austria nor of the Slavs."

And to this policy, which time has shown to have been the wise one, he adhered steadily. He took no part in rising against the Turk, but he worked hard by means of spread of education and information, to attain ultimately the freedom of his country. His death during the Great War is a heavy loss to Albania.

I promised him then that I would do all that lay in my power to bring a knowledge of Albania to the English, and that I would work for its freedom. He offered to pass me on to Gusihje, Djakova, or any other district I wished, and to do all in his power to aid my travels But I had already far exceeded my usual holiday, and appeals to me to return to England were urgent.

I had to tear myself away from the wilderness and I was soon once more steaming up the Lake of Scutari to Rijeka.

CHAPTER TEN
MURDER WILL OUT

I ARRIVED in Cetinje with a Turkish trooper's saddle and a pair of saddle-bags that contained some flintlock pistols and some beautiful ostrich feathers given me by the Mutasarrif of Elbasan and not much else but rags.

The news that I had come right through Albania excited Cetinje vastly. Every English tourist who wanted to go to Scutari was warned by the Montenegrins that it was death to walk outside the town; that murders took place every day in the bazar; any absurd tale, in fact, to blacken the Albanians. The Montenegrins were not best pleased at my exploit, and full of curiosity.

I patched my elbows, clipped the ragged edge of my best skirt, and was then told by Vuko Vuletitch that the Marshal of the Court was waiting below to speak with me.

I descended and found the gentleman in full dress. It was a feast day.

We greeted one another.

"His Royal Highness the Prince wishes to speak with you!" said he with much flourish. "He requests you will name an hour when it is convenient for you to come to the Palace."

It was the first time the Prince had noticed me, I was highly amused, and replied:

"I can come now if His Royal Highness pleases!"

The Marshal of the Court eyed me doubtfully and hesitated. "I can wash my hands," said I firmly, "and that is all; I have no clothes but what I have on." My only other things were in the wash, and I had repaired myself so far as circumstances allowed. The Marshal of the Court returned with the message that His Royal Highness would receive me at once "as a soldier."

I trotted obediently off with him. We arrived at the Palace. It was a full-dress day, and the Montenegrins never let slip an occasion for peacocking. The situation pleased me immensely. The Marshal himself was in his very best white cloth coat and silken sash, gold waistcoat, and all in keeping. Another glittering functionary received me and between the two I proceeded upstairs. At the top of the flight is a large full-length looking-glass, and for the first time for four months I "saw myself as others saw me." Between the two towering glittering beings was a small, wiry, lean object, with flesh burnt copper-colour and garments that had never been anything to boast of, and were now long past their prime. I could have laughed aloud when I saw the Prince in full-dress with rows of medals and orders across his wide chest, awaiting me. It is a popular superstition, fostered by newspapers in the pay of modistes, that in order to get on it is necessary to spend untold sums on dress. But in truth if people really want to get something out of you they do not care what you look like. Nor will any costume in the world assist you if you have nothing to say.

The Prince conducted me to an inner room, greeted me politely, begged me to be seated and then launched into a torrent of questions about my previous years journey to Ipek. He seemed to think that my life had not been worth a para, and that the Rugova route was impossible. "Do you know, Mademoiselle, that what you did was excessively dangerous?"

"Sire," said I, "it was your Montenegrins who made me do it." He made no reply to this, but lamented that for him such a tour was out of the question. And of all things he desired to see the Patriarchia at Ipek and the Church of Dechani and the relics of the Sveti Kralj. He had been told I had secured photographs of these places. If so, would I give him copies?

I promised to send him prints from London. He thanked me, and there was a pause. I wondered if this was what I had been summoned for, and if I now ought to go. Then Nikita looked at me and suddenly began: "I think, Mademoiselle, that you are acquainted with my son-in-law, King Petar of Serbia."

Dear me, thought I, this is delicate ground. "I have not that honour, Sire," I said. Now how far dare I go? I asked myself. Let us proceed with caution. "I was in Serbia, Sire," I continued boldly, "during the lifetime of the—er—late King Alexander." Nikita looked at me. I looked at Nikita. Then he heaved a portentous sigh, a feat for which his huge chest specially fitted him.

"A sad affair, was it not, Mademoiselle?" he asked. And he sighed again.

Now or never, thought I, is the time for kite-flying. I gazed sadly at Nikita; heaved as large a sigh as I was capable of, and said deliberately: "Very sad, Sire—but perhaps necessary!"

The shot told. Nikita brought his hand down with a resounding smack on his blue-knickerbockered thigh and cried aloud with the greatest excitement: "Mon Dieu, but you are right, Mademoiselle! A thousand times right! It was necessary, and it is you alone that understand. Return, I beg you, to England. Explain it to your Foreign Office—to your politicians—to your diplomatists!" His enthusiasm was boundless and torrential. All would now be well, he assured me. Serbia had been saved. If I would go to Belgrade all kinds of facilities would be afforded me.

I was struck dumb by my own success. A reigning Sovereign had given himself away with amazing completeness. I had but dangled the fly and the salmon had gorged it. Such a big fish, too. Nikita, filled with hopes that the result of this interview would be the resumption <of diplomatic relations between England and Serbia, presented me with a fine signed photograph of himself, summoned the Marshal of the Court and instructed him to have it conveyed to the hotel. It was not etiquette, it appeared, for me to carry such a burden myself. The Interview was over.

It was abundantly clear that, in spite of all he had said to journalists, the old man heartily approved of the manner of the death of the last of the Obrenovitches, and had been "behind the scenes" of it.

I had many subsequent interviews with Nikita, but though I strewed many baits, never again caught him out so completely. Some people think that Foreign Affairs can be successfully carried on by Prime Ministers and Secretaries of State who speak nothing but English. I submit that the above information could never have been extracted through an interpreter. For an interpreter gives the other party time to think.

By the end of a week I was back in London. It was not quite a year since the death of Alexander. Nikita had shown plainly that he regarded the event as a very important step in Serb history. And he wanted me to go to Belgrade. But to me the situation was rather obscure. I knew Montenegro was unpopular in Serbia. Perhaps Nikita did not.

For purposes of their own the Montenegrins had risked my life —according to their own statements—by sending me to Ipek. True, I did not then set any value whatever on my life, so was not so brave by a long way as they imagined, but all the same they had had no right to do it. If I went to Belgrade at all, it should not be for an unknown purpose and as emissary of Nikita.

Meanwhile, King Petar was necessarily entirely in the hands of the Pretorian guard, which had put him on the throne and could send him after Alexander if he did not please them. They soon occupied high positions. Colonel Maschin, who had himself helped kill his sister-in-law Draga, was made head of the General Staff, and Colonel Damian Popovitch, the leader of the gang, who has since become notorious for atrocities, even in the Balkans, was given the command of the Belgrade-Danube Division, and King Petar obediently signed an amended Constitution, which greatly curtailed his own power. An attempt on the part of certain officers to resist the regicides was crushed, and several were imprisoned. Serbia was, and remained, under military rule, the object of which was the reconstruction of Great Serbia. The Serbo-Bulgar question rapidly became acute. Prince Ferdinand met King Petar informally in Nish railway station. In October 1904, King Petar visited Sofia. The visit was a failure. Prince Ferdinand was in favour of an autonomous Macedonia. The Serb Press would not hear of such a thing. Pashitch, then Minister for Foreign Affairs, declared that such an autonomy would injure Serbia and be all in favour of Bulgaria. Simitch, diplomatic agent at Sofia, insisted that under such an autonomy Bulgarian annexation was concealed and should that take place, the Serbs would fight till either Serbia or Bulgaria was destroyed. Both men thus admitted that Macedonia was not Serb. But they wanted Bulgar aid to crush the Albanian, in order that Serbia might take Albanian territory. "Heads I win; tails you lose." Bulgaria was to gain nothing. Serbia meant to be top dog. The Serbian Press attacked Prince Nikola so violently that an indignation meeting was held at Cetinje and the populace crowded outside the palace and shouted "Zhivio." The tug between Petrovitch and Karageorgevitch had begun. The regicides had not ended the Obrenovitches to be baulked by the Petrovitches.

A stealthy campaign against Prince Nikola now began, which emanated from Belgrade and had, I am inclined to believe, Russian support.

A ludicrous episode was the arrival in London of Prince Albert Ghika, a Roumanian, who announced himself to the Press as a claimant to the Albanian throne, and was taken seriously even by some quite respectable journals. It was indeed bad luck for him that he timed his visit to correspond with my return from Albania, for I was able to state that, far from being accepted by the whole nation, I had never even heard his name mentioned. In a very amusing interview I had with him I ascertained that he did not know a word of the language of his adopted country. His plans were grandiose, and included Constantinople as capital. "Pourquoi pas?" he asked. It would prevent the Great Powers from quarrelling over it, and therefore make for peace! His curled mustachios, his perfumes, his incomparable aplomb, his airs of a "Serene Highness" formed a magnificent stock-in-trade. But even the fact that he offered me a magnificent salary to be Maid of Honour or Lady-in-Waiting (I forget which) at the Court of Albania did not persuade me to espouse his cause, which disappeared into thin air so soon as the newspapers had a fresh sensation.

Nevertheless Albert Ghika hung around the back doors of the Balkans for some time. It was only in Albania that he was unknown.

CHAPTER ELEVEN
1905

Coming events cast their shadows before.—CAMPBELL.

This holiday was eventful. On the steamer I was addressed politely by an Albanian who had read my name on my bag. He said he had seen me a week before in Venice, and proved it by describing my companions. Said calmly he had purposely shipped on the same boat, knew all about me, but preferred to be known himself as "the Egyptian." He was a storehouse of tales of political intrigue, and yarned till near midnight on the deck as we slid through the phosphorescent sea. Of Ghika and his doings he was well informed. All Ghikas, he said, suffered badly from the same incurable complaint—a hole in the pocket—a disease, alas, common to many other honest men! At any rate Albert Ghika's claim to the Albanian throne had obtained him a rich bride, which was always something. That he really expected to mount that throne was in the highest degree improbable, for he was no fool. "How much has the lady?" I could not enlighten him. "How the English journals accepted him amazes me! But they gave him a reclame enorme. And he had not a sou. Now he has some gold. But no one in Albania knows him, and he has no party there." Followed tales of another "celebrity," Lazarevitch, who claimed descent from Tsar Lazar of Kosovo fame and was, according to "the Egyptian," the finest intriguer in Europe: "not a plot has happened in which he has not had, if not his index, his little finger. He played a large part in the Dreyfus case. And, like Ghika, he has married a rich wife, Only once has he been taken in, and that was by Shaban. You know Shaban? Shaban was really called Dossi. He was employed by Cook in Egypt as a dragoman, and dismissed from that service doubtless for good reasons. He dressed himself in a Gheg costume, got an introduction to Lazarevitch, and said he was an Albanian Bey who wanted to make a Serbo-Albanian alliance against Bulgar pretensions. Lazarevitch jumped at this. The first time he was ever taken in. He gave Shaban several hundred pounds. Shaban had a friend who was a tailor. Faik Bey, who was in London, saw Shaban and denounced him as an impostor. The tailor ran away to Greece with all the money, and was at once arrested there. So Shaban got nothing. Why did the Greeks arrest the tailor? Because of the English gold of course. Probably he was guilty of something or other too. But they would not have troubled about it but for the gold. They got that." He out-Antonied Hope and made Phroso tame compared to the real Balkans. Much more he told and much proved true. But he was obviously a dangerous travelling companion, and when he told me he proposed passing some days with me in the Bocche di Cattaro, I abruptly changed my plan of staying there, hailed a Montenegrin carriage which was waiting on the quay at Cattaro and drove straight to Cetinje.

Later, I received from Paris a gilt-edged letter with a Royal crown upon it from Aladri Kastrioti, the elderly and amiable gentleman who claimed descent from Skenderbeg and toyed with the idea of ascending the Albanian throne himself. He had, in fact, a considerable following in the Northern mountains, for the name of Skenderbeg was one to conjure with, and the Turkish Government prohibited the sale of his picture post cards. He wrote that his secretary, "the Egyptian," had reported his success in making my acquaintance and begged that on my return I would meet him in Paris and discuss matters of importance. This invitation I never accepted.

Cetinje I found bubbling over Albert Ghika. He had come with such good letters of introduction that the Prince had appointed Matanovitch as a sort of guard of honour to him. But when it became apparent that he meant to use Montenegro as a safe spot whence to make trouble across the border, and even began to scatter picture post cards of the future King and Queen of Albania, he was asked to leave the country. Matanovitch was very much chaffed about his share in the expedition.

Orthodox Easter was due. I was told that having had an audience last year it was correct for me to telegraph Easter greetings to Prince Nikola, who was in his winter quarters at Rijeka. In reply came an official intimation that I should call on him at three o'clock next day. I was met by an officer of the Court and taken to the audience. The old man was in the doorway when I arrived, and was very friendly.

He was, I fancy, bored to death at Rijeka, and glad of a visitor from the great world outside. He led me into a small room and insisted on my taking a very large chair, evidently his own seat, while he sat down on one much too small for him, and began very vividly to tell me of his first fight at Vuchidol in 1876 and of the great battle of Grahovo where twelve of his relatives had lost their heads. He was very lively, and there was something extraordinarily old-world, even mediaeval, about him. I felt I was in a by-gone century—at latest with Rob Roy. We must eat together he said, and we had an odd meal of ham, hardboiled eggs, bread and weak tea into which he hospitably insisted on putting five large lumps of sugar with his Royal fingers. He pressed me to eat also the wing of a fowl, but as it was but 3 p.m. this was quite impossible for me. So after hoarse house-keeping whispers to his man, a bottle of Marsala was produced and we drank healths. He questioned me about my Albanian experiences and roared with laughter. He said the Albanians would certainly put me to ransom some day, and promised himself to contribute handsomely. He dug in the pockets of his capacious breeches and fished out some beautifully decorated Easter eggs a peasant had just given him, and presented one to me. Of his people he spoke as though they were all little children. He meant well by them. Truly. But so do many parents, who forget their children are grown up. He meant them to go his way, not theirs. A fatal error. He was very anxious to know how much money I had been paid for my book, and was as inquisitive about my pecuniary situation as the most upcountry of his subjects, and hoped the book would bring hosts of wealthy tourists to the land. I stirred him up by telling him that the Albanians intended some day to make a state larger than Montenegro and take back Antivari and Podgoritza.

"Let them come!" said the old man stoutly. His eyes twinkled and he laughed while he clasped his revolver, confessing he would not be averse to a little war—but there was Europe to be considered. Meanwhile I was to be sure and go to see Grahova and Vuchidol. After a good three-quarters of an hour's talk he saw me to the door and shouted good-bye from the doorstep.

At Nyegushi I engaged as guide one Krsto, recommended me in 1903 at Andrijevitza by a botany professor from Prague, and while our start was preparing went with Kapetan Gjuro Vrbitza and another officer by a track to the mountain's edge whence we could look directly down upon Cattaro. A gun emplacement was made there later. The two Montenegrins amused themselves by hurling stones into Austrian territory—feeling ran then strongly against Austria. For the first time I heard the song:

Franz Josef da Bog ti ubio. Ti si strashno zlo uchinio! (Franz Josef, may God strike thee dead. Thou hast wrought terrible evil.)

Russia was still madly struggling with Japan. It was the Tsar's own fault, said popular opinion. Prince Nikola had offered to send a large Montenegrin army and he had declined it. Consequently only nineteen volunteers, including two of Krsto's own relatives, had gone to Russia's aid. Otherwise "Portartur" would never have fallen. Krsto's cousin was engineer on one of Rozhdjestvcnski's ships. Every one believed England had tried to Sink them by concealing Japanese torpedo boats among the fishing fleet. They, however, kindly absolved me from complicity in the affair, mainly because I had been to Ipek.

France, as Russia's ally, had sprung into high favour and was contemplating the erection of a "nouveau art" Legation. And the new French Minister's little boy put his hands behind his back when introduced to me, and said: "I cannot shake hands with you, Mademoiselle, till you assure me you are not the friend of the Yellow Monkeys." Thus are peace and goodwill taught to children in the "civilized" lands of West Europe.

I started for Vuchidol, which the Prince had expressly desired me to visit, by way of Grahovo. Each village knew of my ride to Ipek, and received me with enthusiasm. Each told the same tale. The rising planned to take place throughout the Balkans in 1904 had been stopped by the misfortunes of the Russo-Japanese War. Montenegro was aghast at the duration of the war, and her faith in Russia as a God Almighty was badly shaken.

Feeling ran high against Bulgaria, for a rumour, started, it was said, by Chedo Miyatovitch, declared that England had promised Constantinople to Prince Ferdinand, and this would interfere with the reconstruction of Great Serbia, which was to be made at all costs. We little thought then the stupendous price the world would pay for it!

There was some dread lest, Russia being now occupied in the Far East, Austria should move. On the way we picked up an old man of the Banyani tribe, over six feet, and hook-nosed. He pointed out landmarks with his long chibouk, carried an old flintlock, and seemed to live in terror of enemies. "Golden pobratim!" he said earnestly to Krsto, "dear brother, listen! My house is but two hours from the frontier. The Austrians can come. Thank God I have this gun! The Tsar of Russia should send plenty of soldiers, then we could live in safety." Nor could we reassure him. He was going to Cetinje to beg the Gospodar to write to the Tsar for troops. "May God slay me, dear brother, but the clanger is great." I stood him a drink and he went tracking over the mountains Cetinje-wards with his antique weapon.

We went on through a land the filth and poverty of which Is unimaginable to those who have never left England. The sterile waterless rocks make it impossible to live with any decency. The worst English slum is luxury in comparison. Barely enough water to drink. None to wash in. One day I had nothing but dirty melted snow out of a hole. Vermin swarmed and no one worried about them. "If we had only as many gold pieces as lice," said folk cheerfully, "this would be the richest land in Europe." The population, in truth, was probably better off in Turkish times, when it lived by sheep-stealing and raiding caravans. Montenegro has never been self-supporting, and since frontier raids were stopped the chief trade of the people had been smuggling tobacco and coffee into Austria. Krsto and his relative were keen smugglers, and knew every nook in the Bocche di Cattaro. Now, in return for various works that she was to do, Italy had been given the tobacco monopoly and a duty was imposed. Montenegro was furious. The vigilance of the Austrian police had made it hard enough to earn a living before. This made this worse. Death to the Italians! God slay Austria! And Russia actually looking on and doing nothing.

We arrived one evening at Crkvitza, near the Austrian frontier. A dree hole; a han filthy beyond all words; no horse fodder, the Kapetan absent and his secretary drunk; a lonely schoolhouse to which some fifty children descended daily from the surrounding mountains. To spare me the horrors of the han, the schoolmaster kindly offered to put me up. But even his house swarmed with bugs and ticks. I rose very early next morning, saddled and packed, and was about to flee from the place, when the secretary came triumphantly waving a telegram and told me I was under arrest. The drink-fuddled creature, thinking to "cut a dash" during his chief's absence, had wired to the police at Nikshitch, "A man dressed as a woman has come from across the Austrian frontier." The reply said, "Detain him till further orders." The telegraph station was eight hours' march distant, but he had sent some one in haste on horseback. There was a terrible row. The populace was on my side. My British passport was, of course, useless. Krsto thought his honour impugned, and I feared he would shoot. Might I return under armed escort to the village of the telegraph office where they knew me? No. All I was allowed to do was to send a man on foot with a telegram for the Minister for Foreign Affairs and await the reply. So I was interned for nearly twenty-four hours in the han and spent the night in a filthy hole with a man, a boy, a woman, a quantity of pigeons, and swarms of lice and bugs. When the reply came from Voyvoda Gavro saying I was free to go where I pleased, the secretary was flabbergasted. It sobered him, and he was afraid of what he had done. I went on to Vuchidol as I had promised, though the Prince little knew what he was letting me in for.

The affair excited Cetinje wildly. Before I left every one had been lamenting that there was now no English Minister in Montenegro. I had been prayed, by Dushan Gregovitch and others, to write to The Times on the subject, to arouse Parliament, and somehow or other get England represented in the country. Now the cry was changed: "God be praised," cried they fervently, "there is no British Minister in Cetinje." "Thanks be to God, there is not even a British Consul." Voyvoda Gavro put his head out of "Foreign Affairs," which was then a cottage in the main street, and shouted for explanations. The dismay was comical. Early next morning an officer pursued me in the street and said the Prince wanted to see me, at once. He was sitting on the top of the steps as he was used to do before the palace was altered, and he too seemed quite overwhelmed with the international complication. Krsto had already given the police a highly coloured account.

The secretary of Crkvitza, the Prince hastened to assure me, would be punished. I said that if he were punished the result would be that when a real spy arrived he would Hot be arrested. For me the affair was a mere travel episode, not worth troubling about.

Then came the crux. The Prince was terrified lest I should write to The Times and shatter his golden dreams of wealthy tourists. The whole Montenegrin Government trembled before the possibility of such a catastrophe. I promised cheerfully not to write to any paper at all. |Nor till now have I mentioned the affairs.

So the matter was settled, to the obvious relief of poor old Nikita, who was most grateful and seemed much surprised that I required no vengeance.

I started again, this time for Nikshitch and the Durmitor, with the intention of going into Turkish territory if possible.

At Rijeka I was taken to the small-arms factory on the river, the primitive machinery being worked by water power. Here were men busy fitting new stocks to old rifles, Russian ones. I was told that one was being prepared for every man in Bosnia and the Herzegovina. When all were ready they would be smuggled in. I was taken aback at this, but found when playing the phonograph in the evening to a large party, that the notion of a not distant war with Austria accompanied by a great Balkan rising was generally accepted. Still more was I surprised to hear talk against the Prince. He and his sons were accused of taking all the best land and doing nothing with it. And the question of the tobacco regie raged. Podgoritza I found greatly changed. The outer world had rushed in on it. The tobacco factory dominated the town. "God willing, we shall burn it down!" said the populace cheerfully. True, it employed many hands, but they complained the pay was low, though they admitted that the girls had never earned anything before. In truth, regular work was a new thing in Montenegro. The end of the days of indefinite coffee- and rakia-drinking and recounting of past battles was now approaching. The middle ages were leaping at one bound into the twentieth century, and the Montenegrin was angry and puzzled.

The Italians had undertaken to construct a railway, quays, and harbour works, and offered fair wages for workmen. The Montenegrins demanded fantastic payment and imagined that by standing out they would get it. To their astonishment the Italians imported gangs of far better workmen and finished the work. Then the Montenegrins cursed the Italians and hated them bitterly. Even Montenegrin officers openly boasted that they did not know the price of the regie tobacco as they smoked only contraband, and feeling ran so high that the Italian Monopol buildings at Antivari were attacked and damaged.

At Podgoritza I met again the Albanian coachman Shan, who had served me very faithfully on my previous visits. He took me to the house of his family. A striking contrast to the Montenegrin houses, it was spick and span and even pretty, for the Albanian has artistic instincts, whereas the Montenegrin has none. Left to himself, his taste is deplorable.

Further signs of change in the land soon showed themselves. Rijeka had already grumbled. At Danilovgiati I was at once approached by a youth, who proudly showed me a Serbian paper containing his portrait and verses by himself. He was lately come from Belgrade, where he was a student, one of the many who have there been made tools of by unscrupulous political intriguers. He indignantly inveighed against the poverty of Montenegro and ascribed every evil to the Prince. I suggested that the Montenegrins themselves were among the laziest on God's earth, and could with energy do very much more with their land. But he blamed "the Government" for everything. No learning, no progress, he declared, was possible. You could not even import the books you wanted. He hurled his accusations broadcast and then, for he took his literary qualifications very seriously, sat down and wrote a verse about me after considerable labour and much sprawling over the table.

Danilovgrad was the home of another reformer, Dr. Marusitch, a Montenegrin who had but recently returned from Manchuria after many years' service as a surgeon in the Russian Army. A wild, enthusiastic creature—good-natured, well-meaning and indiscreet. For Montenegro he was rich. He had just married an extremely beautiful young woman, and the hospitality of the two was unbounded. He at once asked me to stay six months as his guest and write, with his aid, the standard book on Montenegro. Like all who had lived in Russia, he was a hard drinker and tipped down alcohol in alarming quantities. He was a strange mixture of the old world and the new. Took me to see the grave of Bajo Radovitch, who fell in 1876 after having cut off fifteen Turkish heads; admired the bloody feat, but blamed Germany for keeping up militarism. He had no opinion at all of the Montenegrin Government, and poured out a torrent of plans for its reform. He was all for peace, he said, and wanted to rearrange all the world—which badly needed it. I little thought what would be his fate when I wished him goodbye, and promised to look him up next year.

On the road to Nikshitch we came up with the military wagons carrying weapons, mainly revolvers and sword bayonets up-country for distribution. Russia had sent a revolver for each man in the country, and great was the rejoicing. Russia, when she re-armed her forces, usually bestowed the old weapons lavishly on Montenegro. Artillery was soon to follow.

We left the road and struck up-country towards Durmitor, along with a string of pack-horses laden with the Russian weapons which went with an armed escort.

By the way we passed two stones recording recent murders, showing that blood feuds were not yet extinct.

At Zhabljak, Durmitor, I spent two amusing days seeing the distribution of arms. Men flocked in from all parts, were delighted with their new toys, and Russia leapt up in every one's estimation. No ammunition was served out for, as an officer remarked, "It would all be wasted." They conversed on blood and battle and clicked their new revolvers. "How we should like to go over and try them on the Turks," they said. "But we dare not cross the border because of the Powers."

Two chetas (battalions) were armed and had left when a bugle sounded of a sudden. "That means third cheta assemble!" shouted Krsto. All rushed out. Sure enough a telegram had arrived saying "The Turks are over the border! Mobilize at once!"

Every one was delighted. The men hustled into their great-coats. The women stuffed bread and a bottle of rakia into their torbitzas. The officers saddled their own horses, and in a very short time the third cheta was drawn up in line on the hill-top by the church in marching order. The commandant made a speech. They were to behave as Montenegrin heroes. They were not to fire a shot till the word was given, and above all they were to do nothing that would "look crooked in the eyes of Europe." They were a wild lot, in every kind of ragged garment. Had had a few months' drill, so marched in step for the first twenty yards. Then they broke rank, howled a war cry and rushed over the hill like a pack of wolves on the trail, firing their rifles as they went. Their officer followed on horseback and as he topped the brow, turned in his saddle and emptied his revolver over our heads. We sat up all night, every one wild for war. Bandages and carbolic arrived on a mule. There was in fact some fighting on the other side of the border between Albanians and Serbs near Bijelopolje. War, of course, did not ensue. But for some days the frontier was all lined with troops.

Meanwhile I wanted to go on to Plevlje in Turkish territory, and had to wait till the local governor thought safe to let me pass. While waiting I heard here, too, more rumours about the Prince. He was accused of having poisoned the Minister of Justice, who had died suddenly after dining with him. The dead man's family lived here. They said an Austrian doctor had said it was not poison. But there was much talk about it, and folk seemed unconvinced. I never learnt the truth of it. The route at length being open, we crossed the swift Tara at the bottom of a deep gorge on a most primitive ferry of seven planks lashed together in a triangle, and the Turkish gendarmerie on the opposite bank furnished guide and horses. Krsto had to leave his revolver behind, and having never in his life been out without one, was as nervous as a cat and saw brigands in every bush. At which I laughed.

Plevlje then was a strange sight. On one side were modern up-to-date Austrian houses with a park, smart barracks and an inn. On the hills behind it in immense letters of white stone were the initials of Franz Josef. The opposite side of the town was occupied by the Turkish Army, wonderfully smart, as if in competition with Austria, and a Crescent marked the hill on that side. Between the two lay the native town and bazar.

The local Turkish Governor was an Albanian, Suliman Pasha. He was delighted to have an English visitor, explained to me the difficulty of his position, with enemy lands, Austria, Montenegro and Serbia on three sides of the Sanjak, all intriguing to obtain it, and enemy soldiers quartered in the town. Austria he was confident was preparing to move shortly. He believed that even then they had more troops in the Sanjak than was allowed by treaty.

He pressed me to continue my journey to Mitrovitza and to Prizren, where the Russians were, he said, stirring up trouble. But the strict time limit of my holiday made this impossible. The result of the Murzsteg arrangement was, according to him, that Austria and Russia regarded the Peninsula as to be shortly theirs, and were working hard to extend their spheres of influence. Each, under the so-called reform schemes, had put their gendarmerie in the districts they could work from best. They had put England in an unimportant place. England ought to have insisted on being on the frontiers, then the importation of arms could have been prevented. As it was, Austria and Russia were both smuggling arms in by means of their gendarmerie. Russia wanted to provoke a rising of Christians in order to rush in "to save the Christians." Austria wanted to foment differences between Moslem and Catholic, and, being nearest to the spot, hoped Europe would again request her to "restore order" as in Bosnia. "Then she will be one day's march nearer Salonika," said the Pasha. I believe his statements were correct.

I had an introduction to one of the leading Serbs of the town, Filip Gjurashkovitch. The Gjurashkovitch family had left Montenegro owing, as we have seen, to a fierce quarrel with the Petrovitches. Had fled, as usual, to Turkish territory and had, for years, held official positions, Filip had lived in Durazzo, and was strongly in favour of the establishment of an independent Albania, declaring that the trouble with the Albanians was due entirely to Turkish misrule. If given a chance of education they were among the most intelligent of the Peninsula. He emphasized this by pointing out that Suliman Pasha was an Albanian, and only a man of great skill could have kept the peace for twenty years between two rival garrisons both in the same town.

It was Whitsuntide, and several thousand pilgrims arrived at the Troitza Monastery, just outside the town, from Montenegro, Serbia, and even the Herzegovina, as well as from the surrounding villages. Especially a number of schoolmasters assembled, all of whom ran propaganda schools in the district; I thus learnt much of what was going on. The schoolmasters were nearly all Montenegrins and regarded the Sanjak as "their claim." They were furious with Austria, because they had ordered a quantity of the usual propaganda prints, grotesque portraits of Stefan Dushan, Milosh Obilitch, the nine Yugovitches, etc., for their schools in order to preach Great Serbia. Had had them sent by Austrian post so that they might not fall into the hands of the Turks—and the Austrians had stopped them. There was no Russian Consul there to see to it. Nor could Russia be relied on entirely. Two Russian officials had been recently to Miloshevo Monastery, near Prijepolje, and had declared the language spoken there to be Bulgar. And it was the place where St. Sava was buried! They were furious. Russian monks were now firmly established at Detchani. That was all right. None of them wanted reforms introduced into the Turkish Empire, because then there would be no hope of tearing it to pieces. As in Macedonia I found the approved method was to start a massacre and then cry to Europe for help. On all sides I heard again that the great Balkan rising had been stopped by the Russo-Japanese War. The Archimandrite of the Monastery was bitter about Russia. "What does Russia want with Manchuria? She has gone to take distant land that is no affair of hers and has left her brethren in the Balkans unhelped. God's curse is upon her." They were disgusted that Ferdinand of Bulgaria had been guest at the German wedding. He was an arch plotter, but a fool. "He wants to be Tsar of a wide land. But he will not succeed. He has weakened the Serb position by his propaganda, but he will never have Constantinople. Russia would trundle him out. She means to have Constantinople. No one else will." King Petar was Serbia's only hope, but the propaganda against him was active. England's attitude about the murder was incomprehensible to them. Had Alexander not been killed he would have allowed Austria to build and control a railway through Serbia. The Montenegrins jeered at Serbia, "a country that has a new ministry every few months." None of them seemed to think it counted. And none seemed to see the point of all working for a common cause. Whether they were pro- or anti-Petrovitch, they took it for granted Montenegro was to be the head of Great Serbia. For Austria they had nothing but contempt, and said pleasantly that all Austrian officers looked as if about to bear twins. You had only to run in a bayonet and the beer would run out. They had, however, no right to talk of drink, for the pilgrimage was an orgy of rakia, beer and wine.

From Plevlje I rode to Prijepolje, the furthest military outpost of Austria. There were but one hundred Christian houses in it. Nevertheless there was a schoolmaster industriously teaching "Great Serbia" and "patriotism." The Turkish Government was powerless to prevent this revolutionary work, as any interference would have brought protests from the Powers about "persecuting Christians."

The whole of the Sanjak from Mitrovitza to the Austrian frontier was inhabited almost entirely by Serb-speaking Slavs, the bulk of whom were Moslem. Large numbers were descendants of those evicted from Montenegro or Serbia in 1878, and were therefore not well disposed to either land. Krsto was not at all pleased to find that they had changed their habitat for the better and settled in land more fertile than that from which they had been driven. He naively told me he had hoped they had all starved.

Returning to Plevlje I found great excitement about me, as the Austrian authorities had hitherto believed that Plevlje could be reached only by Austrian post cart from the Austrian frontier, accompanied by an armed escort. An Austrian officer and the Consul hurried to interview me. They were polite and friendly, but cross-examined me severely as to the purpose of my visit, and were obviously displeased that an unarmed tourist could come straight across country and wander round without their leave or knowledge. The Consul was a Croat and vehemently anti-Serb. He told me that the Montenegrins had been guilty of starting the recent fighting near Bijelopolje, and that it had been led by a Montenegrin officer.

The Montenegrin version was that the Moslem Albanians drove some sheep on to a Christian grazing-ground; that the Christians drove them off again and so the fight began; that all the Christians there wore Montenegrin caps, and so the tale of the officer was untrue. The Moslems swore to the truth of the officer tale. Judging by the celerity with which the Montenegrin troops were despatched to the frontier I incline to think it was "a put up job."

News came in of the sinking of the Russian fleet by the Japanese. It produced a deep sensation. Formerly every Serb and Montenegrin had jeered at me because we took so long beating the Boers. Now when it appeared that heathens, believed to be black, were at the least inflicting heavy loss on Holy Russia, they felt as though the universe were falling. I noted in my diary: "Out here one feels very keenly the tituppy state of politics. Anything likely to upset the apple-cart should be avoided."

I returned without adventure to Nikshitch, and thence to Nyegushi by a very bad mountain track.

By now it was midsummer and blazing hot. I stayed at Krsto's hut, and slept in a sort of outhouse called the "magazin," built to hold contraband goods by an ancestor. By day the cloudless sky closed down on us like a lid and shut out every breath of air. The little cabbages wilted in yellow rows and the inhabitants of Nyegushi, like true Montenegrins, spent the day smoking and vainly watching for the sign of a cloud, instead of fetching water for their gardens.

At midday the limestone rocks glared and the shadows lay like ink blots. Only at night, when a soft wind stole up from the Bocche di Cattaro, did Nyegushi come to life. Then we gathered on a mound behind Krsto's hut and the neighbours flocked to hear the "monogram" as they persistently called my phonograph. So soon as its raucous voice arose, folk who had gone to bed emerged and joined the party just as they were. But this merely means that they were barefoot and revolverless, for no one undresses in the Near East.

My repertoire was limited, and I played "God Save the King" till I realized what must be the sufferings of the Royal Family. For Montenegro was all agog about King Edward.

When King Edward was last at Marienbad he had met and spoken with Prince Mirko and his wife Princess Natalie. Nor was it surprising, for the Princess was rarely beautiful, her figure as perfect as her face; and her lovely head was poised upon a flawless neck and shoulders. She would have shone in any court in Europe, and it was a hard fate which gave her to the second son of Montenegro. She, poor young thing, was one of the pawns in the game which the Petrovitch dynasty was playing for Great Serbia, and she dreamed of Queendom.

Edward VII admired her and the news flashed through Montenegro. It was in the Glas and the Korbiro (correspondence bureau), the ne plus ultra of fashionable intelligence. Excitement reached boiling-point when it was reported that King Edward in person had seen "our Mirko" and his wife off at the station and promised to call on them in Montenegro. Montenegro felt it had not lived in vain. So the villagers called for "God save the King" endlessly, and under the stars at night tried quite unsuccessfully to learn it, for Montenegrin music is not on our scale and flows weirdly in semitones and less than semitones, and in spite of strenuous efforts our national anthem always trailed off into a hopeless caterwaul. But we all agreed that King Edward would be very much surprised when he heard the song and the "monogram" among the rocks of Nyegushi.

He never heard it. For meanwhile strings were pulling and fortunes changing. I returned to England, leaving the Montenegrins hopeful that he would come some day, and extorting from me a promise to be there with the "monogram".

Briefly, the history of my 1905 holiday may be summed up thus. Russia was powerless, and the dismayed Balkan States could not move without her. Austria had a free hand, and seemed likely to take advantage of Russia's plight. (It should be remembered to her credit that she did not.) There was very marked discontent in Montenegro against the Prince, and it was quite obviously engineered from Serbia, and perhaps from Russia too. The struggle for supremacy between father-in-law and son-in-law, Nikola and Petar, had begun. But Montenegro still believed itself as indubitably the head of Great Serbia. Even the malcontents wanted only to lead Montenegro to Prizren and glory, and were possibly unaware they were being used as cat's paws. Hatred between Serbia and Bulgaria was growing in intensity, and a war-spirit was very evidently stimulated by the fresh arrival of Russian arms in Montenegro.

That the Prince himself was aware of the undercurrent of feeling against him was shown a little later by his sudden bid for popularity. To the surprise of all the land and of the foreign Ministers, including Russia, he granted the Ustav (Constitution) in November, on St. Luke's Day. Montenegro was to elect a Parliament in which each tribe would be represented. He would teach his people self-government before he left them. It was admirably intended. Montenegro, astonished and excited, at once surcharged all the postage stamps.

Prince Nikola had made a bold bid for popularity. But he did not know the web that was already winding around him. On returning to London I found the Serbian, Alexander Jovitchitch, who had been informally representing Serbia since the murder of Alexander, much excited. The British Government, for no visible reason, was coming to the conclusion that all should be forgotten and forgiven, and diplomatic relations resumed with Serbia. As it was inconvenient to have no communication at all, England had adopted a sort of "We really can't ask you to dinner but you may talk with the cook over the area railings" attitude towards Jovitchitch and allowed him to call at the Foreign Office. Now, having suffered long at the back door, he was much hurt to find that on resumption of relations he was to retire in favour of M. Militchevitch, the former Serb Minister, the same who in 1902 had had to clear me of the charge of being a Karageorgevitch. By way of cheering Jovitchitch I said things Serb were indeed looking up. Relations were to be resumed with Serbia, and King Edward had promised to visit Montenegro. Jovitchitch, to my surprise, fired up. He told me sharply that the King would never go to Montenegro. It could not be permitted. "But why?" I asked, astonished. "Because Serbia is the leading state. It would be an insult to the Serb race if King Edward went to Cetinje before Belgrade! It has been represented to him and he has dropped the project."

That King Edward, after all he and the British Government had said about the murders, should now be so sensitive of Serbia's feelings that, to please Petar Karageorgevitch, Edward VII should change his holiday plans, was a little astonishing.

The reason has since then come to light. We were bound to France by the Entente Cordiale, and France was bound to Russia. Petar Karageorgevitch was Russia's choice. Russia had quite decided that Bulgaria, by means of which she had first planned to work, would never voluntarily be her vassal state and act as landbridge to Constantinople, and had therefore, in 1903, definitely preferred Serbia. But she could not support two heads for Great Serbia. One must go. England must not hob-nob with Montenegro. This was the first definite outside sign that there was to be a struggle between Serbia and Montenegro. France's military policy was tied fast to Russia's. And in December of that year—1905—we know now that "military conversations" were begun between France and England. They appear to have been far reaching. If France and England were to concoct military plans together it was clear England must recognize Russia's Balkan agent—Serbia. The situation was the more remarkable, for Edward VII had always been on the best terms with Franz Josef. And it was precisely because Alexander Obrenovitch wished to make alliance with Austria that he was slaughtered. Poor King Edward may have thought he was peace-making, but he little knew the Balkans.

In June 1906, England formally resumed relations with Serbia, an event of far higher import than any one but Russia realized at the time.

It is a date that ends a chapter of Balkan history. Till then Serbia was a petty Balkan state whose history had been punctuated by political murder, who had been aided from time to time by Russia, but quite as often by Austria, and who had usually been recognized as part of the Austrian "sphere." She now formed part of the combine against the Central Powers, and had the support of France, Russia and England.

Montenegro, on the other hand, "the Tsar's only friend," besung by Tennyson, bepraised by Gladstone (mainly, it is true, because neither of these well-meaning gentlemen had ever been there), now fell from her high position. Montenegro had had the praise of England's great men, and the political and financial support of Russia. But from the day when England and France began "military Conversations" the tables were turned. Prince Nikola might strive for popularity with "Constitutions," but, unless a miracle happened, the fate of the Petrovitches was sealed. They would never ascend the throne of Great Serbia.

And the fate of Europe was sealed too.

CHAPTER TWELVE
BOSNIA AND THE HERZEGOVINA

The Lamp of the Past illumines the Present.

The summer of 1906 saw me no longer restricted to two months' travel, but free to go where I pleased for as long as I liked. I planned a great scheme for the study and comparison of the traditions and customs of all the Balkan races, and in August started for Bosnia.

In ancient days all Bosnia and the Herzegovina formed part of Illyria, and was inhabited by the ancestors of the modern Albanian. Thousands of prehistoric graves, similar to those found also in Serbia and Albania, are scattered over the land. A huge cemetery exists at Glasinatz above Serajevo. The multitude of objects found in these graves reveal a very early Iron Age. Bosnia was one of Europe's earliest "Sheffields." Iron tools and bronze ornaments show that their makers were skilled workmen. The ornaments are of particular interest, as many are very similar in design to those still worn by Balkan peasantry, and as the bulk of Balkan silversmiths are Albanians or Vlachs both craft and design would appear to have been handed down from very ancient days.

The Illyrians were great warriors. "The difficulty," says J. B. Bury, the eminent historian of the later Roman Empire, "experienced by the Romans in subduing and incorporating the brave tribes is well known." Briefly, Rome's first punitive expedition to Illyria was in 230 B.C., but the land was not finally annexed till 169 A.D.

The Romans colonized Illyria. Christianity reached the coast early and slowly penetrated inland. Illyria formed part of the Patriarchate of Rome, and Latin became the official language throughout the Peninsula, save in the extreme south and south-east coast-line. Up-country and in the mountains the people evidently retained their own speech, that from which modern Albanian derives. The people in the plains, in direct contact with the Roman settlers, developed a sort of bastard Latin speech and doubtless intermarried largely with the Romans. They and their language exist to-day. They are known as the Kutzovlachs, and are thickly settled on the old Roman routes and the hill-tops. As frequently happens in history, but is invariably forgotten by those who go out to conquer, the marked individuality of the vanquished speedily re-asserted itself and gradually absorbed the victor. The Roman Empire shortly split in twain, and the East was largely ruled by Emperors of native Balkan blood, Diocletian, Constantine the Great, and many of lesser note. Greatest of all was Justinian (527-565), who was of Illyrian birth and succeeded his uncle Justin, a common soldier risen to the purple.

"In four departments," says Bury, "Justinian has won immortal fame. In warfare, in architecture, in law and in Church history." To him the world owes St. Sofia. He and his uncle Justin both strove against the schism between the Roman and Byzantine Churches, and he was powerful enough to carry a measure which tended to unity by modifying, the Synod of Chalcedon without breaking with Rome. And he prided himself upon speaking Latin. Yet there are those to-day who would hand over his Church of the Holy Wisdom to Greek propagandists. He dealt the final blow at Paganism and denounced the Manicheans—of whom we shall hear much later—and enacted severe laws against them.

The history of modern Bosnia begins in Justinian's reign. The Slavs then began to threaten the Empire. Tribes began to drift across the Danube and settle in groups already in the fifth century, but were stopped for a while by the Huns and Ostrogoths, who swept over the Peninsula and infested Illyria and Epirus.

"The departure of the Ostrogoths," says Bury, "was like the opening of a sluice. The Slavs and Bulgars, whom their presence had held back, were let loose on the Empire. . . . The havoc made by these barbarians was so serious that Justinian made new lines of defence." In 548 and 551 A.D. masses of Slavs ravaged the land. "The massacres and cruelties committed by these barbarians," says Bury, "make the readers of Procopius shudder." The readers of the Carnegie report of 1913 do likewise.

Among the fortresses built by Justinian was Singidunum, now Belgrade, which, founded to hold back the Slav, is now his capital. The invading Slavs were pagan, the natives largely Christian. "The Christians," says Presbyter Diocleas, "seeing themselves in great tribulation and persecution, began to gather on the mountains and tried to construct castles and strongholds that they might escape from the hands of the Slavs until God should visit and liberate them." This is probably the origin of the Vlach settlements on hill-tops and the Albanian mountain strongholds. "The year 581," says John of Ephesus, "was famous for the invasion of the accursed Slavonians . . . who captured cities and forts, and devastated and burnt, reducing the people to slavery, and made themselves masters of the country and settled it by main force. Four years have elapsed and still they live in the land . . . and ravage and burn." The Romans and their civilization were swept coastward, and in Dalmatia their civilization never quite died out. In later times the term "Romanes" was used in a special sense to denote the Romans who maintained their independence against the Slavs. Ragusa and Cattaro are some of the towns they founded.

Of the native population many refuged in the Albanian mountains, where they retained their language. Many doubtless remained and were absorbed by the Slavs. Traces, however, of the Illyrian still remain in Bosnia. Tattooing is still common there in many districts. Tattooing is not a Slav custom, but is specially noticed by classic authors as a characteristic of the ancient Balkan tribes. Neither have the Bosnians, as a whole, ever been attached to the Orthodox Church as have the remainder of the Balkan Slavs.

The early history of the Slavs in the Peninsula is obscure. They were a tribal people, and were for some time dominated by the Bulgars. Not till the end of the twelfth century did they unite under their very able line of Nemanja princes and rise to be a power. Even under the Nemanjas the local chieftains were semi-independent, and their inability to cohere proved the undoing of the realm.

Bosnia at an early date—it is said A.D. 940—was ruled by elective Bans. Stefan Nemanja the First Crowned of Serbia, called himself King of Serbia, Dalmatia and Bosnia, but the title seems to have been but nominal. The Bans did as they pleased and intrigued constantly with the Hungarians against the Serbs. The Bosniaks, too, became sharply divided from the Serbs by religion. Already in Justinian's time many of the Slavs near the Dalmatian coast had been converted to Christianity by priests from Rome, and much of the Herzegovina has ever since been Catholic. The mass of the Slavs, however, were pagan till the ninth century, when they were converted by the great mission led by Cyril and Methodius from Salonika.

Manicheism had already, in Justinian's time, taken a strong hold in the Balkan Peninsula. It now became amalgamated with a form of Christianity. A sect known as the Paulicians arose in Samosata in Asia Minor, which combined Manicheism with a peculiar reverence for the teaching of St. Paul. Fiercely persecuted by the Christians, they revolted, joined with the Mahommedans, and wasted much of Asia Minor. The Emperor Constantino Copronymus (A.D. 741), in order to weaken them, transported a great number to Thrace to serve as frontier guards. John I. Zimisces (A.D. 969) settled another large body in the Balkan valleys. Thence their doctrines spread fast. It would be of interest to know how much of their physical qualities were transmitted also. The new faith was known as Bogumil (dear to God) from its reputed Slav leader.

The rapidity with which it spread shows the very slight hold Christianity had as yet taken. The sun and the moon, which figured prominently in it, probably appealed to the old pre-Christian nature-worship of the Slavs. Alexius Comnenus vainly tried to extirpate the heresy by savage persecution. Basil, its high priest, was burnt alive. The sect fled westward and Bosnia became its stronghold. Religion in the Middle Ages was a far greater force than race. Nationality was hardly developed. Bosnia, into which the Orthodox faith seems to have penetrated but little, if at all, was thus cut off from the Serb Empire, for the bulk of the Bosniaks were either Bogumil or Roman Catholic.

We find a great many monuments of the Bogumils scattered through Bosnia and the Herzegovina. Huge monolithic gravestones often curiously carved. The sun, the moon and the cross appear as symbols, and portraits of warriors kilted and armed with bows and arrows and a cuirass, which give a good idea of the chieftain of the Middle Ages. The kilt is still worn by the Albanians.

Of the Bogumil creed not much is known, and that chiefly from its enemies. Catholic and Orthodox alike regarded the heresy with horror. But even its enemies allowed the Bogumils to have been an ascetic and temperate people. They abhorred the use of ikons and images, and unless the subterranean chapel at Jaitza be one, have left no church. Their doctrines spread into west Europe, and by the end of the twelfth century had developed in France into the sect of the Albigenses which was suppressed by the Roman Church with terrible ferocity. It is of interest that the rayed sun and the moon are still found in the armorial bearings of South of France families.

In Bosnia Bogumilism almost superseded all other faiths. In the twelfth century the Catholic Dalmatians and Hungarians in vain tried to suppress it by force. In 1189 Kulin Ban, the ruler of Bosnia, himself turned Bogumil. He recanted under pressure from Rome, but soon relapsed again, and in spite of an Hungarian crusade which ravaged the land, Bogumilism triumphed, the palace of the Catholic Bishop of Kreshevo was burnt and the Catholic episcopacy banished. The Bishop of Bosnia had to reside in Slavonia, and Bogumilism spread into Dalmatia and Croatia.

Bosnia was thus completely divided from the Serb Kingdom of Rashia, which had meanwhile grown up and thrown in its lot with the Orthodox Church. The Bans, in fact, preferred the assistance of the Catholics to the risk of conquest by the Serbs, and in 1340 we find Ban Stefan declaring himself Catholic and agreeing to the establishment of two Bishoprics.

Stefan Dushan, Serbia's greatest Tsar, was now at the height of his power. He succeeded in bringing the south of Bosnia under his control, but the then Ban Stefan Tvrtko (1353) joined with the Venetians and Hungarians against him. Nor was Bosnia as a whole added to Serbia. Tsar Dushan died in 1356 and Tvrtko at once reclaimed his lands, but held them only as a vassal state to Hungary.

The Serb peoples, divided into many small rival principalities, fought each other continuously, though the enemy which was to overwhelm them all was already advancing upon them. The Turk who, be it remembered, had entered Europe at the invitation of the Greeks, to aid them against the attack of Tsar Dushan, had firmly established themselves in the peninsula. Nevertheless the rival native princelings intrigued one against the other, and some even enlisted the help of the Turk instead of banding together against him. The Balkans were an easy prey for any strong foe.

Even after the Turks had beaten the Serbs severely, Stefan Tvrtko, King of Bosnia, seems only to have regarded this as an advantage to himself. He continued extending his realm; had himself crowned "King of Bosnia, Serbia and the coastland" in 1375, and was then the most powerful of the Balkan rulers. As an ally of King Lazar, who ruled over a much reduced Serbia, he, too, sent an army to Kosovo when, far too late, the Balkan people at last united against the Turk. But they lost the day. Union Was impossible to them, and a large part of the Serb Army deserted to the enemy.

Even then the Balkan princelings failed to recognize their danger. Tvrtko, still bent on extending his realm, Instead of opposing the Turks, who did not follow up their victory, gave all his energies to waging war against the Croats and Dalmatians, who at that time were under the King of Hungary. Tvrtko died in 1391, bequeathing a big Bosnia to his heir. But all mediaeval Balkan States were big only during the lifetime of their creator. Tvrtko's brother soon lost the newly acquired Croatian and Dalmatian districts, and Bosnia was further weakened by the breaking off of what is now known as the Herzegovina. It had for long had its own chiefs. One stronger than usual now arose, Sandalj Ranitch. The Turk was almost at the gate, but Sandalj's only object was to make himself a state independent of Bosnia. Kosovo had indeed taught the South Slavs nothing.

The advancing Turk began raiding Bosnia and employed Serbian troops. The Ragusa archives record: "In January 1398, the son of Bajazet, with a great number of Turks and Slavs, entered Bosnia." Stefan Ostoja was now King of Bosnia, but he too seems to have been more intent upon annexing Ragusa than in organizing defence against the Turk. Nor can we stop to unravel the complicated series of quarrels of one Slav prince with another, of their intrigues with Venice, with Hungary, with Ragusa, each playing for his own hand, though the Turks were now established as near as Uskub, and in 1415 invaded Bosnia for the third time. Sigismund, King of Hungary, alone of the neighbouring princes, realized the gravity of the situation and sent an army against the Turks, only to find that the Herzegovina sided with the Turks against him. As a result, we learn from the Ragusa archives, "the whole of Bosnia is laid waste and the barons are preparing to exterminate each other."

Venice meanwhile crept down the coast and occupied much of Dalmatia, while the South Slavs fought each other.

Nationality is the craze of to-day. Religion, in the Middle Ages, played a similar part. Catholic, Orthodox, and Bogumil, hated each other more than they hated the less known Turk. Each was willing to use him against the other.

People of the same race and language then fought each other because they differed about religion. To-day, even holding the same religious views, they fight in the sacred name of nationality. But then, as now, there were a few people who recognized the folly of the fashionable differences. At the Council of Basel in 1431 an effort was made to induce the Balkan chiefs, Catholic, Orthodox and even Bogumil, to send delegates to Basel with a view to ending religious strife and opposing a united front to the Turk.

It was vain. The King of Bosnia, and Stefan, Despot of Serbia, declared war on each other and fought for several years. And Sandalj, Lord of the Herzegovina, sided with the Serbs and bought of the Sultan the right to take Bosnia. They failed to do so, but their efforts certainly helped the final destruction of Slav independence.

Sandalj's successor, Stefan Kosatch, assumed the title Duke of Sava (whence "Herzegovina" the Duchy), became Bogumil and consequently fought both the Orthodox of Serbia and the Catholics of Ragusa. And ever the Turk advanced slowly and always found a Slav chief ready to side with him against a neighbour. At Fotcha, in the Herzegovina, I bought a bracelet of a silversmith, who related that his ancestor was the man who had guided the Turks into the district.

Constantinople fell in 1453, and left the Sultan free to complete the conquest of the Balkans. The Hungarians, led by the great Hunyadi, opposed him. But the Orthodox Serbs, led by their Despot George Brankovitch, whose ancestor had deserted to the Turks at Kosovo, hated Catholicism more than Islam, and sided with the Turk against Hunyadi.

The end soon came. The last King of Bosnia, Stefan Tomashovitch, a Catholic, asked help of the Pope, and endeavoured to raise troops among the Catholics of Dalmatia and Croatia. This enraged his Bogumil subjects, who preferred the Turks. The Sultan's army met little resistance; Stefan was taken prisoner and beheaded by the Turks in 1463, and soon all Bosnia was included in the Turkish Empire. As in other Balkan lands, the rights of the Christians were recognized. The Franciscans were appointed as their spiritual head, and several Franciscan monasteries date from these early days.

The Bogumils in large numbers adopted Islam, with which, in its abhorrence of ikons and images, and in its Monotheism, they were in greater sympathy than with either of the Christian Churches, both of which had persecuted them. But Bogumilism lasted into the nineteenth century, possibly into the twentieth, for a case was reported to me in 1911.

Those Christians who objected to Turkish rule fled south into Montenegro, especially from the Herzegovina, which was finally overthrown by the Turks in 1484.

Nor did the enmity between the Bosniaks and the Serbs cease now that they were under a common foe. Throughout the histories of Serbia and Montenegro we find that the Moslems of Bosnia and the Herzegovina were their bitterest enemies and that the armies, sent against them by the Sultans were very largely recruited from these districts. The sense of nationality did not begin to develop until very much later.

Under the Turk the feudal system of the pre-Turk days continued. We get a clear idea of the pre-Turk social conditions from the laws of Tsar Stefan Dushan, which show the strongly marked class difference of noble and serf. The noble was almost tax-free, but had to supply troops. The serf was tied to the land, and could only leave it with his lord's permission. Different punishments were inflicted upon nobles and serfs, the nobles' being naturally the lighter. So independent was the noble that he could build his own church or monastery in his land and chose its bishop. The serfs were judged by the noble upon whose land they were. They paid taxes; had to give him two days' work a week, and three if he had vineyards; cut hay and corn for him, and so forth. In pre-Turk days the rule of the chieftain seems to have been severe. Under the Turk the system continued, and the "Turk" of many a ballad who oppresses his Christian peasant was in fact the Slav feudal nobleman who, having turned Moslem carried on the ancestral tradition, and to the tyranny of the feudal noble added religious intolerance.

There was little organized government under the Turks. The traditional ballads give us vivid pictures of the heyduks, or brigands. Highway robbery up till, and well into, the nineteenth century was both a lucrative business and a sport which well suited the lazy but adventurous spirit of the people. It perpetuated in fact the everlasting raids of one noble against another in pre-Turk days. To this day a Montenegrin "junak" delights in pillaging a village. But continuous work is abhorrent to him.

Armed Turkish patrols guarded the main trade routes between Ragusa, Constantinople and Vienna. They cleared the route from time to time, and then woe to the captured heyduk, whether Moslem or Christian. Heavy the ransom to buy his freedom. But brigandage was rampant before the Turk came, and, as we have seen, the history of the Peninsula was one of incessant bloodshed and disorder. The Turk, in fact, showed more toleration for his Balkan subjects than they did for each other. Each aimed at the extermination of the other. Probably, had not the Turk overwhelmed them all, one or other would have ultimately predominated, and absorbed or exterminated the rest. Under the Turk all survived. He slapped them each impartially and allowed no one to exterminate the other. Nor was their hatred of the Turk ever great enough to cause them to combine against him till 1912, and then they were at each other's throats again so soon as he was removed.

Though, as we have seen, Montenegro was recruited by refugees from Bosnia, the converse also holds good. Many a Serb and Montenegrin flying from bloodvengeance, many a Slav criminal flying from Austrian justice, refuged in Turkish territory and turned Moslem. Nor when, at the beginning of the nineteenth century, the Serbs struck for independence did Bosnia join them. The Slav Vezir and the Pashas of Bosnia led great armies against them. By then the whole situation had changed, however. The ebb-tide of the Turk had begun. Austria and Russia in the eighteenth century had already decided upon the partition of his lands. Russia thought and cared only for Constantinople and the way there. Bosnia was recognized as Austria's sphere. The long wars and the liberation of the Serbs had effects in Bosnia and the Herzegovina. Revolts, largely agrarian, of the Christians began to take place. The big landowners, though Slavs, were Moslems. Their peasants were largely Christian. In 1849 a great rising was followed by the flight of thousands of Christian peasants into Austria, who in time of stress has often been the South Slav's only friend. The Herzegovinians, encouraged and incited by the Montenegrins on their borders, rose frequently, and it was their great rising of 1875 which started the Russo-Turkish War of 1877.

Before declaring war, however, Russia came to an agreement with Austria about Bosnia. It was understood that Austria should receive Bosnia on condition that she took no part in the war. Russia did not include this in the Treaty of San Stefano, but the scheme received the strongest support at the Congress of Berlin. The aim of both England and Germany was to hold back the ever forward-pressing Slav forces. Great Britain pledged herself to Austria previous to the Congress. "Le Gouvernement de Sa Majeste Britannique s'engage a soutenir tout proposition concernant la Bosnie que le Gouvernement Austro-Hongroise (sic) jugera a propos de faire au Congres."

Austria was offered Bosnia without reservation, and could then and there have annexed it. It was only doubt on Austria's part which led her to choose "administration" in place of annexation. The decision of the Congress at once caused trouble. The mass of the Bosnian Moslems violently opposed separation from Turkey, and the Herzegovinians, who had risen with a view to union with Montenegro, were equally opposed to Austria. The Austrian Army in 1878 met with great resistance, and only after heavy losses and four months' fighting finally subdued the land. The Herzegovinians declared to me that they only laid down their arms at the request of the Prince of Montenegro, under the understanding that Austrian administration was to be but temporary, but under the terms of the Treaty no time-limit was mentioned.

That the arrangement was intended by the Powers to be permanent appears from the text now (1919) published from the Vienna archives under date June 18, 1881, whereby the Courts of Russia, Germany and Austria-Hungary agree that "Austria shall annex these two provinces at the moment she judges opportune." This agreement was renewed in 1884. That the Powers considered the provinces as definitely annexed is shown by the fact that when in 1881 Austria introduced military conscription and recruited regiments for her own army no objection was made, nor did any Power intervene when Austria put down by force the resultant insurrection. On the contrary they most sternly ordered the Prince of Montenegro to prevent his men from rushing to the aid of the insurgents. Nor did Europe make any protest when the capitulations were abolished by Austria, though the land was nominally still a Turkish province. And Austrian coinage soon entirely replaced Turkish money.

Up till this time it is important to note that Russia, was taking no steps with regard to claiming Bosnia for her Pan-Slav schemes. Her immediate aim was Constantinople, and she had planned to obtain it by means of a large Bulgaria, which should be a vassal state. But Bulgaria soon struck for complete independence and showed that she would never be Russia's puppet, and elected Prince Ferdinand in defiance of the Tsar with the express intention of breaking away from Russian influence.

Russia therefore finally turned towards the Great Serbian Idea, which otherwise she would probably not have taken up till the annexation of Constantinople had been accomplished.

Till now, Russia had recognized the Montenegrin dynasty as the leader of Great Serbism. She now turned towards Serbia. It was in a far better geographical position and could supply a much larger army, and Montenegro could still be used as a tool.

The result of this was that when in 1897 the Emperor Franz Josef and Goluchowski went to Petersburg and asked for a confirmation of the agreement of 1881, "that the territorial advantages recognized to Austria-Hungary by the Berlin Treaty are and remain acquired by Austria-Hungary and therefore the possession of Bosnia-Herzegovina and the Sanjak of Novibazar cannot form matters of discussion; the Austro-Hungarian Government reserving to itself the right of substituting for the actual title of occupation and garrisoning, that of annexation."

Russia had now other plans and replied "the annexation of the two provinces would give rise to more extensive questions which would necessitate a special examination in time and place."

And in the summer of that very year the Tsar received Petar Karageorgevitch, the exiled claimant to the Serbian throne, and started upon her Great Serbian intrigue.

CHAPTER THIRTEEN
BOSNIA IN 1906. THE PLOT THICKENS

In the summer of 1906, when I visited Bosnia, the plot was already far advanced. Petar Karageorgevitch was on the throne of Serbia, and Russia, who had had a bad set-back in the Far East, was again turning Balkanwards.

To visit Bosnia a visa was necessary, a sure sign that a land suffers from "unrest." To obtain it I went to the Austrian Embassy. The young gentleman who attended to passports was out, and I was bidden sit on a bench with a number of rather poverty-stricken Austrians. When the gentleman appeared he was vexed to find so much work, and refused most of the applicants roughly. Their papers were incorrect or he was dissatisfied with their reasons for wishing to return home. One "cheeked" him considerably in German, and I laughed. It therefore never occurred to him that I was English. I am in fact, when travelling, rarely taken for English, which is often convenient. He addressed me sharply in German: "You want to go to Bosnia?"

"Yes, please." He took me for a Bosnian, and I let him do it.

"When did you leave Bosnia?"

"In the summer of 1900."

"What have you been doing in London?"

"Writing and other things."

This alarmed him and he said sternly: "You must tell me exactly why you left Bosnia."

"Because I am English," I said politely, "and it was time to come home."

I pressed my passport upon him, which he had been too haughty to look at before. Then there was hurrying and scurrying and orders and abuse of the doorkeeper and much confusion, and I was conducted to a drawing-room and apologized to (for having been treated as an Austrian subject) and given the visa. I enjoyed the episode immensely, and incidentally learnt how the official mind regarded Bosniaks. My previous experience in Serbia caused me to go in search of a new-laid Serbian visa also, in case I wished to cross the frontier. Militchevitch this time was very friendly, joked about the awful bill for cypher telegrams which I had run up for the Serbian Government in 1902, and promised to send me some introductions to leading Bosniaks.

At Trieste great events were in progress. The Emperor Franz Joseph was to hold big military manoeuvres at Trebinje in the Herzegovina and a naval review at Ragusa. The air was full of political electricity, flags and decorations, and the coasting steamer was full of police spies. All papers and passports were scrutinized carefully at each landing-stage. The Kaiser had not visited Dalmatia for very many years, and the populace was delighted. Dalmatia complained bitterly that money was poured into Bosnia and nothing done for her. Now things no doubt would look up.

Then we touched at Lesina and learnt that the Kaiser was unwell and that his heir presumptive, the Archduke Franz Ferdinand, would replace him.

"I know what is the matter with him," said the captain to me: "he has political fever. Something has happened."

The tale ran round that the Kaiser had intended after the manoeuvres to announce the annexation of Bosnia-Herzegovina. But that Abdul Hamid, apt at expedients, had learnt this fact, and had sent Franz Josef a polite message regretting that he was unable in person to receive His Majesty on this, his first visit to a Turkish province, but assuring him that his reception should be in every way suitable. Se non vero, ben trovato. Possibly true, for it came out later that Goluchowski actually broached the subject to Russia in the summer of 1906 and Russia raised objections, and may very probably have informed Abdul.

The news caused great disappointment. The old Kaiser was genuinely respected and even loved. Towns that were poor had spent much to do him honour. Perhaps this was one of the "tides in the affairs of men" and nations, that can be taken once and once only. The change of feeling was marked at all our stopping-places. It was very late when we reached Ragusa, and a gauntlet of police had to be run. The town was crammed. Next day the great grey warships lay off the coast and the army was arriving, disembarking and marching up to Trebinje. No stranger might go there without a special pass. I did not ask for one, as in such cases one sees only what one is meant to see, which is misleading. So I got up at 4 a.m. and went to look at the army. It was put to an unusual test in Europe, as it had to rely largely on mule transport. Having done much pack-saddle travel myself, I noted with interest that the Bosniak regiments were the only ones who knew how to "pack-saddle." With most of the others the saddles rolled under at once, or halfway up the road, which is worse. The army marched off early. I then made the acquaintance of a pretty girl, who was engaged to one of the officers, and from her later heard all that happened. This I supplemented by sitting in the cafe when the officers came back and hearing their curses. The men were dead-beat. The water supply had broken down, so had the food. The burning limestone karst had been too much for the men from the plains, and they broke down badly. Only the Croats and Bosniaks had stood the test. The manoeuvres were a failure.

The arrival of the Archduke and suite was very quiet. Ragusa was decorated entirely with Slav colours. Only on the Government offices did the yellow and black of Austria appear. At three in the afternoon the Archduke Franz Ferdinand was to drive through the town, whose broad main street is a fine background for a procession. It was crammed with a gay throng, and the national dress of Ragusa can be very gay indeed. All were talking and laughing.

Then came the solemn strains of "Gott erhalte Franz den Kaiser," the finest of all national anthems, and a sudden hush fell on the crowd. A silence absolute and unbroken that continued till the unhappy man, who sat motionless and erect, his face as blanched as a corpse, drove out of the further gate of the town. Then the crowd burst into one huge laugh. So complete was the demonstration that it was certainly pre-arranged.

"Write to the papers! write to the papers!" cried several who knew me, in high glee. Then Prince Danilo passed, and the crowd cried "Zhivio!"

I met The Times correspondent and said: "Well, that was a display. You have something to write about now!" But he replied that as we were on friendly terms with Austria he should certainly not report it. Nor did the papers to which I wrote think fit to publish this highly significant affair. Thus is the trend of Foreign Affairs hidden from the public.

Editors might as well often do without their correspondents, for they tell them beforehand what to emphasize, or cut the important news out of their telegrams.

The Archduke arrived with a portmanteau full of medals, and took them all away with him again. His only enthusiastic reception was from the deputation of Albanian Bishops and other ecclesiasts who came from Scutari to greet him. He was a brave man, for after the demonstration he went into the town on foot almost unescorted, and during the drive, though he must have expected a bomb every moment, he showed no loss of self-control save the blanching of his face. From Ragusa I went to Serajevo. I took the phonograph to collect songs, and wished specially to collect tattoo patterns and see the Bogumil and all other local historical remains, but was badly hampered, nor is it my purpose here to describe things anthropological. Had I been left to my own devices I should doubtless have made larger collections and seen less of the political situation. But the Austrian police, like the Serbian in 1902, insisted on rubbing my nose in it.

Travel in the interior was forbidden without a special pass. The British Consul was absent, and had referred me to his Italian colleague who muddled the business badly, whether because he was stupid or for reasons of his own, I did not find out. A little of both, I think. I was asked to call at a certain hour on the Governor of Serajevo. He was a Croat, spoke German to me and told me it was the wrong time of year to travel in Bosnia. Much surprised, I said I had wintered in Macedonia and could stand anything. He then spoke Serb, and I foolishly replied in the same tongue. I told him all I wanted was the permit, and that I could shift for myself. He objected that the food was bad; native houses dirty; winter near —such a journey as I proposed among the people in short impossible. I replied I was used to bugs, lice and fleas, could sleep on the ground and eat anything. All I wanted was a pony and a respectable guide. He stated that unfortunately there were no guides in Bosnia, so I said if I could have a pony I would find the way myself by map. Remembering my trump card at the Serb Legation, I asked if the country were in too dangerous a state. He hastened to say it was not. At last, countered at every point, he offered to lend me his man-servant for a fortnight; could not spare him longer. I should then have seen enough and could return to England. I said I could not so inconvenience him; that I could not get any work done in the time and that I thought of staying months not weeks. He said he would think it over and I was to call again. Next time he was all smiles and had a map ready. "Here," he said, "is your route. Here is a letter"—he pointed to a large pile—"for the Bezirksvorsteher of every place. You will present it on your arrival and do nothing till the authorities have arranged for you. The tour will take three weeks, and then you will go back to England." It was a great disappointment to me. You cannot get a native to tell you folk-tales while you draw the interior of his hut, if a policeman is sitting waiting till it is done. Nor can you live with a family and see its habits. Just as I had plodded round Serbia in spite of the police, so I would not be put off Bosnia, but to this day I regret the great amount of most interesting material that was there at my hand and which I could not gather. Bosnia was a mine of old-world lore and belief. As in Serbia, however, it was obvious that there was something the authorities wanted to conceal. And as "DORA" had not yet been born in England the affair seemed to me unutterably silly and tiresome. The first part of the journey I was, for all practical purposes, under arrest. Met on arrival everywhere by a most polite young official, who told me his whole time was at my disposal. "This is a mosque," he said, "this is a Turkish coffee-house. We will have a cup of coffee. This is the Catholic Church, or Orthodox, as the case might be." We inspected the school, and took a walk in the environs. "Now you have seen all. I will go with you to the post office and get a place for you on the diligence to-morrow. It starts at eight." The evening was spent in the hotel where all the Beamters had their meals. I tried to get information about local customs. Sometimes my hosts supplied them. More often the topic bored them. We talked of Vienna and London. After a good deal of this I reflected I was losing time and money. Every one was politeness and kindness itself. But I missed the long evenings in Albanian or Montenegrin huts round the fire; the talk and the doings. The Austrian official who sighed only for the Opera or the Ringstrasse and thought himself an exile wearied me. But as I was not allowed to study the native I had to study him. I startled some of them one night when they asked me as usual, how I liked Bosnia, by telling them that so far I had seen none of it, nothing but the Austrian occupation. This sort of thing went on a bit longer. Then on the Herzegovinian frontier I accidentally picked up an official to whom I had no letter of introduction. A cheery, enterprising individual who said he did not know to which of the many races of the Empire he belonged—and did not care. Was a geologist and a bit of an antiquarian. Took me up an 8,000 foot mountain and incidentally almost killed me. For on the desolate summit we surprised a chamois at close quarters, which snuffed us, gathered its feet and jumped over what looked like a precipice, though it had footholds for chamois. My new friend insisted on following it, as the shortest way down. When we were on a slippery grass slope so steep I could see the bottom of the valley a thousand feet below between my own boots, and the native servant lad refused to further risk his life, I too struck, and the chase was given up. When we arrived at a gendarmerie outpost on the night of the second day, and I was nearly dead-beat after seventeen hours' continuous struggle over many rocks and other obstacles, he confessed he had had no idea of the way. The stolid gendarmerie captain was appalled. "But if the Fraulein had died?" he asked. "Ah, but I knew she was English!" cried the other, "they can do these things. She will be all right to-morrow." He was delighted with the exploit, and suggested all kinds of places I should go to. I told him about my route and my previous experiences. He roared with laughter. Said it was silly nonsense. Some of the Serajevo people were too stupid for words. "Have you a passport? And it is in order. Very well. You are a British subject. They dare not stop you. Why should they? They ought to be glad to get tourists, and they won't if they go on like this. Burn all those letters and go where you please."

He made me a list of places where I should find Bogumil monuments, tattooed people, Roman remains and so forth. Told me that in his opinion Austria was wasting time and money in the provinces. The changes were too quick for the people; they preferred the old Turkish tracks and pack beasts to carts and the new roads, and that they suspected everything new. He himself got on with the people excellently, took me into several houses where they had portraits of Prince Nikola of Montenegro, and chaffed them about wanting to join that land. "They are all of them plotting across the border," he said, laughing. "They would far rather pig along like the Montenegrins. I've tried hard to persuade them to use iron ploughs. Our government supplies them at less than cost price. But they won't. They say, 'No, it is a Schwab thing.' We have spent no end of money trying to improve the live stock: bulls, stallions, rams, boars of the finest breeds. We sent a splendid boar last year to a village in charge of a man who was supposed to be reliable. And when Christmas came he killed it, roasted it and asked all the village to a feast. It was worth a lot of money. He only said that there was so much meat on it, it seemed a pity to let it live! It will take them several generations to get new ideas. Why worry. All this talk of going to Salonika is folly. This place is too much for us." His own job were beautiful irrigation works which kept a whole district fertile through the heats of summer. "But," he laughed, "the people are not a bit pleased. They say that in the old days it rained when it was God's will. They have quite forgotten they lost most of their crops every year from the drought. This is a Schwab thing, so they think it bad." On parting with him I took his advice and went where I liked. I was "shadowed" a good deal and my correspondence was generally ten days late, but otherwise was not interfered with. Living in native houses and going as guest to festivities, weddings, etc., as I had done in other Balkan lands was, however, impossible. It would have got my hosts into trouble. As it was, the wife of an official was very angry when I said I could get a meal in any village. For she declared she and her husband had even been refused coffee, the people all vowing they had none.

The reason for all the fuss was that the authorities were trying to hide the fact that the country was going through a very bad crisis, which was further exacerbated by the rumoured annexation; the open talk of an advance towards Salonika; and the renewed political activity of Russia and Serbia, which had now got England installed again at Belgrade.

Speaking Serb, I found without difficulty that there was a very strong Serb propaganda being worked from Belgrade among the Orthodox, who at that time formed nearly two-fifths of the native population. Next in number were the Moslems and after them the Catholics, lastly several thousand Spanish Jews. Orthodox, Moslem and Catholic native populations were entirely Slavonic. There was an acute division between the Orthodox and the other two parties.

The Catholics and even some of the Moslems called themselves Croat, and hated the term Serb. I had heard a report that in Croatia a reconciliation between Serb and Croat had taken place. None was to be seen in Bosnia. Only in the Herzegovina did the Catholic natives wish union with Montenegro.

The bulk of the Moslems looked longingly towards Turkey. The Orthodox, on the other hand, were violently pro-Serb, and feelings between Austria and Serbia had risen to fever heat.

Towards the end of 1905, Pashitch, then Prime Minister of Serbia, though already working hard against Bulgaria in Macedonia, signed a secret commercial convention with that country providing for the free interchange of goods with the exception of certain specified objects, and binding the two to a monetary convention and assimilation of weights and measures. As both countries produced much the same articles the arrangement did not appear to be likely to stimulate trade and as the racial hatred and rivalry of the two over the unsettled Macedonian scheme was extreme, the permanence of the arrangement was in any case doubtful.

Serbia was in dire need of a loan, and was on the point of concluding one for 70,000,000 francs. Part of this was to be supplied by the Vienna Bank, and both Serbia and Bulgaria were negotiating new commercial treaties with Austria. Serbia thought best therefore to keep the transaction with Bulgaria quiet. But just as business was almost concluded with Austria, a Bulgarian newspaper blurted out the Bulgar-Serb convention. The Austria-Hungarian Government demanded at once to see the document, and all business came to a standstill. Nor was this surprising, for Petar I, Pashitch and the regicide group were notoriously Russia's proteges, and any secret arrangement on their part was likely to be directed against Austria.

Austria closed her frontier to Serbian live stock.

Serbia was on the bubble. England had stipulated that the regicides were to be retired from power, as a condition of resuming diplomatic relations. (A stipulation that showed either that the Foreign Office little knew the Balkans, or that it knew very well that the treaty was a farce and did not care.) The regicide gang was infuriated and plotted the assassination of their opponents who wished by legal means to settle the question. But, as was delicately expressed by The Times correspondent, "it is stated that the police authorities refused to afford facilities for the execution of the plot, which consequently failed." Pity indeed that the police of Serbia did not remain "conscientious objectors" to plots of assassination. And about the same time when Vladan Georgevitch was sentenced to six months' imprisonment for "revealing state secrets," in The End of a Dynasty, the author in court denounced King Petar as the humble instrument of Russian policy.

Austria insisted on modifications to the Serbo-Bulgar convention; Turkey too demanded an alteration.

But by the time I arrived in Bosnia this affair was thrown quite into the shade by a new step on Serbia's part. She decided to purchase the artillery for her reconstructed army from the Creusot works in France. This so infuriated Austria that she declared a complete boycott of all Serbian goods. Serbia retorted and the frontiers were absolutely closed; so tightly indeed that along the Serbian frontier I found the officials complained of a meat shortage, and a great trade in smuggled fowls was run at night.

Feeling ran very high. Bosnia being under military occupation naturally bristled with officers and men. The officers talked very freely. Not once did I ever hear the Serbo-Bulgar convention mentioned. It was always the guns. They said it was not a question of trade in armaments. That did not matter. It was the question of policy. Serbia showed plainly now to all the world that she was ranged on the side of Russia and France against the Central Powers. "She has joined the Franco-Russian combine against us." They were quite right too, though being then unaccustomed to war, I thought their suspicions unreasonable. And neither I nor they knew that this step had followed immediately on the commencement of "military conversations" between France and England. But that this arming of Serbia was directly connected with the ringing-in policy of France and Russia is now obvious. Poor Edward VII may have thought he was peace-making, when he let Petar Karageorgevitch's gory past be forgotten and forgiven, and agreed to give up his visit to Montenegro so as not to wound that monarch's sensitive feelings—but he little knew the Balkans.

Scarcely one of the Austrian military or civil authorities I spoke with had ever visited Serbia or Montenegro. They all regarded the two as semi-savage lands used as tools against them by Russia. When I arrived at Vishegrad, close on the Serb frontier, feeling was running high. Serbia showed no sign of giving way as had been expected. I told the officials their boycott was bound to fail, as you cannot starve out a people whose main assets are maize and pigs. "You will see I am right. They will simply go on eating pigs till you are tired." The Bezirksvorsteher was annoyed at this, but interested. I said "Get me a horse and a guide, and I will go into Serbia and see." He retorted It was impossible as the frontier was closed, but he hired me the horse and a very black gypsy, a wild enough creature, and I went.

Was halted at the border blockhouse, which the black gypsy thought unpassable, but the Serbs were rather pleased to be inspected, telephoned through to Uzhitza, and I rode on. An amusing sidelight was the surprise of the gypsy at finding the same language both sides of the border. "But they talk Bosniak!" he cried.

An aged peasant on horseback joined me and asked so many questions about London that I thought he knew something about it till he asked "Is it a free country?"

He was puzzled when I said, "Yes."

"But it is under Austria," he protested.

"No, no," said I, "it is a free country."

"Thank God," said the old boy, "and I believed it was under Austria. Bogati—so many people are under Austria. But London is not."

In Serbia I found I had guessed right. "In spite of the horrible curse, nobody seemed a penny the worse." Uzhitza was in high spirits and reminisced my visit of 1902. They referred with triumph to the murder of Alexander. Since that, everything had been going splendidly. The army was everything and all possible money was to be spent on it. If Alexander had lived he would have made an alliance with Austria and have stinted the army. The army and Great Serbia was the cry. They were all for Russia. As for the wretched Draga, the ladies told me that she had received them at some function or another with powder all over her face. Imagine having to kiss the hand of such a fallen woman! (Fashions have changed now, or England would be a female slaughterhouse.) All the officers killed in her defence were stated to have been her paramours. Nothing was too bad for her. King Petar was described as one who would never interfere with the army. There was much enthusiasm over the resumed relations with England. It was obvious that no one believed that the regicides would really go; their departure was a mere matter of form. As for the boycott, they laughed and told funny tales. A bride had ordered her whole trousseau at Vienna. The wedding was fixed. But the frontier was closed. Her girl friends gallantly went to Vienna in their oldest garments; changed and came back, rather stout but triumphant, clothed in the whole trousseau. As for export, by the aid of France and England they would export to Egypt and Marseilles via Salonika. The French artillery would come in by the same route. French artillery they intended to have.

I was much interested, but as I had brought no baggage could not go further into Serbia. The Mayor gave me a mounted gendarme as escort to the frontier.

This impressed the Vishegrad authorities much, as did the fact that I had got across the frontier at all. The Bezirksvorsteher asked at once what I had learnt in Serbia, and if the frontier would soon be open.

"I do not know," said I.

"What do you think?" said he.

"I think not."

"Our Minister at Belgrade is of the same opinion," he replied. In truth the officers who had protested that Serbia had now openly joined the Russo-French combine were right. And what is more, through our Entente with France, we too now, consciously or not, were tools used by Russia for the making of Great Serbia and furthering Pan-Slav ambition. Serbia began to feel it safe to pull long noses at Austria. That the Austrians on the other hand regarded their occupation of Bosnia as permanent was clear. No nation merely on a temporary job of "putting things straight" would have expended the vast sums and effort needed to bring a half-wild Turkish province in twenty-eight years up to a high state of material well-being. The mountain roads are second to none in Europe. Mines, agriculture and every possible industry were being developed regardless of expense, by up-to-date methods.

"The officials," I noted in my diary, "give one the impression of being over-worked." Everything was centralized and had to go through the Konak. They wrestled with a mass of detail and mostly felt like exiles in a wild land. The large majority were Slavs—either Poles, Croats or Bosniaks, and these got on much better with the populace than the Magyars or Germans, of whom I met a few. The mistake of the Government was in trying to go too fast. A leap in twenty-eight years from the twelfth century or thereabouts to the twentieth was too much. The peasant intensely conservative by nature resented every change. "Better that a village should fall than a custom" is a South Slav proverb which I have heard quoted with approval. An astonishing amount of work had been done and admirably done. Future generations will profit by it. But the peasant who had had all his ideas and habits upheaved had had time to forget the oppression of the Turk, but remembered, with kindness, his slop-dawdle tolerance, This happens, I believe, in every land "freed" from the Turk. The people vaguely expect an earthly paradise where every one will do as he pleases, and find to their dismay that you can no longer evade the sheep-tax by tipping the hodja to let you put your flock on "vakuf" land. The Christian loses his privilege and has to serve in the army which he hates. He cannot run to a foreign consul for support against his Moslem neighbour, nor earn good pay by acting as spy for one Power or another. He complained bitterly that the Turkish Government never made roads or mended bridges, When he finds, however, that the new foreign government expects him to contribute to their making by giving labour, or paying tax, he is furious. "Liberty" for most Balkan Christians means liberty to massacre Moslems and take their property. The Bosnian Orthodox peasant found precisely the same law applied to him and the Moslems. The strict impartiality observed by the Austrian Government towards all three sects caused the wrath of all. "What," said a Catholic fiercely, "can you think of our Government when I tell you that a priest baptized and converted three Moslem lads, and the Government actually made him send them back to their parents and censured him because they were not of age? Not of age, if you please, and so their souls are not to be saved!"

The Moslem was equally furious with the equality treatment, for he was no longer top-dog.

The most remarkable work of the Austrian Government gave perhaps the most offence. It was the medical. The Bosniak, in appearance, is often a giant. But his appearance is deceptive. Stripped of his numerous waistcoats his chest measurement, as the military doctors informed me, is so poor that a larger percentage of Bosniaks were rejected from the army than in most of the other recruiting districts of Austria-Hungary. As in all South Slav lands, tuberculosis raged. "Thirty per cent, affected, without counting an apex" as a Bosnian doctor told me. And scattered over the country, but especially virulent on the eastern districts along the Serbian frontier, was syphilis. In some parts this was so rampant that the Government posted on the village walls and in the schools, notices warning persons never to drink from a glass after some one else, or wipe with the same towel, and other advice. All of which went against the custom of the people. Against tuberculosis the schools waged an anti-spitting war. A child who spat on the floor had to clean it up, which was considered a great indignity and gave great offence. Compulsory cleaning of streets to a population who regarded the street as the proper receptacle for all garbage was a further source of trouble. That the medical work produced a great improvement, that malaria, by drainage, petroleum on the ponds, and quininizing of the Population was stamped out in some districts and got in hand in others counted for nothing. They "were not our custom," they were "Schwab."

The forests also were a source of friction. In old days the peasant cut what he pleased, where he pleased. His goats browsed the saplings and they grew up crooked. But they made firewood and it did not matter. No replanting ever took place. When all the wood was cut on a hillside the winter rains washed away the whole of the soil and left bare rock. A pity—but the will of God, sighed the peasant, and he went on to fell the next wood.

Forestry laws infuriated him, and his disregard of them infuriated the forestry officer. A goat-tax (slight for the poor owner of a couple of goats) was instituted, rising according to number, to a sum which made the keeping of a large herd impossible. An official, to whom I remarked on what seemed to me the paucity of flocks, said, "We do not let them keep goats and they won't keep sheep. For my own part I should relax the goat laws for a while at least; they cause such resentment. But the central authorities will not do it. We have to rely largely on the sale of timber to run the country. It is one of the most valuable assets."

All officials agreed in finding the people very difficult to move; very childlike in their ideas and very slow to adopt new ones. A few hated and loathed them.

It was, however, not the officials but the private residents who were on bad terms with the native population, families who had come for business purposes from civilized and comfortable Austrian towns, and who would not take the trouble to learn Slav except just enough for their marketing. I had never before been in a land under foreign occupation, and commented on this attitude to some officers. They jeered at me and said, "You have evidently never been to Egypt. Wait till you have seen your own people there."

I was annoyed at the time. But when some years later I went to Egypt I found the English attitude to the native worse and repented of my comments about Bosnia. One race in truth cannot see with the eyes of another.

The Austrian official really tried to adapt the law to native ideas, and when unable to unravel complicated questions of native usage, even summoned the ancient council of "the good men" to decide according to local custom. A good deal of blood-vengeance still went on, but with the knife; firearms were strictly forbidden, and very few licences for them issued. This was a source of great discontent, for the carrying of arms to the South Slav peasant means manhood. The Christian's idea of liberty is to carry arms. And the fact that the Moslem also was debarred from so doing in no way consoled him. In one respect the lack of firearms was a real hardship, for Bosnia swarmed with wild pig which devastated the crops. When the corn was standing, peasants sat up all night drumming on petroleum tins around the fields to drive off beasts. There were enough wolves also to harry the flocks. An Austrian official killed ten in one night with strychnine during my visit. But the natives complained bitterly that the Government did not permit them to shoot wild beasts and did not keep them down itself.

There was, I was told, very little stealing but, in the forest districts where the woodcutters all carried long handled hatchets, a blow with which was invariably fatal, there was a good deal of slaughter, as in a quarrel a man struck with whatever was handy. Only if the attack proved to be cold-blooded and pre-arranged was capital punishment inflicted. Otherwise imprisonment up to twelve years according to the circumstances.

Wages were low. The peasant was very poor. Very high wages were obtainable in America, and thousands emigrated thither. They ascribed this to Austrian rule, but the same thing was happening in Montenegro, where the Government was vainly trying to stop emigration by refusing passports. It was simply an economic question of supply and demand. Labour was wanted in America at any price. The emigration had the same effect in Bosnia as in Montenegro. A large surplus of women remained behind, and the birth-rate of illegitimate children rose high and, as is perhaps inevitable with a military occupation, prostitution was common. This, though, was not the only cause of immorality in both Montenegro and Bosnia. In old days all the women of the family were the property of the men of the family, who had the right to shoot at sight any man tampering with a wife or daughter of a family group. A blood vengeance so started might mean twenty lives. The risks were not to be lightly taken. The emancipation of women and the restriction of firearms produced new complications.

The Austrians were rather pleased to see emigrants leaving the land, and said they hoped they would never come back, so that they could be replaced by a better population. They were anxious to consolidate their position in Bosnia as fast as possible, so as to be ready for a forward move. "Nach Salonik" was a favourite topic of conversation. A friendly chemist at Fotcha even invited me to have tea with him under the Austrian flag at Salonika, that day three years, that is October 1909, by which time he fully expected to be established there. He considered the Government had been shamefully slow. They ought already to be well on the way there. I travelled by train from Ragusa to Mostar with a General and his daughter. She, who had just arrived, looked with wonder at the bare grey rocks we passed and asked, "Why ever did we take all these stones, father?"

"Part of the price we paid Europe for Salonika, my dear!" he replied.

I wintered at Serajevo, and by taking my phonograph to the Moslem coffee-houses gained some popularity, for there was but one other such instrument in Serajevo, and you had to pay to hear it. The Moslems, I soon learnt, wanted only the Padishah and hoped for the return of the Turk. Several had lived long years in Egypt. But when I told them I meant to go there they very earnestly begged me not to. All the English were very soon to be driven out or done away with, and the company unanimously agreed that it would be a very great pity that I, who had been so kind as to play the "monogram" to them for nothing, should be killed out there. I asked them to tell me truthfully what it was that the English did that was so bad. They replied very reasonably: "Everything. Nothing you do is as we do. You make yourselves fine houses and streets in Cairo. Why do you not make them in your own land and leave our land to us? We hate your things. The land is now not our land. It is all Alia Franga." You do not like our ways. We do not like yours. Go and leave our land to us."

We should say just the same thing, only less politely, were we "occupied" by the Japanese. They were kind enough to say that the English were not so bad as the Schwabs, but I fear this was only out of gratitude for phonograph favours.

In a private room upstairs they sang me a special ballad of the Greco-Turkish War of 1897, which began by describing how Prince George of Greece and the British Consul and some other European officials drank beer together and when they had drunk too much, planned a treacherous attack upon the Turks. It was a long song and took four hours to sing—with refreshments in the middle. I did not stay to the end. Every one, of course, believed in the guilt of the British Consul.

At Serajevo I got, too, into a very Nationalist Orthodox set through the Nationalist school kept by Miss Irby. The pro-Serb party was all Orthodox, wildly anti-Turk and furiously anti-Catholic. All that was Latinski was abhorrent, and every vice and crime was imputed to the Catholic clergy. They were represented as fiends in human shape, who stole people's children and baptized them into the Roman Church. I had found similar fanaticism among the Montenegrin peasants, but did not expect it among the educated Bosnian officials and their wives.

They made no secret of being in communication with Serbia, told of their expedients to smuggle in papers and dodge the police authorities. And when the windows were carefully shut used to sing "Onamo, onamo," and other forbidden Nationalist songs. In one respect I found the Orthodox exactly like the Moslems. They wanted to be top-dog and suppress the others. A pretty school mistress complained to me bitterly of the authorities who had put her to teach in a purely Catholic district, "where I can do no propaganda at all." She wanted a Parliament for Bosnia, and assured me that as the Orthodox party was the largest they would then be able to shout the others down, from the gallery, and was naively surprised when I told her that this was forbidden in England, which she had thought was a free country. She had been taken once to the Budapest Parliament for the express purpose of screeching all the time certain members spoke. The debate ended in a free fight, and she had been hoarse for days.

This idea of freedom is, of course, not unknown in England. It is the only one existing across the Adriatic. An ardent Great Serbian once explained: "When Great Serbia is made we mean to have religious equality everywhere. For instance, in Ragusa there are two monasteries, both Catholic. This is unjust. When it is ours, one will be Orthodox and one Catholic."

"Which do you mean to rob then, the Franciscans or the Dominicans?" he was asked. "Rob!" he said, much hurt. "We are going to make religious equality. One must be Orthodox and one Catholic." And this he continued to repeat, though it was urged that in this case one or the other order must be deprived of its monastery, and that, moreover, the vast majority of Ragusa is Catholic.

But Liberty is a glorious thing, and I found the Orthodox heartily approved of Alexander's murder as one step towards it.

By now I had learned that even officials in Austrian employ were working against the Austrian Government. A friend of mine, who was also much interested in things South Slavonic, wrote at this time and suggested I should join the Slovenski Jug Society then recently formed. But as it was made clear to me that these so-called patriotic associations were plotting against the Austrian Government I decided that I, as a British subject, should steer clear of them, more especially as one could not tell to what lengths they would go. I had been on the brink of the plot for the destruction of Alexander Obrenovitch, a sufficiently alarming precedent, so I declined to become a member of the Slovenski Jug, preferring a front seat at the drama to being possibly dragged onto the stage.

As one of my objects in this journey was to see Christmas customs in a peasant house I determined to leave for Montenegro, where I could do so easily, and left the tense political atmosphere of Bosnia with some relief.

CHAPTER FOURTEEN
1907

Blindly and bloodily we drift.—MASEFIELD.

The thirteen days' difference between the Old and New Style enabled me to spend Christmas 1906 at Serajevo, and celebrate it a second time in old Serb fashion in Krsto's hut at Nyegushi in January 1907. Montenegro lay deep under snow, all mountain tracks buried. Life in the villages was rough and severe. We celebrated Christmas, the New Year, the Blessing of the Waters, and St. Sava. But by leaving Bosnia I had not found peace. The undercurrent of discontent with the government was more marked than last year. Even in Nyegushi, the birthplace of the Prince, there were growlings. What was done with all the money? The most hateful and wearisome work in all the world was guarding flocks on the mountain. Therefore a herdsman should be paid more than a chinovnik (official). Nevertheless every youth aspired to be a chinovnik, because then you could retire early with a pension. Many men had lately returned from America with pockets full of cash. They preached that the duty of a government was to make "jobs." They used the English word, and their audience had not the least idea what "jobs" meant, except that it was a highly desirable something which brought in money. America was a republic, and in America there were "jobs." Therefore, if you had a republic you would have "jobs." The new Parliament roused no enthusiasm. The Prince could veto its decisions, and its members had but childish notions. The old idea of local soviets was not extinct, nor their rivalry with the tribe next door. Many a member consequently thought it his duty to his constituents to veto a road for another district, until his own had been supplied, without seeing that at this rate nothing could be done. Dr. Marusitch was clamouring to remove the capital to

Danilovgrad, and make other sweeping changes. Tomanovitch, the Prime Minister, and his son, aide-de-camp to the Prince, were hated and reported to have sinister influence. Those still faithful to the Gospodar blamed him for giving up his official power. Cetinje, however, was excited over a new subject. A manager from Earl's Court had come to invite Montenegro to take part in a Balkan States Exhibition. Highly flattered, Montenegro had signed the agreement without the ghost of idea what to do or how to do it. The show was to open in May. Montenegro, of course, could not possibly be ready by then, so I was asked by the committee to write a letter informing the management that the exhibition must be postponed till July, or whenever Montenegro was ready. I explained that this was no use in England. Montenegro must be ready—or drop out. They argued: "But when the London people hear there is going to be an exhibition they will change their season to suit it." I retorted: "Whenever I want you to do something you say: 'Nije nash obitchaj!'" (It is not our custom). "Now we say this to you." And I hustled them. Petar Plamenatz was the Secretary for Home Affairs. He was to give me facts—imports, exports, education, post, telegraph, etc.—for an article on Montenegro for the catalogue. Every morning he said: "To-morrow without fail I will give you all the figures." And every evening: "Mon Dieu, it is impossible. I am tired!" He had two hours free at midday and all his evenings. At the last minute, when told the thing must go to press, he said: "But why all this anxiety about facts, Mademoiselle? Write what you please. I am sure it will be charming!" I wrote an essay, which necessarily contained no point of commercial importance, and insisted that he must hear it before it was sent as an official Montenegrin production. "But I have a headache," said Petar. "What does that matter?" said I, and I made him hear it. He said it was admirable, and added no single fact. And he was one of the Intelligentzia upon whom the fate of Europe later depended.

At this time I was daily teaching English to one of the schoolmasters, an interesting task, as it showed me the total lack of discipline there is in the education of the average Near Eastern. He had a good deal of brain power and a certain amount of information, but was totally unable to make himself do anything he disliked, even when he knew it to be necessary. Would not begin with simple things because he was not a child. And when he could not understand difficult ones, flung the papers on the floor and stamped on them, vowing he would never do English again. I smiled and said: "Very well. Don't. It does not matter to me. Goodbye." To which he would exclaim: "Good God, what fish blood. But with your sangfroid you are a born Professor. I lose my temper with my class twenty times a day." He had the impossible Near Eastern ideas of Liberty. Briefly: "Do as you please, and damn the rest!" Was an ardent "Great Serbian," but was not a Montenegrin, and when "freedom" was attained hoped to force Montenegro into the correct path. His idea of education was primitive. He despised every form of game, exercise, and gymnastics as waste of time, and had never done any himself. "That is why you are so absurdly neurotic and you have never learnt to keep your temper." I chaffed him. He retorted: "Fishblood, fishblood." An interesting specimen of the Intelligentzia.

Meanwhile Prince Nikola became anxious about Earl's Court. He sent for me, took a gold medal from his breeches pocket, and gave it to me with the request that I would go to England, see the managers of the exhibition, and keep an eye on the exhibition when opened. A staff of Montenegrins was to come over and manage the section. Meanwhile, in order that it should become widely known, he thought it would be a good thing if I told all my friends there was going to be an exhibition, and ask them to tell theirs. Thus the news might be spread through London.

That exhibition would take a volume in itself. Briefly, Bulgaria, Serbia, and Montenegro were represented. Montenegro, with characteristic laisser faire, never appointed a commissary at all, and the work all fell on me. Fortunately, in fact, for I was the buffer state between Serbia and Bulgaria, who were at daggers-drawn. At the necessary meetings the Serb Commissioner talked German and Serb into one of my ears, while the Bulgar shouted French and Bulgar into the other, and the English manager at intervals begged me to "tell him what was the matter." Even when invited out for a day in the country the Serb and Bulgar peasants refused to dance together. John Bull did his best to work up an anti-Serb demonstration more than once. But though we balanced on the edge of hostilities, the Balkan War did not break out at Earl's Court.

I have often thought since it was a pity the Foreign Office did not study our methods.

The five Montenegrins who came "to help" were far too proud to do any work at all, or associate with any of the others. They looked on the Bulgars as foreigners, and despised the Serbs.

Montenegro's attitude was shown by Petar Plamenatz, who arrived for a week's visit as special Commissioner for Montenegro just in time for the opening ceremony, when I had done the whole preliminary work of arranging the show.

Lord Fitzmaurice invited all the Balkan representatives to lunch. I translated the invitation to Petar. "I shall not go," said he. "I have a headache."

"That makes nothing," said I, "you are here to represent Montenegro. This invitation is an honour, and I accept it for you." Petar was surprised. He had naively imagined that as Commissioner for Montenegro it was he who conferred the honour upon Lord Fitzmaurice. He went, however. I asked how the party had gone off.

"It was really extraordinary," said Petar. "Do you know that of all the Balkan representatives, I was the only one who knew how to conduct myself in a comme il faut manner!" The next invitation, a dinner, he flatly refused to accept. I was still more resolved that if I had to "run" the exhibition for Montenegro, Petar should continue to behave comme il faut. He dodged and excused vainly. I wrung the truth from him. He had no clean shirt. It is the only time I ever bought an evening shirt for a gentleman.

Petar left after the most strenuous week of his life. Nothing, however, would induce his five compatriots to do anything at all, and just as they thought they had demonstrated that as the finest representatives of the South Slav stock, their mission in life was to exist and look beautiful, to their intense surprise the management sent them home.

Meanwhile, our inability to obtain any reply to business questions from Montenegro was explained by the sudden news of the discovery of a plot to assassinate Prince Nikola, and, it was said, his family, too. Our five Montenegrins received letters from home full of the wildest details, which they all believed, showing that the country was in a whirl, and that the Exhibition must be steered! without any further aid from the homeland. Numbers! of arrests had been made. Russia was said to be implicated in the plot, for the girls of the Russian Institute had trampled on the Prince's portrait at the bidding of Sofia Petrovna, its head!

After this the whole work of the Montenegrin section was wasted. Not one of the trade openings we found—some very good—were taken up, and no letters were replied to.

Montenegro, though she did not realize it, had in truth reached the turning-point of her history. She was no longer the recognized leader of the Great Serbian movement. During the years when Serbia was "in Coventry" Montenegro had done nothing to strengthen her position, save some futile posing to journalists as "the one good boy." Now Serbia, with Russia behind her, was to the fore. Montenegro's tide was about to ebb. I wrote strongly to the Montenegrin Government that it was most necessary to appoint a representative in London. I would not myself go on doing the work of a consul Without authority or pay. Preferably they should send a Montenegrin. If not, I suggested two Englishmen willing to do the work, one of whom they appointed next year.

It was a step in advance, but it was too late. Serbia, completely whitewashed, re-established a Legation and a commercial agency, and began an energetic propaganda.

Meanwhile an event of world-wide importance Took place. On August 31, 1907, the Anglo-Russian agreement was signed. The Anglo-Russian difficulties of the Middle East were arranged, and Russia was free to turn all her attention towards Constantinople.

She was lavishly supplied with French gold, and could count on French military support. France was already arming and aiding her Balkan ally, Serbia. And Russia, without doubt, was aware of the "military conversations" of France and England. Possibly the agreement with Russia was one outcome of them. It is noteworthy that though England had "agreed" with Russia, so little did she realize the possibilities of the Near East, that we were the only Great Power which had no permanent representative in Montenegro, and no representative at all on the East of the Balkan peninsula, save Mr. Summa, our Albanian Vice-consul at Scutari.

Austria retorted to the steps being taken by the Russo-French group by obtaining from the Sultan permission to build a railway from Uvatz, on the Bosnian frontier, to Mitrovitza, which would link up Serajevo with Salonika.

The Balkan railway question had been rankling for years. The Slav wanted an east-and-west line to connect with the Adriatic. The Teuton a north-south one to reach the Aegean. Neither would allow the other's plan to mature. I used to get much amusement in mixed company by proposing various railway lines and hearing the violent denunciations or applause that followed, according to the political aims of those present.

The Turks have been freely blamed for neither constructing railways nor allowing others to do so. But to be fair, one is bound to admit that they knew very well such lines would be used for strategical purposes, and they lived in terror of the Slav Adriatic line. Before judging Abdul Hamid harshly, let us consider at what period we should have allowed Russia to build and control a line across India "to advance trade."

The year 1908 opened with the railway question. Russia and Serbia furious about the Uvatz-Mitrovitza scheme. The Morning Post, it is of interest to note, was markedly pro-Austrian.

I remembered four points: (1) The Austrians' boast that they would be in Salonika by 1909; (2) The Pasha of Plevlje's statement that Austria had more troops in the Sanjak than she was entitled to; (3) The oft-repeated statement of Serb and Montenegrin that the Austrian gendarmerie officers superintending "reforms" in Macedonia smuggled in arms; (4) That Serbs and Montenegrins were also arming and carrying on a sharp Great Serbian propaganda in Bosnia, the Herzegovina, and the Sanjak.

In the great race Austria now seemed a neck ahead, riding Uvatz to Salonika.

CHAPTER FIFTEEN
1908. A FATEFUL YEAR

Europe was now definitely divided into two camps, each arming against the other. Plots thickened, and events crowded on one another. So knotted did the Balkan threads become, it is hard to untwine them. One thing must be remembered, and that is that at the centre of the knot was always Constantinople. To which Power or group should it belong?

I arrived in Cetinje at the end of April to find things about as bad as they could be. Depression was general, and the place in a hush of terror. Every one hastened to warn me against every one else. The Prince was due next day on his return from Petersburg, whence great things were expected, and a general holiday was proclaimed in honour of the event. Mourning added to the general gloom, for the two infant sons of Prince Mirko, the only direct heirs to the throne, had died within a month or two of each other of tubercular meningitis. Baby Stefan had been playfully called Stefan Dushan II, with the hope that he would reign at Prizren—and he was dead. All hope of a child to Prince Danilo had been given up; much had died with Baby Stefan. Some even hinted at foul play, but this suspicion was quite groundless, for tuberculosis was rapidly spreading in the land; it is worth mentioning only as showing the mental state of the country.

On the other side were murmurs deep and sinister against the Prince and his line, the first growl of a storm. The prisons were full. Folk whispered of many untried prisoners. Some Who had befriended me in former years were not only in prison, but in heavy irons —Gjurovitch, who had been a minister, and poor garrulous Dr. Marusitch. His wife had snatched her husband's revolver and fired at the gendarme who arrested him. The peasants of Drobnjak had tried to prevent the arrest of Serb agents who were distributing revolutionary leaflets, printed in Belgrade.

Soldiers were sent to enforce the arrests. Some had refused to act, and had had some heavy sentences inflicted on them. It was all part of the Great Serbian movement. The Montenegrin Government would send no more students to Belgrade to be corrupted.

The very morning after my arrival Tomanovitch, the Prime Minister, sent for me. He was extremely anxious and nervous, and asked what the English papers said about the plot against Prince Nikola. I told him the English Press had said little beyond reporting unrest in Montenegro. He hurried to deny there was any, and said he wished me to know the truth. Prince Nikola had behaved with the greatest moderation, and had even permitted Dr. Marusitch to visit his sick child. The plot against the Prince had been planned by wicked enemies from outside. What did I intend writing to the papers on the subject?

I had been but a few hours in Cetinje, but perceived the affair was a bad one, and as I knew people on both sides it would be hard to avoid being dragged into it. I replied therefore that I had written nothing, and intended writing nothing to the papers, and wished to take no part in Montenegro's internal affairs. He was visibly relieved and thanked me. We parted on friendly terms, he assuring me that he wanted me to know the "truth." So did every one else. And it was always different. One side said that so soon as the people had had a voice, a wild scramble for place and power had ensued; that "freedom of the Press" had loosed such a flood of scurrility, abuse, and libel that it had to be suppressed by force; that finding themselves thwarted, a gang of malcontents had plotted to assassinate the Prince—some said Prince Danilo, too—and to seize power themselves; that they had been in communication with Russia and Serbia, and had arranged the affair in the latter country; that severe example should be made, and wholesale executions take place.

On the other hand, folk said that the Prince, furiously jealous of power, had offered the "Constitution" merely as a pretence to Europe that he was up-to-date, and had so arranged as to retain autocracy; that he purposely suppressed knowledge, kept out literature, and encouraged only the narrowest education in order to retain power and keep folk ignorant; that those arrested were the cream of the land, all the most advanced spirits, all those who were for civilization; that even schoolboys had been hunted down like wild beasts and thrown into prison as political offenders; that no one's life was safe; that spies were everywhere, who curried favour with the Petrovitches by the numbers they arrested; that the prisoners were miserably maltreated. The more moderate declared the Prince to be helpless in a "ring;" that by rashly giving the Constitution he had deprived himself largely of power, and no longer knew what went on; that, till he gave up administering justice eight years before, he had been "the father of his flock," and knew all about everything. Now he had lost touch and would never regain it. They hoped for a general amnesty of all prisoners. The Prince's return from Russia was melancholy. He was reported to be suffering from a feverish attack, and the Princess, too, was very unwell. His journey was believed to have been a failure.

The Russians of Cetinje received me with extraordinary enthusiasm. Filled with joy for the Anglo-Russian agreement, Sofia Petrovna, of the Russian Institute, kissed me over and over again. The Institute was a feature of Cetinje, and Sofia Petrovna was its queen. It was the Pan-Slav centre of the whole district, where Slav girls, brought in from Turkish and Austrian districts—girls from Prizren, girls from Bosnia and Dalmatia, as well as Montenegrin girls, were brought up to Serbism and belief in Holy Russia. Mademoiselle was stout, ruddy, And amazingly energetic; autocratic, but good-natured. Her lean, restless-eyed subordinate, Alexandrovna, however, drove the pupils the way they should go with pitiless severity, and perhaps as a result the girls of the Institute were all said to leave it finished intriguers.

The glory of Holy Russia was what Sofia Petrovna lived for. Russia and England were now united, and she dreamed dreams and saw visions. Russia's path was clear. Her dominion over all Europe and all Asia merely a matter of time. Sofia was enchanted. "Ah, my dear! What is your Empire? Your ambitions are nothing to ours. Nothing, nothing. Till now you have stood in our path. Now we shall march together. Russia is God's agent. You will give us your practicalness. We shall give you our beautiful religion. For at present you know you have none!" Borne on a wave of enthusiasm, she pressed me to spend Good Friday and Easter Sunday at the Institute and take part in the celebrations.

The gathering was very Russian. I was astonished at the difference made by the Anglo-Russian agreement. Hitherto the Legation had been distantly polite. Had sometimes asked questions, but never supplied information. Now nothing could exceed their friendliness. Together England and Russia were to fight Germany, and I said in vain I had no wish to. "Your commerce necessitates it," they declared. They considered Austria's railway scheme to Salonika as a direct insult "which we shall never permit." About Montenegro they despaired. The Prince was riding to ruin. All Russians who visited him were pained to find him surrounded with Austrian Slavs, Gregovitch, Tomanovitch, Ramadanovitch, even his doctor, Perisitch—all from Austria. The very servants in the palaces often Austrian or German. The arrests had been directed by senseless fear; he had alienated the sympathy of the best in the land; could brook no rival; had quarrelled with his Petrovitch relations; listened only to flatterers who directed him against Russia. Finally, they blamed him severely for the Constitution, which he had promulgated! without consulting Russia.. Even she—Sofia Petrovna—who had given twenty years of her life to Montenegro and spared no pains; even she was now the victim of anti-Russian intrigue, and accused of the childish folly of bidding her girls trample on the Prince's portrait! Her girls—in a school paid for largely by the Dowager Tsaritsa! Oh, it was too much. And the Prince had believed it, and informed her that never again would the Royal Family visit the school (nor, in fact, did they). Tears stood in the poor lady's eyes. Her school had been the meeting-place of the intelligentzia. Ministers, priests, and officials had sought her advice. Now persons wishing to curry favour with the Prince had maligned her.

A lying, treacherous race, said one of the Russians. But poor Sofia, through her tears, said they were foolish and misled. Both she and the Secretary of Legation wanted me to ask, for an audience with the Prince, but I decided not to be mixed in anybody's plots, so merely left a card at the Palace, where I learnt that the Prince was still very unwell. A report of a conversation between Vesnitch, Serbian Minister in Paris, and Izvolsky, October 1908 (see Bogitchcvitch, xvii), throws light on what had occurred. "You must," said Izvolsky, "however, soon come to an understanding with Montenegro. The scandalous discord which exists between Belgrade and Cetinje must be cleared off the carpet. We have most urgently pressed this on Prince Nikola when he was in Petersburg." The Prince, we may surmise, went to ask Russian support, received no sympathy, began to realize he was no longer Russia's "only friend," and was filled with sick anxiety.

The Montenegrins, too, were much excited about the Anglo-Russian agreement. Vuko Vuletitch said cheerfully: "Now you can fight Germany." And the usual group round the hotel door cried: "Of course you will. For what else is this Entente?

You must fight soon, or you will lose all your trade." They looked forward to an Anglo-Russian Paradise, where the Teuton ceased from troubling. I fear it is not so joyful as they anticipated.

Vuko Vukotitch was as sore as Sofia Petrovna. He, too, had been accused of anti-Petrovitch sympathies, and threatened with the boycott of his hotel. He was seeking influential marriages for his many daughters. The eldest, Madame Rizoff, as wife of the Bulgarian diplomatic agent, was already playing a part in politics. Rumour said he had been on the point of affiancing another to one of the men now in prison.

I decided that Cetinje was no place for me, and that I would carry out my long deferred plan of a tour in the Albanian mountains. Sofia Petrovna pressed upon me an introduction to M. Lobatcheff, the Russian Vice-Consul at Scutari, and thither I went, leaving Cetinje to stew in its own juice. It was anthropology I wanted, not plots.

My work and travels in High Albania I have told elsewhere. I shall here only indicate the political happenings, for I did not escape them by going from Montenegro. In the Balkans you may change your mind any number of times, but you never change your sky full of Power-clouds.

All Europe was represented at Scutari, as in Cetinje, but by Consuls, not Ministers. A difference mainly in name, for they were there for the same purpose, and in Turkish territory even a Vice-Consul, if of an energetic and bullying nature, had almost as much influence as a Minister Plenipotentiary. For the Turks lived in terror of the Great Powers who squatted round the edge waiting an opportunity to pounce, and allowed consuls to do things unthinkable in any other land. During the late war America was roused to frenzy because the German representatives there tried to work a German propaganda. But for over a century the representative of every Power that wanted a bit of Turkey, not only worked ceaselessly by similar means, but had a private post office by which to convey and distribute the correspondence of any revolutionaries his country was supporting; had spies everywhere, and could, should any of his minions be caught red-handed by the Turkish authorities, obtain and demand their release, if not by fair means, then by foul. The Turks could not even close a brothel, if protected, as it frequently was, by a Great Power.

In Scutari, in 1908, Austria and Italy were both working strenuously to obtain influence over Albania. Austria had had a long start. Italy was now a good second. One made a hospital, the other replied with a home for the aged. One played a dispensary, the other an infant school, and so on, regardless of expense. Russia, who hoped ultimately to obtain Albanian lands for the Serbs, made a very bad third, for the Slav element in Scutari and its district was so small as to be practically negligible, and she could not work, as did her rivals, by means of churches and schools. There were but a few Slav families, mainly those whose ancestors had fled from Montenegro or the Herzegovina to escape from bloodvengeance, with a sprinkling of late comers who were "wanted" by the Montenegrin police. A tiny school and church were all they could fill. M. Lobatcheff and Petar Plamenatz, however, gave all their energies to working on this element and keeping it as discontented as possible.

Lobatcheff was very friendly to me. Being introduced by the Russians in Cetinje, I was expected to supply and convey information. The politics of the little consular world are funny. I found that the fact that he—Lobatcheff—representing All the Russias, had as a mere Vice-Consul to walk behind Petar Plamenatz, representing All Montenegro as a Consul-General, rankled most bitterly. He, too, like the Russian Legation at Cetinje, made no concealment of his belief that Montenegro had taken the wrong turning, and was on the down grade; said the Prince, after the wholesale arrests of last summer, would never regain his position and popularity. But I would not be attached to the Russian consulate, nor to any other party, and made the acquaintance also of the attache to the Austrian Consulate, a charming and cultivated Viennese, who was my very good friend.

Austria was represented by an arch-plotter, Consul-General Krai, who worked the pro-Austrian propaganda; the same man who was in Monastir when I was there in 1903-4, and he did not like my reappearance in Scutari. Count Mancinelli represented Italy. France had not in 1908 begun her pro-Slav intrigues in Albania, and had but a feeble representative, who picked quarrels with the Austrian attache over the latter's bulldog. But as in the Near East even a consular dog is suspected of politics, this may, for all I know, have been the first sproutling of France's subsequent conduct.

The Austrian Consulate-General, with Krai at its head, was easily top-dog in

Scutari then. The Slavs punned on his name: "Krai hoche bit' Kralj!" (Krai wants to be king). Especially he looked on the mountains as an Austrian preserve, and sent parties of Austrians there. The Turkish Government, acutely suspicious of "tourists," consequently forbade all strangers to travel inland—pretending danger. Just before my arrival, an Englishman, who arrived with letters to the Vali from our Embassy at Constantinople, had been refused a permit to travel inland, and had gone for a tour in Montenegro instead.

Our dear old Albanian Vice-Consul, M. Nikola Summa, however, said that if I would go without permission the tour could be easily managed. And so it was. The now notorious Essad Pasha, then Bey, was head of the Scutari gendarmerie, and I dodged his patrols successfully in the grey dawn.

Essad, known through the land as "the tyrant of Tirana," had till recently commanded gendarmerie at Janina. By his unscrupulous extortions and his quarrels he had made the place too hot to hold him, and had been transferred to Scutari, where he was very unpopular. The tale current about him was that he had married a second wife because his first had not borne him a son; that he lived in terror of being poisoned by the discarded lady, and Scutari cheerfully wished her speedy success.

Head of the family of Toptani of Tirana, he was known to be very ambitious, and was therefore employed by the Turkish Government, who thought it safer to make a friend than a foe of him. His elder brother, Gani Bey, had been murdered in Constantinople some years earlier, by a son of the Grand Vezir by order, it was said, of Abdul Hamid. The murder had been dramatically avenged by Gjujo Fais, one of Gani's serving men, who shot the assassin in broad daylight on the Galata bridge. A spirited ballad, one of the most popular in the land, describes this feat. Gjujo's life was spared, but 'in 1908 he was still in prison, and Essad was despised for having left his brother to be avenged by a servant. Essad took vengeance later, as we shall see.

In the Albanian mountains, as in Bosnia, it was impossible not to wonder at the great work done by Austria. Every Catholic tribe had its neat and usually well-caredfor church, whose priest lived hard by in a house rough, it is true, but superior in its arrangements to the average native dwelling.

Europe had entrusted Austria with the care of the Catholics of North Albania. She had trained priests, built and maintained churches and hospices, had built the Cathedral of Scutari, and established and protected the first Albanian schools of the

North. Austria had carried out Europe's behest well.

With but few exceptions all the mountain priests were Albanians, and almost all had had part of their training in Austria. In knowledge and intelligence they were much ahead of the almost untrained "popas" of Montenegro, who had never been beyond their own borders. In the case of the higher ecclesiastical orders the difference was even more marked, for they included many very cultivated and able men.

The Catholic quarter of Scutari had greatly advanced since my first visit in 1901. New shops and businesses had been opened, and the streets repaved. I made the acquaintance of many of the townsfolk, and was struck by-the far higher standard of cleanliness to be found here than in Cetinje.

The idea that the Montenegrin could teach civilization to the Albanian was patently absurd.

Scutari was hotly excited over the bomb affair of Cetinje. The trial of the prisoners, who had been in close confinement for nearly a year, came on in May. Scutari, as a whole, expressed disgust for the Montenegrins: "Nikita," folk said, "is our enemy. But he has done well for Montenegro. If God had given us a Prince like him we should have known how to value him." Petar Plamenatz left Scutari to defend the prisoners, and his consular colleagues—including Lobatcheff—foretold that all would receive heavy sentences, for they had no great opinion of Petar's powers.

The trial proved highly sensational. The fact that a good deal of evidence was given by a Bosnian journalist—one Nastitch—who was proved later in the Frledjung trial to be a discreditable witness, has led to the erroneous opinion in some quarters that the plot was a bogus affair. But the plot was a very genuine one, as I learnt beyond all doubt from my own observations, from details given me by relatives of some of the men implicated, and other Montenegrin sources. It was, in fact, the first round in the death-or-victory struggle for supremacy between the Karageorgevitches and the Petrovitches, the prize for which was to be the headship of Great Serbia.

I had learnt already in 1905 the growing ill-feeling against Prince Nikola, and had remarked that his most bitter critics had lived in Russia or Serbia.

There was also talk of a widespread secret society, known as the Club. A club in the Near East means something revolutionary. The people of Andrijevitza, who told me later on in hushed whispers about the "Clubashi," were amazed to hear that in London the police permitted clubs to exist in the best thoroughfares. The Clubashi went round the country spreading Great Serbian propaganda. Its headquarters were in Belgrade, where it worked by inciting the numerous Montenegrin students to revolution. The brother of one of these students, and the son of one of the arrested men, both gave me details. The students met in an eating-house at Belgrade, since notorious, "At the sign of the Green Garland" (Zelenom Vjencu). Great Serbia could not have two heads. The Petrovitches were therefore to be rendered impotent. All the powder and ammunition magazines of Montenegro were to be simultaneously seized, and the Prince was to be killed, or—and many preferred this—terrorized into abdication. Nikola was represented by the propagandists as the tyrant that stood in Great Serbia's path. Any one who has passed hours and days in Near Eastern eating-houses and cafes knows the ceaseless political altercations which go on and the violence of the sentiments habitually expressed, heightened ever by one glass more of rakia, "josh jedan!" The South Slav is a born orator, and sweeps away himself and his listeners on a flood of eloquence. I have seen livid wrath over mere trivialities. Had our Foreign Office but graduated in a Balkan pot-house its outlook on things Near Eastern would have been greatly extended.

The plot against Prince Nikola failed, for one of the said students had doubts about it and wrote to his brother, who held an official position in Montenegro, hinting at sinister events. The recipient told me that he feared at first that his brother was mixed in the affair, and wrote a very strong remonstrance. In return the boy supplied the Montenegrin Government with full details as to the routes by which the conspirators would enter the country with their bombs.

They were all arrested on arrival. Some came via Cattaro, others overland to Andrijevitza, for the Vassojevitch tribe, together with the Bratonitchitch and the Drobnjaci, were deeply dipped in the plot, and in touch with the propaganda worked by Serb komitadjis in the district between Serbia and Montenegro. Vassojevitch paid heavily. Three of her finest youths were condemned to be publicly shot. The whole population, including even the mothers of the condemned, were ordered to witness the execution, and to the further anguish of the relatives the bodies were buried "like dogs" by the wayside.

Such was the plot. The question was: Who was behind the Montenegrin students in Belgrade, and who supplied the bombs? These came from the Royal Serbian arsenal at Kraguyevatz, where, in 1902, I had heard so much of Karageorgism. It was asserted at the trial that Prince George of Serbia had been concerned in obtaining them. That they were brought from Serbia by Montenegrins was proven. It was then clearly the duty of the Serbian Government to investigate into a conspiracy planned on its own soil against a neighbour state and punish the supplier of Government bombs. It not only, however, refused to extradite certain Montenegrin students, who were suspect, but it made no arrests, asserted violently it knew nothing of the plot, took no steps to obtain information, and withdrew its representative from Montenegro.

To one who, like myself, knew from personal experience that you cannot even draw a cow or buy a carpet in Serbia without the knowledge of the Serbian police, the conduct of the Serbian Government was entirely unconvincing, and the obvious reply to Serbia's "We know nothing," was "But it is your business to know and to take such steps as to make it impossible in the future for a gang of students in a pot-house in the capital to plot the murder of a neighbour sovereign, and to obtain Government bombs for the purpose. Who superintends the foreign students in your capital?"

Pashitch, when interviewed on the subject, replied only that Montenegro had made demands for extradition "completely incompatible with our constitution and laws, and so they could not be fulfilled." He was Prime Minister during part of this troublous time, but did nothing to make peace between the two rival Serb nations.

Montenegro claimed that even before the discovery of the plot Belgrade knew that something was happening, as Serb papers had been carrying on an anti-Petrovitch propaganda openly, and had reported that the Montenegrin students of Belgrade University had read a proclamation calling on Montenegrins to revolt.

Of the accused, several turned informers against others, and asked for pardon. Others begged for light sentences, but did not deny guilt. The ex-Minister Gjurovitch denied all complicity, and so did poor Marusitch, but his wild and loudly expressed plans for turning Montenegro upside down and inside out went hopelessly against him. Both men got heavy sentences.

Lobatcheff, the Russian Vice-Consul, was furious at the arrest of Marusitch, the ex-Russian military surgeon, declared him a harmless chatterbox, and said Prince

Nikola had lost his head. So had all Montenegro. Neither party knew which would come out "top-dog"; each suspected the other, and spies and treachery were rampant. Prince Nikola leapt at any evidence that would help him crush his enemies, and Nastitch, the spy, took advantage of his terror to help widen the gap that already yawned between Serbia and Montenegro. The Prince was terrified. Not only was his life threatened, but even if that were spared he dreaded losing the one thing for which he had lived and striven—the throne of Great Serbia. That Austria, as some have stated, should have planned the coup is very improbable. For one thing, its object was to strengthen Serbia by joining the two states under one dynasty. Not even Sofia Petrovna nor Lobatcheff, both red-hot believers in Holy Russia and haters of Austria, ever even suggested to me that Austria was the cause: they ascribed it all to Nikola's own folly, and were pro-Serb. That Austria should try to take advantage of the complication was but natural.

Among the accused who got crushingly heavy sentences of imprisonment in irons was Radovitch, since well known as one of Nikola's fiercest opponents. He was known as a "Clubashi," and as an engineer had built the prison at Podgoritza, to which he was now doomed. "My God, why did I build cells like this?" is said to have been his cry on entering, for the prison was inhuman in its arrangements.

"True or false," I noted in my diary at the time, "the charge against the Crown Prince George of Serbia will probably split Serbia and Montenegro. ... I hope old Nikola's reign won't end in fiasco."

By the time the trial was ended much else had happened. In June King Edward and the Tsar had met at Reval. England and Russia had indeed "agreed." And things were acute in Morocco. The junior staff of the Austrian consulate chaffed me, and asked when we meant to fight Germany. I declared "Never." My friend the attache assured me that if we went on in the way we were going we should be obliged to have military conscription. The Macedonian question now was acute. England was believed to have arranged with Russia to take active steps in Turkey. We discussed it endlessly. The attache used to dine with me, and we agreed that our respective countries were guilty. If the Powers wished, they could establish order easily. No Power wanted order. Each was seeking its own interests. Never has there been more hypocritical humbug talked by both great and small Powers than over Macedonia. They handed moral letters about law and order to the Turk with one hand, and with the other distributed revolutionary funds to effectually prevent the establishment of either. Each group preferred to burn up the whole place rather than let the other get a bit of it.

The ethics of the situation were illustrated by Lobatcheff, who asked me whether I thought Montenegro safe for tourists. On my replying that I had had no difficulties, he told me that a Czech had very recently been murdered there for his money, and his body cut to pieces and hidden. The Montenegrin peasants had declared that, contrary to their advice, he had gone over the Albanian frontier, and the remains had only been accidentally discovered. Lobatcheff had had the details from Dr. Perisitch, the Prince's physician, who had made the post mortem.

Next day the Austrian attache came laughing, and told how some Czech tourists had just arrived, and at once bought and put on fezzes as a protection against the "fanatical inhabitants," who, so they had been told in Cetinje, had lately murdered a Czech. I gave him Lobatcheff's report, which put a very different complexion on the matter. When it was too late Lobatcheff came to beg me to consider the tale of the murder as strictly confidential. The Austrians were on no account to hear of it! Nor could I make him see that it was only fair to warn others beside Russians and English. In fact Lobatcheff's ideas were little less crude than those of Montenegro. Like the Cetinje folk, he expected that the result of the Anglo-Russian agreement would be that Russia would get all she wanted, and was vexed that I took up the cause of the Albanians. The more I saw of the Albanians and of the Slav intrigues for their destruction, the more I thought Albania worthy of help. The enterprising and industrious Albanian was worth a dozen of the conceited idle Montenegrins. Except Prince Nikola and the hotelier Vuke Vuletitch, it was hard to find a Montenegrin in Cetinje who used his brains—if he had any. An educated Albanian is often a highly cultivated man, whereas even Lobatcheff was forced to admit that Paris and Petersburg could not make more of a Montenegrin than a Petar Plamenatz or a Marusitch. Nor was the Austrian Consul Kral better pleased with my Albanian travels. It was reported to him that whereas the mountains had formerly been pro-Austrian, they had become, since my visit, entirely pro-English. He concluded, ridiculously enough, that I was sent by the British Government, and made a long report to Vienna about me, as I ascertained later. I was unaware then of the activity being shown by the Franco-Russian combine and England, and thought his anxiety overdone. To an outside observer, however, Anglo-Russian activity also seemed perilous. Baron Greindl, Belgian Minister at Berlin at that very time, wrote (July 4, Letter 49): "I asked the Secretary of State yesterday ... if he had not yet received the English proposals with regard to reforms in Macedonia. ... . I said that another point seemed disquieting to me, viz. the way in which the preliminary pourparlers were conducted between London and St. Petersburg to the exclusion of Austria-Hungary, whose interests were of the most importance in Balkan affairs."

That Krai spied my movements is perhaps under these circumstances not surprising, more especially as Lobatcheff, who hated him, called out derisively to him at a friendly gathering of all the Consuls: "Have not you found out what the Englishwoman is here for yet?" which made matters worse.

The political tension was felt even in the remote corners of the Albanian mountains. Tribesmen vaguely expected war. An Austrian advance in the Sanjak was rumoured.

I was up in the mountains when the astounding news arrived that there had been a Turkish revolution. It was incredible. I hastened to Scutari. Not one Consulate as yet had any information, except that a Constitution had been proclaimed. Scutari was wildly excited. The foreign representatives were sceptical and contemptuous. The thing was impossible. Not till Sunday, August 2nd, did the official proclamations and rejoicing begin. Then all North Albania was wild with joy. Moslem and Christian united. It was believed that Europe had intervened, and the Turk would rule no more. The mountain men swarmed down in their best, were feasted by the town, shouted "Long live Constituzi," and fired their rifles till not a cartridge was left in the town. Yet with over two thousand armed men in the town for two days and nights, and no police force to cope with an outbreak, not a single disorder occurred. Every one was far too happy to do wrong, and enjoyed themselves wholeheartedly. Even the French Consul and Lobatcheff, who did not conceal their anti-Albanian feelings, said: "Mon Dieu! what a people this would be if they had a just ruler!"

The Mirdites were cautious. Their Abbot, Premi Dochi, waited to see which way the wind blew before committing his flock. In reply to the newly-appointed Vali, who asked why the Mirdites did not come to take the oath of fealty, he replied that when he was allowed to return from exile to Mirdita, he promised that he would concern himself solely with spiritual affairs, and was therefore powerless;

that the only head the Mirdites recognized was Prenk Bib Doda, their chief, who was unfortunately in exile still at Constantinople. He alone could put matters right. It was an astute move. The Young Turks at once sent Prenk home.

On September 30th Prenk Pasha rode up into Mirdita and was received by his delighted people. I went with him, and witnessed the wildly magnificent scene. Mirdita believed no Turkish promises. They had never seen "a Constituzi"; they did not know if they would like it, and thought it was a "flam of the devil." Nor were they pleased to see the two Young Turk representatives, Halil and Khiassim Beys. It took all the eloquence of the Abbot to talk them over, and only after long deliberations did they consent to swear a "besa" (peace oath) till Ash Wednesday, 1909, stipulating at the same time for the retention of their old privileges and their old laws.

Premi Dochi's successful scheme for the restoration to Mirdita of Prenk Bib Doda was a masterpiece, which might have well led to the autonomy of Albania. Had Prenk been a born leader of men, not only Mirdita but all the mountain tribes would have rallied to him. But alas! there was nothing of the leader in him. Thirty years of enforced idleness and exile had turned him from a rebel youth into a stout and amiable elderly gentleman, with a considerable sense of humour, but devoid of all capacity or even desire, to rule.

The Abbot's trump card was not an ace—it was not even a knave.

Meanwhile the Austrian Consulate was bubbling with rumours of a quarrel at Ischl between King Edward VII and the Emperor Franz Josef. It was said that King Edward had rudely walked out of the Royal box at the theatre where he was the Emperor's guest, in the middle of the performance, and had given as an excuse that the performance was improper. The consular youths refused to believe any play could be too highly flavoured for the King of England, judging by pieces which they knew he had witnessed, and declared there had been a political quarrel. This was later officially denied. In any: case the result was the same—friction and misunderstanding between the two countries—and it is evident that King Edward's journeys to Reval cannot have pleased Franz Josef.

Nor was there any sign that the Turkish Constitution would be a success. The Albanian Moslems were soon furious to find that instead of giving them freedom, it meant that they would all now have to give military service. The districts of Ipek,

Prizren, Djakova, Upper Dibra, Scutari, and others who had hitherto been exempt, declared that they had not fought the Turk for years in order to be conquered now. The Christians, who had believed that "Constituzi" meant the Turk was going, were horrified. Nothing would induce them to fight for the Turks. Already in September I found distrust of the Turk all through Kosovo vilayet. The Moslems who had gathered at Ferizovitch and demanded Constitution of Abdul Hamid saw they had been tricked. They declared they had been summoned to fight Austria, and said they were ready to do that, but they would never allow themselves to be dictated to by the Turks.

I talked with the two Young Turk officers, Halil and Khiassim Bey, at Scutari. They were hopelessly ignorant. Knew, in fact, no more about a Constitution than did the up-country mountain men. It was a sort of magic word which was to put all right. They were arranging to be photographed in new uniforms with plenty of gold braid, and were childishly happy. When I said: "But you have the Bulgar question, the Greek, the Serb, and Albanian questions all to solve in Europe alone—surely those are more important than new uniforms," they replied: "These questions no longer exist. We have made a law. All are now Ottomans!"

"You may make a law that a cat is a dog," said I, "but it will remain a cat."

They expressed horror that I should compare human beings to animals, and Halil persisted: "It will be like England. In England you have the people of Scotland and Ireland. But they are all English. A man from Scotland, for example, would not say 'I am Scotch.'"

"But he would," I persisted. "If you call an Irishman, English, he will probably knock you down." They were surprised and incredulous. They had no plans, no ideas. That no one wanted to be an Ottoman, and that, contracted to "Ot" the word was used as a term of contempt to denote "Turk" by the town Christians was unknown to them. Albania was, in fact, for the Young Turks, the most important of its European possessions, for, well handled, it might have remained loyal to the Turk against the dreaded Slav. But Constantinople did nothing to achieve this. And Scutari was infuriated because, though the prisoners had been released in honour of the Constitution throughout the land, the doors of Scutari prisons were still closed. Folk began to say: "The Young Turk is as bad as the Old."

I took a long journey up into Kosovo vilayet to districts which had previously been practically closed to travellers for many years, visiting Djakova, Prizren, Prishtina, Mitrovitza, and the plain of Kosovo. Here it seemed obvious that the new regime must fail. The Serbs everywhere were in very much of a minority, and their headmen —the Bishop of Prizren, the Archimandrite of Grachanitza, the master of the Serb theological school at Prizren, and others frankly lamented the Turkish revolution, and looked on it only as a frustration of all their schemes. A well-governed Turkey was the last thing they wished for, as it would prevent the creation of Great Serbia. Prizren itself was so overwhelmingly Albanian that the Serbian College, with its students brought even from Montenegro and other non-Turk lands, seemed ridiculously artificial.

Nor were the Albanians any longer pleased about the revolution. They meant to accept nothing that would bring them further under Turkish power. As for the Turkish authorities, they were still under the magic of the blessed word "Constitution," and in order that foreigners should be so too, sent gendarmes ahead to prepare a group of "peasants rejoicing under the Constitution" at Djakova, ready for the arrival of some French delegates.

I was back in Scutari when, on October 5th, came the startling news that Ferdinand of Bulgaria had proclaimed himself Tsar of independent Bulgaria. This confirmed the Christians of the town in their rooted belief that all that was going on was arranged by the Great Powers for the purpose of entirely overthrowing the Turk.

Tuesday, October 6th, the Austrian attache had supper with me, and was bubbling with excitement. He had a great piece of news, but it might not yet be told. I was to try and guess< He would tell me so soon as possible. Wednesday and Thursday passed, and on Friday early, in rushed my old Marko crying: "War is declared by Serbia, Russia, Montenegro, and Turkey against Austria!" Why, he did not know. Running out to learn, I met the attache beaming: "We have annexed Bosnia and the Herzegovina!" he said. "Then you have done a dashed silly thing!" said I. He was greatly surprised, and promised to come to dinner with me and fight it out. I went to the Montenegrin Consulate and found Petar Plamenatz almost in tears with a red-hot proclamation of Prince Nikola's in his hands, calling on all Serbs of all countries to unite and denounce the breaking of the Berlin Treaty, and laying great stress on the fact that all his ancestors were buried in the Herzegovina, which was now seized by Austria. Petar was of opinion that war was inevitable, otherwise all the plans of the Serbs for Great Serbia were ruined. Serbs and Montenegrins must act as brothers.

Excitement in the town was further heated by the arrival of the French Minister from Belgrade, who interviewed the newly-arrived Prenk Bib Doda, and the wildest things were reported and believed, even that England, Germany, and Austria had combined to crush the Slavs. Folk discussed which Power would land there. Prizren was said to have declared itself independent. And one of the political prisoners of the Cetinje bomb affair, who had been condemned to fifteen years, escaped and took refuge in Scutari. In the general excitement I never learnt his name, and he left for Serbia.

The Austrian attache duly came to dinner, and explained that it was absolutely necessary to annex Bosnia as the Young Turks were preparing for the general elections. The two provinces were nominally part of the Turkish Empire, and the Turks would claim that they should be represented in their Parliament. Europe had never intended the provinces to revert to Turkey; they had been entirely Austrian for thirty years, and the change was in name only. It would also make it possible to give the provinces a liberal and civilian government, a thing not possible when it was a question only of a military occupation. I countered with: "Let sleeping dogs lie." Europe would never have taken it from Austria, and if it had been agreed that Austria should retire from part she would have been necessarily heavily compensated. He replied: "Ah, but you don't know something we know, and which has expedited the affair. England is on the point of annexing Egypt. The same problem faces you there." I did not believe this possible, and declared that we were pledged to the Egyptians to restore the land to them. I believed, then, we should keep our word. He laughed, and said he had certain information that we should annex it. Nor would he agree, when I persisted, that Austria had made a mistake in not bringing the question up before the signatory Powers. We discussed the anti-Austrian propaganda, which I had found rife in Bosnian He believed it to have been largely due to the uncertainty of the position, and declared that, faced with the fait accompli, the Serbs would drop the intrigues which kept up the agitation, and that a civilian government and a constitution would speedily ameliorate everything.

Austria was already withdrawing the officers' families from the Sanjak, and complete evacuation would follow. She dropped also the Uvatz-Mitrovitza railway scheme which the Young Turks seemed not over-willing to permit.

Moslem wrath, fierce against Austria, was further excited by the arrival of malcontent Moslems from the annexed provinces, who had thrown up their businesses and emigrated to the Young Turks. A curio-dealer from Mostar, whom I knew, was among them He and his friends had all believed that the Turkish revolution meant that Bosnia-Herzegovina would be the Sultan's once more. I asked why there had been no rising, and he explained humorously that, except his wife's scissors, he had no weapon to rise with. The "Schwabs" had called in all knives big enough to fight with, some weeks before the annexation was proclaimed.

A Moslem demonstration took place outside the Austrian consulate. The consular staff sent for Browning pistols, and insisted on ordering one for me, too, as declared my lodgings outside the town were dangerous. There was a whirlpool of contrary currents. Just before the Turkish revolution took place Essad Bey, who was aware of what was going on but, characteristically, meant to keep clear till he knew which was the winning side, applied for leave to go abroad for his health, which appeared excellent, and abroad he remained till Young Turk victory was certain.

In the first frenzy of joy, over what they believed to be the coming reign of liberty and justice, one of the cries of the townsfolk had been: "Now if Essad ever dares come back they will hang him, and give back all the lands and monies he has stolen!" Essad, however, outwitted the Young Turks as easily as he later outwitted the British Foreign Office. Whatever happened, he would be "butter-side uppermost." He announced that he, too, was a Young Turk, and returned in triumph as a member of the Committee of Union and Progress. This did more in Scutari to shake all faith in the new regime than anything else. Excitement grew. War was expected at any moment. Serbia and Montenegro were reported to have mobilized, and all frontiers were armed. On October 28th I find in my diary: "Had urgent appeal to go to Belgrade, but decided not—I don't want to get badly mixed in their politics." The Montenegrins were all for war, and the wildest reports reached us of Prince George of Serbia's efforts to precipitate it.

Russia, still reeling from her Japanese thrashing and torn with internal troubles, could do nothing. That was plain to every one but the South Slavs.

Baron Nopcsa, the Hungarian traveller, whose knowledge of Albanian matters is unrivalled, returned from a tour in the mountains. He was violently anti-Serb, and, in reply to my hope that war would be avoided, said very earnestly: "It can't be. Russia Is rapidly recovering. The Slavs mean our destruction; it is now or never for us. Our one chance is to crush them before they become too strong." I suggested there was room for both. He maintained there was not. "Let the Slav once get the upper hand, and there will be room for no one else. You had better remember that!" As a choice of evils, he favoured union with Germany against the common foe.

The pro-Serb attitude of England astonished every one except the "Great Serbians," who did not think it strong enough, and hoped for British naval support at least. To the Austrians it was incomprehensible that England should have made such a complete volte-face since 1878. The Czech consul-general, the Croatian secretary, and the Dalmatian doctor—all Slavs—were dead against Serbia and-all her claims. And in spite of the surprise expressed by England it appeared that the question of Bosnia's status had been discussed with England almost immediately after the proclamation of the Young Turk revolution. For a Reuter telegram had reported: "August 12, Vienna. . . . it was agreed at the conference between Baron Aehrenthal and Sir Charles Hardinge at Ischl to-day that any developments arising in Bosnia and the Herzegovina from the constitutional changes in Turkey should be considered as purely internal matters affecting Austria-Hungary and not involving any question of international policy." Sir Charles Hardinge, who had come in company with King Edward VII, at once returned to England.

The Moslems regarded the annexation as a Christian attack on Islam, and, as it was Ramazan, demonstrated loudly at night in the Christian quarter of Scutari. The Turkish Government boycotted all Austrian goods, and as the bulk of Scutari's imports came from Trieste the town felt this severely. The attache told me that England was believed to be behind this boycott for commercial purposes, and that as Austria manufactured a great deal expressly for the Turkish market a prolonged boycott must spell ruin. How easily we thought it spelt in those days!

Montenegro, meanwhile, went rabid because her special envoy to Belgrade, Yanko Vukotitch, cousin to the Princess, was stopped, and, it was said, searched on Austrian territory. Things were touch and go. The Montenegrin army was preparing to fall on Cattaro. War seemed inevitable, for England's attitude caused the Montenegrins to believe that they had only to begin and British aid was certain.

Imaginative people actually saw the Mediterranean fleet coming up the Adriatic. They were spoiling for a fight. I was sure our bark was far worse than our bite was likely to be, but was very anxious, for we had no British representative in Cetinje to advise moderation, and, while we went on barking, Montenegro might bite. Montenegrin and Austrian troops faced each other on the frontier, and a rifle fired by a man full of rakia might set the whole ablaze.

People at home did not know how close the spark and the powder lay. If war ensued, it would mean the end of Turkey in Europe. In spite of tension between Christian and Moslem, the Albanians remembered that blood is thicker than water, and were very anxious to consolidate their position by adopting a common alphabet for all Albania. This, owing to Turkish prohibitions, had previously been impossible. For Italy and Austria, who printed school books in Albanian, did so for their own purposes, and not to encourage nationality, and so each used a different alphabet and changed it not infrequently.

A great national meeting of representatives of all Albania was held at Monastir, which the Albanians then reckoned as one of their towns. The Latin alphabet was chosen, a common system of orthography adopted, and the frontiers of Albanian territory discussed. The Turks, alarmed at the growth of Albanian Nationalism, again began restrictions, and hurried to arrange for the election to Parliament of such members only as were pro-Turk. As I wrote at the time: "The so-called election is no election at all. The tyrant of Tirana, Essad Bey, a man who is greatly detested, and has an awful reputation, is to be member for Tirana, elected' by the peasants who are terrified of him. Even Scutari is surprised he has succeeded in making them do it. He is head of the gendarmerie, and this gives him great power." It has been said that in an emergency you can always trust a Turk to do the wrong thing. Every mistake possible to make in Albania, the Young Turks made, and while they still rubbed Albania up the wrong way, Austria was still boycotted. Kral himself tried vainly to unload a barge of sugar. And still Serbia, Montenegro, and Austria showed their teeth on the frontier. The Crown Prince George of Serbia was reported to be about to assume the command of the army as a second Stefan Dushan. But his rush to Petersburg and appeal to the Tsar met with rebuff and refusal. Russia was not yet ready for another war, as Lobatcheff sadly admitted.

We became used to reports several times a week that war had begun somewhere or other. But the town was in a fever of excitement when, towards the middle of November, we heard that the British fleet had arrived in the Adriatic, and that the Admiral was about to visit Scutari. "War for certain! Albania is saved!" cried folk. The hotel reported that the Admiral and suite had engaged rooms, and were coming via Cetinje. The British fleet must be in the Bocche di Cattaro! The Vali decided to send a band and a guard of honour to meet him. I suggested that Edward VII was coming in person, but people were past seeing jokes. Our Vice-Consul had had no news at all, and was agitated. All day the Admiral and British fleet were expected. The Crimea would be repeated, and Turkey saved. Next day brought forth—a British charge d'affaires and five ladies who had merely come for fun to see the bazar, and were overpowered by finding themselves officially received. All Scutari, perhaps all Turkey, tense and tremulous, waited to see what steps Great Britain would take. And its representative, all unaware of what political fever in the Balkans is, saw the bazar, had tea at the Austrian Consulate, and went back again to Cetinje, escorted to the boat by a Turkish guard. Then the storm broke! What did Great Britain mean? Scutari was amazed, perplexed, bewildered; wild rumours flew. An Anglo-Austrian Alliance—a break with Russia—a slap in the face for the Turks. Nothing was too crazy to be believed and repeated. A knock came at my door. In came Lobatcheff in full uniform. He said that his Tsar had been insulted in his person. Was fizzling with excitement. Had I any information for him? Had the British Government reversed its policy? What was the object of this mission to Scutari? And so on—red hot. I told him there was nothing to be excited about. "An English official had come for a holiday. That was all. Did he suppose that a diplomat on business would bring a party of ladies?" But the Russian had got all his bristles up. "That I decline to believe," he said. "I have too high an idea of the skill of your Foreign Office to believe they would send a man at such a moment to visit the bazar for no purpose!" And it took me ever so long to talk him round. Having settled Russia and got rid of him, in came Mr. Summa, our Vice-Consul, also deeply troubled. The Vali had asked him for an explanation of the policy of Great Britain. He, too, was of opinion that the Foreign Office could not have concocted such a plan as a visit to the bazar, except for some deep and obscure purpose. The Young Turks having made a Constitution, naturally expected Great Britain, also a Constitutional country, etc. etc. Why had not the British envoy visited the Vali? In fact, you could hardly blow your nose in

Scutari without being suspected of political intentions.

Then came a message from Petar Plamenatz, who was ill, and wished to see me. The Slav kettle gets hot in a minute. Petar, who was not such a big pot as he imagined, was boiling over. His Prince, his country, and—worst of all—himself, had all been insulted. Why had he, who was Consul-General for Montenegro, not been called on? With Petar, as usual, I was very firm. "This gentleman," said I, "doubtless heard of your illness in Cetinje. He came here as a tourist, and so naturally did not wish to disturb you. Why should he, when he came not on official business, but merely to see the bazar?" Petar was squashed. The whole episode illustrates the fact, which few people in West Europe appreciate, namely, that in the Near East politics are a nervous disease.

I left for Cetinje shortly afterwards. My last letter said: "The war-clouds are thickening. The people here who foretell the future in sheep's bladebones and fowls' breastbones have foretold nothing but blood for weeks. ... It is said that by the end of four months Austria will occupy the Sanjak as far as Mitrovitza."

"To save us," say the Albanians, "if the Serbs are allowed to have it, it will at once be Russian. We should be lost, and our religion crushed. If Montenegro declared war the Albanians will at once reoccupy Dulcigno; that forced cession of Dulcigno, engineered by Gladstone, has done more to keep up hatred here than anything else."

"I gather from the Press cuttings that none of the reviewers like my idea that the Constitution can't last. But so far as I can make out, only the English and the French papers believe—or pretend to believe—in it." To me it seemed, indeed, clear that the Young Turk regime was bound to fail. No one but the Young Turks wanted it, and they had started it at least thirty years too late. Territorial aggrandizement was what Greece, Bulgaria, Serbia, and Montenegro wanted. Russia and Austria, too, were both burning to "free Christians from the Turkish yoke." And if Turkey reformed herself into an earthly Paradise, the lands those Christians lived in would be lost for ever.

Then came talk of withdrawing the international gendarmerie from Macedonia. This I could not believe possible. "England will never do anything so crazy!" I declared.

"She will though," said the Austrian Consulate, "and so soon as the Young Turks have enough rope they will hang themselves." And sure enough the gendarmerie was withdrawn, and the Young Turk let loose to go as he pleased. In Cetinje I found popular opinion furious both with the Young Turks and with Austria. Either and each would prevent the formation of Great Serbia. All were for war, and still believed England would support them if they began. I went to the drinkshops as being the centres from which to distribute information, and told gendarmes, soldiers, and pot-house visitors generally that England Would not go to war for them.

"But," they declared, "your own Prime Minister in Parliament has said: 'We will never allow the Treaty of Berlin to be violated.' Our guns are on the frontier pointing at Cattaro. It is war!"

"Oh, they tell a lot of lies in our Parliament," said I. "Don't believe them. We are not going to fight. You will get no help."

I was exceedingly afraid some fool would start firing, for they were getting tired of doing nothing on the frontier in the cold. All the Corps Diplomatique, save Austria, interviewed me, anxious to hear how the Constitution was working in Albania. None of them had any belief in it. The French Minister even said it would require twenty Napoleons to solve Turkey's many problems, and the Turks had not one.

The Prince sent for me, and I saw he, too, expected war, for he questioned me about the Red Cross, and asked me whether I could get medical aid from England.

The steamer in which I left Cattaro was empty of goods because of the boycott, and of passengers because of the political situation. There was a non-commissioned Austrian officer with me in the second class. As the boat left the shore he said fervently: "Gott sei dank! Gott sei dank! I have got away. The war will begin very soon now, and every one in Cattaro will be killed, like a rat in a trap. We shall win in the end. But Cattaro will fall at once. I have been there for weeks with the guns pointed on us day and night. Gott bewahre!" He, like Baron Nopesa, believed it to be a case of "Now or never!" Austria must fight. If she waited a few years the Slav combine would be too strong.

"We have the whole of the German army with us," said the officer, "and you could do nothing to stop us."

Probably he was correct. In 1908 Russia was quite impotent, and the Central Powers might have won.

But Germany insisted on peace.

I arrived in London, and was amazed to find for the first time people who believed in the Young Turks. They would listen to no facts, and would not believe me when I said that the Turkish Empire, as it stood, would probably barely survive one Parliament. A prophecy which was almost exactly fulfilled.

CHAPTER SIXTEEN
1909

An accident and a long illness forced me to spend 1909 in London. In March came a significant change in Serbia. Prince George, the Crown Prince, in a fit of uncontrolled rage, amounting to mania, kicked his valet down some stone steps and killed him. Rumours of the Prince's strange and violent conduct had long been rife. He escaped trial by renouncing all rights to succession to the throne, and his brother, Prince Alexander, became heir. Alexander was said to have the support of the regicide officers' party, the Black Hand. George, too, had his partisans, who declared that if he were as mad as his great-grandfather, old Karageorge, so much the better, he would lead Serbia to glory.

In March, too, came the counter-revolution against the Young Turk regime. I had learnt from a letter from Albania that this was about to take place. It failed, to my regret, for I hoped that its success would result in the landing of international forces, and that international control might solve the Balkan problem peacefully. I believed then that rule by the Western Powers would be better than that of the Turks. Now that we Know that these so-called civilized Powers will starve millions, and bomb helpless crowds, in order to obtain land and supremacy, many of us blush for the criticisms we once showered on the state of Macedonia.

The Young Turk won in 1909, and Abdul Hamid was called on to abdicate. Essad Pasha (formerly Bey) the ex-gendarmerie commander at Scutari, was now hand in glove with the Young Turks. He played, in fact, on whichever side he thought to gain something for himself. He managed to be one of the three who took the fatal message to the terrified Sultan, and spoke the words: "Abdul, the nation hath pronounced thee deposed!" Thus dramatically avenging the murder of his brother Gani fifteen years before, very completely. Abdul went, and with him went the Empire.

He had lived a life of terror, and played a long game of "bluff." But those who knew him intimately declare that his success with the Powers depended more on the way they outwitted each other than on his skill as a diplomatist. Recent revelations have shown us that the much talked of intrigues of the East are child's play compared to the plans built by the West.

Hitherto all that went wrong in Turkey was ascribed to Abdul Hamid. The Young Turks had now no scapegoat, and were in a perilous position with foes within and without. They resolved, therefore, that the only way to consolidate the Empire was to forcibly Ottomanize the population as fast as possible. But it was too late by many years for this. The Balkan States had expended huge sums on propaganda in Turkish territory, and knew that if their oft-repeated demands for reform were carried out, all their plans for territorial aggrandizement would be ruined. They fitted out bands and hurried on propaganda. The Serbs had started the Narodna Odbrana society, and opened a school in which officers trained komitadji bands, taught bomb throwing, train wrecking, mining, and shooting, to volunteers. These were designed primarily for attack on Austria to avenge the annexation of Bosnia. They acted also with ferocity in Macedonia against the Bulgars. Serbia, whose propaganda in Macedonia was very recent, tried to make up now, by planting schools and sending forth komitadjis.

Austria early in 1909 dropped her North and South railway scheme. But the Slavs clamoured still for an East and West line, and Russia backed them, and Prince Nikola still cried out about his ancestors, who, for the time, remained buried in the Herzegovina. Russia demanded that the Dardanelles should now be opened to her warships. It came out that when Baron von Aehrenthal met Izvolsky—Russian Minister for Foreign Affairs—at Buchlau in September 1908, Izvolsky had agreed to the Austrian annexation of Bosnia in exchange for the opening of the Dardanelles. He may have believed this would automatically follow any violation of the Berlin Treaty. But he was outwitted. Would that he had always been! After much argle-bargle Europe decided to accept the fait accompli in Bosnia, and not to reassemble the signatory Powers. Serbia did not receive the corridor she demanded through the Sanjak, and signed an agreement accepting the changed state of Bosnia. Prince Nikola, in consideration of his lost and buried ancestors, obtained certain concessions in the status of Antivari. Russia, as war was impossible for her, did all she could to maintain peace, even undertaking a large share of the pecuniary compensation demanded of Bulgaria by the Turks. To Serbia she counselled moderation, but, as we have learnt from recently published documents, pledged herself to support Serbia later on. On March 6, 1909, the Serb representative in Petersburg informed Belgrade: "Chamjakow informed me very confidentially that . . . in the audience which took place on Monday the Tsar said that the situation was terrible, for Russia was unprepared for war, and the defeat of Russia would be the ruin of Slavdom . . . In answer to the question what attitude Russia would assume in case Austria should attack Serbia, the President of the Duma said: We did something no other State has done up till now. We proclaimed to the Whole world that we are not in a position to make war, but we shall consider any attempt to coerce Serbia as the beginning of a European conflagration, in which we cannot at present join. But it will flame up in the future when we are in a position to have our way." (Telegram xvi, Bogitchevitch). Russia thus very clearly told Serbia so early as 1909 that so soon as Russia was ready, Serbia had but to provoke Austria to retaliation and the European war, from which Russia hoped to obtain so much, would at once blaze up. "You press the button, and we'll do the rest."

As one result of the Bosnian crisis, Izvolsky lost his popularity. In 1910 he was retired from the post of Minister for Foreign Affairs, which he had held since 1906, and went to Paris as Russian ambassador, where he toiled unremittingly at inciting France to co-operate in his schemes. Already in October 1908 he had thus instructed M. Vesnitch, Serb Minister in Paris: "Russia has hitherto supported Serbia, and will continue to support her, however and wherever she can. You must come to an understanding soon with Montenegro. . . . Further, you must come to an understanding with, Bulgaria, and in this we shall honestly support you. We no longer desire a Great Bulgaria. Such an idea we now look on as a mistake" (i.e. it would block the route to Constantinople). This is the first official proof we have of Russia's plan to construct a Balkan League for her own use, from which it is clear Bulgaria was to derive no benefit. Before going to Paris, Izvolsky laid yet another stick ready to kindle the European blaze. In October 1909 he made an agreement with Italy, whose hatred of Austria was increasing, by which Italy and Russia "bind themselves to a mutually benevolent attitude, the former in regard to Russia's interests in the Dardanelles, and the latter in regard to Italy's interests in Tripoli and the Cyrenaica." Italy, in fact, under cover of military manoeuvres, made extensive military preparations against Austria in 1909, while hostilities over Bosnia were possible. Baron Nopcsa told me bitterly in 1910: "We shall never again rely on Italy. She mobilized against us last year." That his statement was true was confirmed to me later by Mr. Wadham Peacock, who told me he had been at that time in Verona, seen active preparations, and heard the approaching war against Austria freely discussed by Italian officers.

The Albanians hastened to consolidate their position by holding two important National Congresses at Dibra and Elbasan, at which a scheme for national education was discussed, and the formation of Courts of Justice, road-making, and the purpose to which taxes were to be applied. These, they insisted, were to be used for national works. The Young Turks would give no pledge to this effect, and foolishly tried to extort a tax to pay for the Bulgar rising of 1903. They ordered also the disarming of Albania, and sent a large force into Kosovo vilayet for this purpose.

The Albanians, led by that very gallant chieftain, Isa Boletin, rose, and fierce fighting ensued, which, had the Turks but known it, was the beginning of the end. They hopelessly alienated the Albanians, the one race whom they might have had as ally.

Another important event was the trial at Agram of a number of Serbs and Croats accused of conspiracy with Serbia against the Austro-Hungarian Government. Thirty-three were condemned to various terms of imprisonment, but were released on appeal, and brought a countercharge of libel against Dr. Fried Jung, a Journalist, for asserting in the Neue Freie Presse that they had been subsidized by Belgrade, and advocating that Belgrade should be purged of a nest of conspirators. Pashitch, Spalaikovitch, and the Slovenski Jug (founded in 1904), and others were accused. There was no question of Friedjung's bona fides. He founded his article upon what he believed to be genuine documents, and on the evidence of Nastitch, the Bosnian, who had given sensational evidence at the Cetinje bomb trial. Nastitch proved to be a professional spy, and the evidence forged. Friedjung lost his case, and the sentences of the condemned men were annulled. But his contention that plots against Austria were being made in Belgrade has been proved undoubtedly true by later events. The accused denied everything at the trial, but so soon as war broke out in 1914 the Serbo-Croat party appeared with ready-made plans, and Supilo, who had most vehemently protested his innocence, appeared as a recognized leader. The trial, in truth, resembles the case of The Times v. Parnell. The Times, like Friedjung, lost its case not because the charge was false, but because all the evidence produced was forged. That Parnell was intimately acquainted with and connected with all the anti-English work going on in Ireland is now well known. Friedjung was correct. Belgrade winked at the anti-Austrian work that was going on. The komitadji school was taught by Serb officers. Evidence was not easy to get, for, as it was explained to me by the pro-Serb party in Bosnia, in 1906, nothing of importance was written down, and the Austrians searched the post vainly. And the fact that they told me the Slovenski Jug was directed against Austria prevented me from joining it. Friedjung's failure proves only the folly of employing a stupid spy, not the innocence of the accused. Pashitch, after war began, never ceased trumpeting his schemes for Great Serbia. He grudges even now a few snippets to Italy, without whose aid it might not have been made. To assert that Pashitch, who, with his set, had worked to make Great Serbia ever since they had removed the Obrenovitch from its path in 1903, was innocent of plotting against Austria in 1909-10, is to ask for too much credulity. Had not Russia already said the road to Constantinople lay through Vienna?

England had previously been uneasy about the regicides, and had demanded their dismissal from the Serb army, but now ceased to trouble about them. They were probably needed to teach in the bandit school of the Narodna Odbrana. And henceforth they held important posts. The original gang of some fifty murderers, officers and civilians, developed into a formidable society called the Tsrna Ruka (Black Hand), which became a government within a government. The Black Hand was responsible to none. Many members of the Government were reported to belong to it, a convenient Jekyll and Hyde arrangement, by means of which crimes of all kind could be committed, for which the Government took no responsibility, and of which it denied all knowledge. King Petar having been put on the throne by this gang, had naturally no power over them, and Prince Alexander was reported to have joined the society. Talk there was about it all enough to lead one to think "No smoke without fire." Members of the Tsrna Ruka joined the police force, and so secured their plans against police interference. By means of a paper called Premont they preach violent chauvinism, and advocated savage methods. Damian Popovitch, the head assassin, held an important post. Efforts on the part of politicians, who disapproved of its methods, to break up the society failed. Unexplained deaths took place. The Black Hand brooked no interference.

CHAPTER SEVENTEEN
1910

Ill and crippled with sciatica, but hopeless of recovery in England, I managed to get to Scutari in April 1910, hoping there to find a sun-cure, and at least to learn what was happening.

Things had gone from bad to worse. No one now believed in "Constitution." The attitude of the populace on the Sultan's accession day showed this. No reforms or improvements had as yet been even begun. People said: "We will not give money to the Turks to buy gold braid for officers and guns to kill us with."

Lobatcheff had gone to Mitrovitza to hold it as a Slav outpost. My friend, the attache, had left after having almost fought a duel with the French Consul over his bulldog. Dushan Gregovitch represented Montenegro. Italy and Austria were redoubling their efforts to win over the Albanians by showering "benefits" upon them, although each had formally agreed not to countenance the partition of Albania, and the Nationalist Albanians were making strides in spite of the efforts of enemies. At the time of the Young Turk revolution some thirty Albanian papers were being published abroad. Now, as the Constitution promised freedom of the Press, printing was going on all over Albania, and the new alphabet was universally adopted. The Albanian girls' school at Koritza was filled to overflowing. The South strove to throw off Greek influence, and at Elbasan a school for training teachers was opened with mixed Moslem and Christian staff. As the Albanian poet had sung, it was a case of:

> Awake, Albanians, awake!
> Let not mosques nor churches divide you.
> The true religion of the Albanian is his national ideal.

Nationalism gained in Scutari by the death of the old Austrian Archbishop, and the elevation in his place of Mgr. Serreggi, an Albanian patriot.

Fighting was going on in Kosovo vilayet, but the Christians of Scutari firmly believed that Austria, as protector of the Catholics, would never allow the Turkish army to enter the Catholic districts. In the town the Turks pursued a foolish policy. Only one per cent, of the Christians understood Turkish, and about 20 per cent, of the Moslems, and but few could read or write it. Nevertheless the Turks gave out all notices in Turkish, and the people did not even trouble to ask their meaning.

Then came a grave event. One Sunday morning my old Marko, in whose house I lodged, announced solemnly: "Last night Teresi had a terrible dream about you. To-day you will have important news from England. God grant nothing bad has happened to your noble family." I chaffed the old man, saying: "There is no post to-day!" And then came a knock at the door, and the old blue kavas from the British Consulate handed me a note from M. Summa. "I regret to inform you of the death of our beloved Sovereign, Edward VII, which I have just learnt by telegraph from Salonika." Teresi's reputation as a dreamer became immense.

King Edward VII, in a short reign, had largely contributed towards bringing Great Britain from a state of "splendid isolation" into a tangle of—to me—very doubtful associates. I wrote: "The King's death knocks out one's ideas of what sort of a position England is going to hold. . . . Poor George ascends the throne in an awfully difficult time, with internal and foreign politics both in a regular tangle. A far more difficult beginning than Edward had. For, then, we had not upset the whole balance of power in Asia and Europe by making that alliance with Japan. I always hated it. The result . . . the predominance of Germany in Europe, is going to cost us dear. And when Japan has got all she can out of us, she will turn round and bite."

And in the same week I noted: "The newly-appointed British Minister is coming here to-morrow. Thank goodness there is no acute political crisis on now, as there was when the last man came." Mr. and Mrs. Beaumont arrived, and there followed in pursuit of them a King's messenger, who bore the assent of the British Government to Prince Nikola's desire to proclaim himself king.

His position now hurt badly. The Petrovitches were the oldest Balkan dynasty, and were the lowest in rank. The Montenegrins were divided as to the desirability of the change. Prince Danilo and his set were said to favour it strongly. The thing was decided upon suddenly, and the country consented. "I expect some Power engineered it," says my diary. And soon the rumour was very certain that the step had been taken by the advice and with the agreement of King Ferdinand of Bulgaria. "Which do you love best—me or Ferdinand?" Prince Nikola had asked me suddenly, when I last visited him. "You, of course, Sire!" said I, and wondered at the time why he had Ferdinand on the brain.

That the Turkish Empire would now soon break up, was the general belief, and Kings Ferdinand and Nikola would divide the peninsula. Bulgaria would obtain her Alsace-Lorraine, Macedonia, and Nikita would reign over Great Serbia from Prizren.

Fighting continued in Kosovo vilayet. Meanwhile I was carried dangerously ill to the Austrian hospital, and lay helpless between bouts of agony and injections of morphine. The Albanians came and wept over me, and prayed for advice and help. When I was nearly screaming with pain they implored me to make an effort and write for them to the Foreign Office and the papers, for the Turkish army was approaching. I was dragged to a sitting position, managed to write two letters, and fainted with the pain. Vain agony. Nothing could break the journalistic ring which forbade any criticism of the Young Turks. A foolish policy, for it led them to believe their actions beyond criticism, and helped their undoing. The more they blundered, the more Italy, and Austria, and Russia rejoiced. They expected the Withdrawal of the international gendarmerie to send the Turks downhill with a crash. England, probably, was not guilty of withdrawing for that reason, but was much less well informed, because more sparsely represented, than the other Powers. And we were already tangled in Russia's plans, and did not know what they were.

The Turks sent over increased forces and artillery into Kosovo vilayet, and Scutari learnt with dismay that in spite of the valour of the Kosovo men they were being forced back and back, and the Turkish army was approaching Scutari.

Prenk Pasha, who had been made a member of the Committee of Union and Progress, had promised the Turks safe-conduct through Mirdita. This was in strict conformity with the policy explained to me by the Abbot Premi Dochi in 1904, viz. that the Turk must be maintained until Albania was sufficiently organized to stand alone, otherwise the Slav, the more relentless foe, would fall upon her. The other Catholic tribes were wildly dismayed, and the headmen ran from one consulate to another begging advice. None was given them. They were far too poorly armed to resist, and in July 1910 the Turkish army entered Scutari and ordered the populace to give up its arms. They did so quietly. The Christians had few to give. The Moslems feared, by rising, to provoke an Austrian intervention.

I was too ill to be taken out to see what was going on, and, to my great disappointment, was still unable to move when the celebration on the occasion of Nikita's elevation to kingship took place in August.

Montenegro had raised a loan from England the year before, and had expended the whole of it in making electric light in Cetinje and building a Government house of superlative ugliness, and so vast that it seemed obviously intended to administer a much larger territory than Montenegro.

Scutari was excited about Montenegrin doings. Foreign visitors flocked to Cetinje to assist at the fete. Bulgaria was represented by King Ferdinand himself, Serbia, only by the Crown Prince, and he, said rumour, decided to come only at the last minute. Conclusions about a Bulgar-Montenegrin combine were freely drawn. One point both Montenegrins and Albanians agreed upon, "A king must have a kingdom. The Powers would not otherwise have allowed him to be king. Soon there will be war!"

While still in hospital I received an English paper, with illustrations of the launch of a Dreadnought. The doctor, a Dalmatian Slav, looked at them sadly. "Why do you do these things?" he asked. "You are forcing on war. You will ruin Austria. We admire everything English, except your Dreadnoughts. Each time you build one, we of the Triple Alliance are forced to build one too. We Austrians have no colonies, and never want any. We need no navy. We are already overtaxed, and the breaking-point must come one day. You eat us up with your terrible wealth. To my mind all Europe is mad. We have one common danger—the peoples of Africa and Asia, who are developing rapidly. If we want to save European civilization we must federate against the common foe. If ever there is a war in Europe —and God forbid—it will be the suicide of the white races. They will fight to extermination, and the day of the coloured people will dawn. We shall deserve our fate. It will be the result of our own folly."

Where he is now I know not. His words come back to me always. After three months I emerged from the hospital, well but weak, into a dismayed and depressed

Scutari. The Turks were trying to hamper nationalism by ordering Albanian to be printed in Arabic characters, and making Turkish compulsory in the schools. They had roused fierce anger, too, by publicly flogging some offenders, a punishment regarded in Albania as so shameful and humiliating that it bred sympathy for the victim and hatred for the inflicter. Has it, perhaps, the same result in India and Egypt?

Our next news was that Montenegro's feelings were woefully hurt. Nikola had Just been made king—but Montenegro was the only state in Europe on which the special mission to announce the death of King Edward and the accession of King George had not called. Montenegro had spent much on sending Prince Danilo to attend the funeral, and Princess Militza is distantly related to Queen Mary. The omission rankled very badly. It would be interesting to know who suggested that King Nikola should be left out.

Having achieved kingship, Nikola soon began to act. So soon as the Turks had persuaded the Albanians to disarm, they began to make a census of all fit for military service. This the Christians swore they would never give, and were furious with Austria for not intervening. The Moslems, too, vowed they would not serve outside Albania. And before any one knew what was going to happen a number of the Gruda tribe went over the border into Montenegro. Numbers of the Hoti and Shkreli followed. Scutari was astounded. The Austrians were furious, and vowed Russia had paid for it. The Turks clapped on further anti-Albanian laws, and most of the papers were suppressed. The Koritza girls' school was closed, and news of arrests came from all over the country. The Turks circulated copies of the Arabic alphabet, and ordered its use, and the Albanians burnt them.

To escape the winter I went to Egypt, nor will I detail my six months' stay there, except to note that it entirely changed my ideas about the Austrian occupation of Bosnia. My diary towards the close of my stay notes: "I wouldn't be a native under British rule at any price. They may 'do a lot of good to you,' but, dear God! they do let you know their contempt for you, and drive your inferiority into you. Any one with any spunk would rather go to hell his own way than be chivied to heaven by such odiously superior beasts. . . . The Moslems are not grateful for 'benefits' they do not want, and the Christians are discontented and annoyed, as in Bosnia." During the winter I heard from Albania that a fresh revolt was planning;

that General Garibaldi had promised arms and men, and that it would break out in the spring. Before leaving Egypt for Europe I stayed at Alexandria, and saw my friend the attache, who was now a full-blown Austrian consul, and retracted the criticisms I had made to him on Austria in Bosnia.

At Constantinople, I learnt that the Albanian revolution had broken out. Popovitch, the Montenegrin Minister, complained bitterly that his Government gave him no information, and left him to answer the Turks' charges of complicity as best he could. He was so anxious about the affair that it was obvious Montenegro was "dipped" in whatever was happening, and he begged me to go straight to the scene of action.

CHAPTER EIGHTEEN
1911 AND THE INSURRECTION OF THE CATHOLICS

I arrived in Cetinje on May 5th, and found Italy had built a Legation bigger than that of Austria. France had erected a gay villa in the main street. Great Britain still only parlour-boarded at the hotel for a few months in the year. The elephantine Vladni Dom (Government House) dominated the town, and two ridiculous new houses in the "new art" style had been built in the main street out of the "pickings" so folk said, of the British loan, the whole of which had been spent on useless ostentation. I had hoped that it would have been used for irrigating, or otherwise developing the land, and promptly sold out my few shares in disgust—and at par. I wonder how many other people got out as cheaply?

Vuko Vuletitich was swollen with pride over his daughter, who, as Madame Rizoff, held a great position as wife of the Bulgarian Minister in Rome and was known as "la bella Montenegrina." Through Rizoff I was told Montenegro hoped to attain to much.

I had been so disgusted over the bomb affair in 1908 that I had fully intended not to visit Montenegro again. I was sick of the web of intrigue which entangled the land. But now it seemed that only from Montenegro could I watch the case for Albania.

I was summoned to the palace, and received by the whole royal family, who were very gay, and did not conceal the fact that they expected and wanted war, and bade me go to Podgoritza, where the Queen's cousin, General Yamko Vukotitch, was in command of affairs.

The details of the insurrection I have told in my book, The Struggle for Scutari.

Here I will narrate only those political facts which fear of injuring my informants compelled me then to withhold.

Briefly: the insurrection was planned by King Nikola as part of his effort to obtain a kingdom. Taking advantage of the unrest caused by Young Turk rule, he used as his lever old Sokol Batzi, a worthy man of the Gruda tribe, who had fought against the Turks in 1877, and therefore taken Montenegrin nationality. Nikola rewarded him suitably, and Sokol, in return, served him with dog-like fidelity. To Sokol, much respected by the tribesmen, Nikola entrusted the task of inducing the Albanian Catholics to migrate in numbers into Montenegro, promising them that if they would revolt against the Turks their wives and children should have shelter and protection till their land was freed from the Turks, and that they should receive sufficient arms and ammunition. Nikola himself promised independence to the tribesmen. Sokol was a simple-minded old fellow. Bitterly did he and his family repent later of the way they had let themselves be made cat's paws of. A considerable sum of money was collected in Montenegro to finance the revolution. An Austrian Slav doctor was engaged, and a rough hospital prepared, and a store of maize purchased. These preparations went on through the winter. Montenegro's protests, to Europe, of her innocence were lies which were black even for diplomacy, As for the interview which Prince Danilo gave to the Morning Post, it was a shameless tissue of falsehoods. He declared that Montenegro had supplied no arms or ammunition to the insurgents, when at that very time his cousin, Yanko Vukotitch, was distributing weapons and directing the military operations under my eyes.

Even worse was his statement: "It grieves my heart to see these brave mountaineers die for the liberty of having their own schools for their children." When not one single Albanian school was permitted in Montenegro; forcible Slavizing was going on in the Kuchi and Triepshl tribes, and the Catholic Albanians of Podgoritza were not allowed to make a floor to their church and had to kneel on the bare gravel.

At Podgoritza I soon saw that the Montenegrins wanted war. King Nikola hoped thus to mend his damaged prestige. Mobilization began. On July 11th Yanko told me all was ready, and he could take Scutari in ten days. He offered to take me there on a gun carriage. The artillery tracks to the mountains were completed, and the big guns were going up. Ox-carts creaked past at night, taking up the ammunition. The

Turks, it was said with glee, dared not withdraw troops from the Bulgar frontier, and were hampered with revolts elsewhere. Soon, however, large Turkish forces arrived. It was clear the untrained Maltsors could not stand against the overpowering numbers. Too late they saw they had been tricked by the Montenegrins, and cried to the Powers. At their request I helped draw up a letter to Sir Edward Grey, explaining their situation and their wishes, and we sent it. King Nikola, who was posing to the Powers as the victim of the Albanian insurrection, was very angry when he heard of this, and suspected me of instigating it. But I did not. The Maltsors, too, were tricked by General Garibaldi, who had promised to aid them and did not do so. They had expected the South of Albania to rise also. Had it done so, I believe the Powers would have been obliged to recognize the Albanian question, and much future war might have been spared. But, unfortunately, the South believed in Ismail Kemal, and he worked on which ever side paid him. He was then in league with a Corfiote Greek, one Androutzos, who boasted to me in a letter that he and Ismail had advised the South against rising, and had "saved Albania." A few risings took place, but not enough to make a mark in Europe.

Meanwhile Montenegro still expected war, and to every protest I made that Montenegro could not fight the Turks single-handed I was always told that Bulgarian help was certain. The army was anxious to begin, for it was mobilized, and the revolt had cost more than had been expected. But for the fund I raised the wretched refugees would have suffered yet more bitterly. Montenegro cared nothing for them. All she wanted was territory. Great Serbia was discussed with singular cold-bloodedness, one of the schoolmasters saying at the dinner-table that it would never be "made till the Petrovitches and the Karageorgevitches are sent after the Obrenovitches." And King Nikola's tactics were severely criticised. Either make war or demobilize—the country could not stand the strain. I was warned not to trust Stanko Markovitch, the Governor of Podgoritza, a sinister figure enough, who had been raised suddenly to this height from being master in a primary school, for "services rendered." "The King's poisoner," said folk. "Beware!"

Foreign correspondents swarmed, and Russian officers came and reconnoitred the frontier. The Turks occupied all the strategical posts. Russia was not ready for war, and would not have it. Suddenly the Maltsors were told Montenegro could do no more for them, and they were to make peace, and go back to their burnt and pillaged homes. Never has a people been more shamelessly betrayed. King Nikola had used the poor creatures as a cat's paw, had failed, and now brutally cast them out, and pretended to the Powers that Montenegro was innocent. By brutal threats the Maltsors were induced to accept the Turkish terms. But they stipulated I was to return with them and stay the winter. This I undertook to do, and before leaving was told by some one who had just had audience with the King that owing to pressure from the Powers he had been forced to postpone war till next year, but that Montenegrin troops would occupy the strategical points so soon as the Turkish troops withdrew, and I was to be ready. The Montenegrin army was, in fact, never quite demobilized, and the King badgered the Powers continually to order the withdrawal of the Turkish troops "which threatened his frontier." Great Britain realized that Montenegro was a spot which needed watching, and sent Count de Salis there as Minister. High time, too.

I went to Scutari worn out with toil, responsibility, and the heat which stood at 104 in the shade. France was now represented by a Levantine Pole. Krajewsky, bitterly anti-Austrian, and very active.

English sympathy for the Maltsors had been aroused, and Mr. Nevinson came out to report on the state of things and help me to organize relief work. In order to close the Turkish frontier the Montenegrins declared cholera in Scutari, though we saw no signs of it, and quarantine was declared. We were cut off from news, and when distributing quinine in the fever districts round Alessio learnt suddenly that Italy had declared war, and was bombarding Tripoli. It was a bolt from the blue. Italy had no casus belli, but as we have seen, Izvolsky had arranged the affair two years before and no Power protested, save that Austria forbade Italy to land in Albania. Krajewsky became violently pro-Turk. Scutari rightly judged the war as the first step towards the break-up of Turkey. The Turks behaved with admirable tolerance. None of the Italians of the town were Interfered with, and though war broke out on September 30th the Italian Minister did not leave till October 23rd. Mr. Nevinson returned to London, and I was left to carry on relief work.

All I could do to prevent the tribesmen being again cheated by Montenegro I did. Petar Plamenatz, now consul, tried hard to buy their help in the coming war by promising arms and liberty. Montenegro intended no annexation, he said. "Nikita himself had promised," said the tribesmen. But I now would not believe

King Nikola, even if he swore on the body of St. Peter Cetinski. His actions were suspicious.

For the first time for many years he visited his Austrian rentiers, and was warned by the Entente Ministers. "England," said Plamenatz, "was firm; France mild, and Russia very disagreeable."

Montenegro was evidently in touch with Bulgaria. Plamenatz told me that the bomb thrown into a mosque at Istib to excite reprisals or force the Turks to declare War, had been expressly prepared in Sofia, and anxiously awaited results.

Serbia and Montenegro were now on the worst terms. On December 24th, the season of peace and goodwill, Plamenatz, in a rage, showed me a telegram just received by the Orthodox priest of Scutari. The Patriarchia had been persuaded to appoint one Dochitch, a Montenegrin of Moracha, to the Bishopric of Prizren, in place of Nicephor, dismissed for drunkenness and other inappropriate conduct. Montenegro triumphed, and looked on Prizren as hers. The Serbs were furious; the priests of Kosovo refused to recognize him, and had telegraphed to the two priests of Scutari and Vraka to do so, too. They, being Montenegrin, were all for Dochitch, and their tiny flocks supported them.

Any Serbo-Montenegrin agreement seemed, then, quite impossible, and Petar fulminated against Serb infamy.

CHAPTER NINETEEN
1912. THE FIRST DROPS OF THE THUNDERSTORM

1912 dawned ominously. Montenegro worked ceaselessly to rouse the Maltsors, promising them that they should receive sufficient arms and, this time, gain freedom. Meanwhile the Turks carried out their agreement to feed the late insurgents very well. But Petar Plamenatz never ceased quibbling over the French translation of the terms, and inciting the tribesmen to quite impossible demands. Repeated messages brought me varying dates for the commencement of hostilities. Montenegro meant war. But Montenegro could not wage it alone. Which Power was shoving her? I was fairly certain that Bulgaria and Montenegro had some sort of an engagement, and learnt later I was right.

Baron de Kruyff, Dutch correspondent and head of the Foreign Journalists Society which visited Podgoritza in 1911, told me that when he left Montenegro in June (1911) King Nikola, on hearing he was going to Sofia, asked him to convey a letter thither, addressed to a private individual, and to open it on crossing the frontier. On doing so he found it contained another addressed to King Ferdinand, with instructions to deliver it into the King's hands. He had an audience, and did so. The letter contained the first proposals for a Bulgar-Montenegrin agreement, by means of which each monarch should aid the other to achieve his ambitions, and Nikola hoped to reign at Prizren. King Ferdinand favoured de Kruyff with a long audience, and asked him to convey the reply. De Kruyff objected that his sudden return to Cetinje without obvious reason would excite suspicion. It was therefore arranged that he should meet Popovitch as Montenegrin envoy in Trieste. Which he did. I wonder if Russia knew this? I fancy not.

Russia was now working for a Balkan Alliance, which, though primarily directed against Austria, had for its ultimate goal the acquisition of Constantinople. Nicholas II of Russia, like Nikola I of Montenegro, was obsessed with a city. Russia was recuperating rapidly. She was financed by France, and sure of military aid. She had entangled England. The secular enmity of the Balkan peoples was the one weak spot in her plan. To amend this she transferred Hartwig, Russian Minister in Teheran, to Belgrade.

He had successfully worked the ruin of Persia. He was now to compass that of Turkey. Hartwig was a man to stick at nothing. Dr. Dillon tells us that his methods were so abominable that even the Russian Foreign Office protested. "People asked how he dared oppose the Foreign Office on which he depended. The answer was that he was encouraged, and put up to it by the Tsar. When at last M. Izvolsky extracted permission to recall the rebellious minister, Nicholas II decorated him, and told him that his was the only policy Russia could pursue with dignity and profit. . . . Thereupon he entrusted Hartwig with the most important post in the Balkans."

De Schelking, secretary to the Russian Legation in Berlin, gives a picture of Hartwig's immense influence: "Shortly after his arrival in Belgrade, Hartwig created a most exceptional position for himself. The King, Prince Alexander, Pashitch, none of these made any decisions without consulting him first. . . . Every morning his study was besieged by Serbian statesmen who came to ask advice" (The Game of Diplomacy). It is amusing to compare de Schelking's account with an order from Pashitch, November 14, 1912: "Take notice: Our Ministers in Foreign lands are to be informed that Hartwig has not visited the King, and that he comes to the Foreign Office less than any of the other Ministers." According to de Schelking he had no need to visit anybody. But I fancy Kings Ferdinand and Nikola made their plans without consulting him. Nor can they be blamed for so doing.

The alleged object of Hartwig's Balkan alliance was to protect the Balkan peoples from further annexation. It was, however, difficult to unite Bulgaria and Serbia, and would have been harder yet had King Ferdinand known that Russia had already told Serbia that she had no use for a Big Bulgaria. Perhaps neither the Serbo-Bulgar nor the Bulgar-Greek alliances would have been effected, but for the co-operation of Mr. J. B. Bourchier, whose honesty was beyond all doubt, and who was trusted where a Balkan envoy would not have been. He too, unfortunately, was unaware that Bulgaria's fate was already sealed by Russia, and that England was too deeply tangled in Russian intrigue to be able to stand for justice.

The Serbo-Bulgar alliance was signed on February 29, 1912, and was to be in force till December 1920. The two parties were "unconditionally and without reservation to mutually aid each other with all the forces of the State if one or more other States should attack one of these countries" and "to support one another with all force should any one of the Great Powers make the attempt to forcibly acquire even temporarily any territory situate in the Balkans, and at present under Turkish suzerainty." Russia meant none but herself to put a finger in the Balkan pie.

Russia seems to have been doubtful about Montenegro, for the Serb minister in Petersburg reports (February 17, 1912): "As regards the visit of the King of Montenegro, and as regards Austro-Hungarian relations . . . in pursuance of what was intended King Nikola was given some energetic counsel to pursue a quiet line of conduct, and not to let himself in for any adventures." Serbia now was on very friendly terms with the Greeks and helping them to kill Bulgar komitadjis in Macedonia. Montenegro, feeling secure in her arrangements with Bulgaria, was induced to declare alliance with Serbia. The Bulgar-Greek alliance, the hardest to make, was finally negotiated.

These things were all secret, but the air was tense with them. We were told we should know definitely if it were peace or war when King Nikola returned from Petersburg in February. Prince Danilo at the same time went to Sofia. We were told to be ready for war in April. Gavrilovitch, who was Serb Minister at Cetinje, came to Scutari with young M. Cambon, a significant combination, and was visibly relieved when I told him I was doing all I could to keep peace in the mountains Serbia, as we know now, was acting strictly as Russia's tool, as shown by official documents, and Russia wished to postpone the Balkan crash till she was ready. But having made the Balkan Alliance, it took the bit in its teeth. Daily I saw Montenegro shoving towards war, and the Turks steadily fortifying Scutari.

On March 10th Petar Plamenatz was suddenly transferred to Constantinople, and replaced by Jovan Jovitchevitch, who naively said he had been instructed to ask me for maps and information. Petar went to Constantinople, as he afterwards boasted, for the express purpose of declaring war. "Ma guerre a moi!" he called it. "Car c'est moi qui l'a fait."

At the last moment, when war was seething, Hadji Avdil, Minister of the Interior, started with a Reform Commission through Turkey. But he only precipitated the end. A narrow-minded man, filled with inordinate conceit of his own importance, he passed with difficulty through Kosovo vilayet and arrived in Scutari on March 10th. Instead of pacifying the excited Maltsors, he refused to meet them on any terms which they considered safe. And he left matters far worse than he found them. That he, too, expected war was evident, for he appointed the military commandant Hussein Riza as Vali.

The Albanians of Kosovo again rose in revolt. Ise Boletin again led them. They triumphed everywhere, and this time entered Uskub, where their conduct was admitted to have been exemplary by the Foreign Consuls. The Turks, finding that the Albanians were about to march on Monastir, called a truce, and agreed to recognize the four vilayets of Janina, Scutari, Kosovo, and part of Monastir, as an autonomous Albanian province. The immediate result of the Albanian victory was the overthrow of the chauvinistic Young Turk party and the appointment of a more moderate Cabinet. The effect of this coup on the Balkans was electric. Each Balkan State had pegged out for itself a slice of Albania. Delenda est Albania was the one point on which they agreed. Heedless of Russia, they hastened to make war before Albania should have time to consolidate.

War preparations hurried on. Montenegro worked upon the discontent caused by Hadji Avdil. King Nikola had returned from Russia, but had not fixed the date of war as we had expected. I thought perhaps Italy was shoving, in order to assist her war in Tripoli, which still dragged on. But in a few weeks' visit to Rome I had a long talk with San Giuliano, and perceived clearly that Italy was not urging Montenegro.

There seemed but one possible explanation, and that was that an understanding had been come to between Greece and Bulgaria, and that Montenegro therefore felt certain of the co-operation of the whole of the Bulgar army. In Rome, Popovitch, the Montenegrin Minister, had told me, when announcing that General Martinovitch had been made War Minister: "This means war."

Returned to Scutari, I went straight to the Greek consul and in the middle of a chat on nothing particular, asked: "A propos, Monsieur, is it true your Government has signed a treaty of alliance with Bulgaria against Turkey!" The poor little man almost leapt from his chair. "Mademoiselle!" he stammered, "you are surely aware there are things political of which one may not speak." I begged him to say no more. More was unnecessary. War I knew was now certain. The secret alliance had, in fact, been signed on May 16th.

Next day a frontier fight took place, provoked by Montenegro. It lasted seven hours. Every one cried: "It is war!" The Montenegrin Consul was greatly agitated. He knew what his country was doing, and cried: "Mon Dieu, Mademoiselle, I hope you will not write a book for five years! You know too much."

To avoid being besieged in Scutari I left for Podgoritza at once, and found Podgoritza so certain of war that I was begged to stay and see the first shot fired. Why war was then postponed I never made out. Perhaps Montenegro had to wait for Bulgaria.

Cetinje also expected war, and asked me to collect funds for the wounded. The King begged me to prevent the Maltsors rising yet, which showed me he again intended to make a tool of them. Kol Mirashi, one of the pluckiest of the Maltsor patriots, told me they all knew this, and meant to rise at once to show Europe they were fighting for independence, and not for Montenegro.

I said: "Why not keep quiet and develop autonomy?" He replied: "Impossible. The Montenegrin-Austrian plan is now complete, and will soon be in motion. We must act independently. King Nikola went to Russia for help. They refused him. So he has joined with Austria."

The Russian visit had been a fiasco. Lazar Mioushkovitch, who, with Dushan Gregovitch, had accompanied the King, told me: "It was terrible." Dushan Gregovitch—good looking, and remarkable rather for high stakes at bridge than common-sense—rashly allowed himself to be interviewed. Montenegro's grandiose schemes for conquest appeared next day in the papers. "The Tsar was furious. He threatened us even with annihilation! The King told him Dushan was known to be a liar, but it was of no use. It is finished! We have no more to expect from Russia!"

But war preparations hurried on. And some of the Bank employees told me that the King had raised a loan in Vienna "in order to start an Agricultural Bank!" They smiled.

Montenegro now tried to force the Turks to declare war by provoking two bad frontier fights near Kolashin and Andrijevitza, each time burning several Turkish blockhouses, and going far over the frontier. The Powers ordered the recall of the Montenegrin troops on August 5th, or they would have occupied the whole Berani district. I went to Andrijevitza on August 27th and stayed there a month. The big guns had already been taken up and were on the frontier, and ammunition was widely distributed, not only to Montenegrins, but also to the Serbs from Turkish territory, who came over the border at night. General Yanko Vukotitch was in command. There was a hospital full of wounded, and Andrijevitza was furious with the Government for having broken faith. They had been promised assistance, and had expected this fight to be followed at once by war. The whole district was strongly anti-Petrovitch, and in close touch with Serbia. Veshovitch, the frontier commandant, even said— when I suggested that a declaration of war might be followed by the re-occupation of the Sanjak by Austria, and a possible attack on Montenegro: "What then? Anything would be better than the Government we have down there!" and pointed Cetinjewards. Jovan Plamenatz assured me emphatically that Austria would not attack them. And he counted for certain on Bulgar support. The Turks, however, displayed great restraint, and did not declare war. Veshovitch then told me that as neither the efforts of Bulgaria nor Montenegro could force them to it, Montenegro herself would begin. He had bombs ready to spring another Turkish blockhouse, and so soon as he had finished the big bread-oven for the army would do so, and cross the border. Sniping, as I saw myself, was already going on daily.

A strange tale has been circulated that Montenegro mobilized but four days before war broke out. The above facts show this to be quite a mistake. Montenegro had been preparing over a year, and could have begun in July.

I hastened to Cetinje to tell Count de Salis what was happening. He replied that the Powers were doing nothing useful, and he feared it was now too late.

I went to the Russia Institut. It was October 3rd. Sofia Petrovna was happy and excited at the prospect of war; foretold the end of the Turk and the triumph of the Holy Orthodox Church, to which she was heart and soul passionately attached. While we were discussing the situation, in hurried Yougourieff, one of the Russian officers attached to the Legation, and superintending the Military Cadet School financed by Russia, who, though she was no longer supporting Nikola, was actively training young Montenegrins as cannon-fodder.

He stopped short on seeing me; hesitated; said something in Russian. Seeing

I was de trop, I rose to go. Sofia Petrovna bade me stay. "Mademoiselle," she said, "knows the whole political situation. You can speak before her."

He asked me doubtfully: "Will you promise not to send off what I say to a newspaper?" I promised.

He sat down and began hotly in French to Sofia: "The Montenegrins are absolutely mad! You must use all your influence to stop them. They must not make this war! We have already told them so most severely. They are mad, I tell you—we cannot and must not have war now."

Sofia disagreed vehemently. All was ready. Things could not go on like this. "But I tell you," said Yougourieff excitedly, "absolutely there must be no Balkan war without Russia. And we are not ready." Sofia persisted: "My friend—we shall intervene. We said we would not in 1877—and we did. We shall now."

He became very serious. "I tell you this is not 1877. We cannot intervene. Unless Austria intervenes, which God forbid, we have no excuse for war. And nothing is yet ready. We are working as fast as possible, but there is much yet to do. These people must wait!" He was in deadly earnest, and plainly speaking the truth.

I asked quite suddenly: "And when will you be ready, Monsieur?"

"In two years from now, Mademoiselle, we shall be absolutely ready for our great war!"

It was October 3rd, 1912. Russia began her great war on August 1, 1914. Yougourieff was only two months out. No wonder he made me promise not to publish his remarks.

We learn now, from a report by Gruitch, Serbian Minister in London, September 8, 1911, to the Serbian Foreign Office, that the date was known to others as well. Speaking of the agreement about Morocco, he says: "The agreement has one result, that war will be postponed three or four years. . . . Both France and her allies are of opinion that the war—even at the expense of great sacrifice, must be postponed to a later time, that it to say, until the year 1914-15" (see Bogitchevitch, xi). No wonder that Gavrilovitch and young Cambon approved of my peace policy, and that Yougourieff was emphatic.

I went to General Yanko Vukotitch's house. Rakia was flowing. He, madame, his secretary, and others were in high feather. Yanko explained the plan of campaign to me. He was to lead the main division to Prizren. The two other divisions under Brigadier Boshkovitch and General Martinovitch, were to attack Scutari, and, having taken it, to join the triumphant Yanko at Prizren. No mention was made of when the other Balkan States were to come in. Bulgarian support was certain. Madame Yanko begged me to go with her husband and photograph his entry into Prizren.

The whole campaign, it appeared, was expected only to last a few weeks, and only 150 beds had been made ready at the hospital. The Montenegrins honestly believed that theirs was the finest army for its size in Europe.

General Martinovitch told me to go off to Podgoritza if I wanted to see the first shot fired. When I arrived there on October 6th all was ready and waiting. Another proof that the "four days' mobilization" tale is an error.

King Nikola had made up his outstanding quarrel with his relatives, and the Royal Voyvodas, Marko, Sharko, Bozho, and Gjuro all arrived. On the night of the 8th all sang: "Let me see Prizren!"

There was wild excitement. No one mentioned the Serbs. I asked, "What is the Serb army like?" They roared with laughter. "Oni chuvahjuf svinje Gospodjitza!" (They are swineherds, lady!) Next morning at 8 a.m. Prince Petar fired a gun into a Turkish camp across the frontier.

The tale of the war has already been told. Here only a few significant facts need telling.

Montenegro expected by rushing the first into war to occupy all the coveted districts, including Prizren, before Serbia was ready. Bulgaria would beat back the Turks, and Ferdinand and Nikita share the bulk of the peninsula. The Montenegrins recked nothing of the Serbs, but they miserably miscalculated. The Serbs reached Prizren before they did.

It is possible that Bulgaria and Montenegro, in fact, forced on the war. Both knew they would gain nothing by waiting for Russia. And if two of the Balkan States insisted on war the other two were bound to come in.

Montenegro's plan failed. Her first startling successes were due to the fact that the Maltsor risings had largely cleared the way for her. But as the Montenegrins began at once to treat Albanian territory as their own, and even loot Catholic Albanian houses, tension between the Maltsors and Montenegrins arose and increased. The Maltsors flung away the Montenegrin caps dealt out to them, withdrew in numbers, and soon consulted me as to whether they should attack the Montenegrins in the rear and cut them off. I begged them not to, as I then believed in the honesty of the Powers, and thought Albania would get justice. I regret it now.

South Albania also perceived that the self-styled "liberators" who poured in from Greece were but brigands intent on gain and murder, and on November 28, 1912, Ismail Kemal, who was in Constantinople when war broke out, managed with difficulty to return to his native town Valona, where he hoisted the National flag, proclaimed the independence of Albania, and formed a provisional government. It was hoped that by thus showing that Albania wanted freedom, and detached herself completely from the Turks, she would be respected by Europe. For the Balkan Allies had stated they were at war only with the Turks.

Official notification of Albania's resolve was sent to the Powers, and the Albanians hoped for sympathy, for it was they who in fact had aimed the first blow at Young Turk tyranny. The Greeks and Montenegrins and Serbs, far from sympathizing with Albania's wish for freedom, were incensed by it. The Greeks blockaded Valona, and cut the telegraph. The yacht of the Duc le Monpensier, however, ran the blockade, and took off Ismail Kemal, Gurikuchi, and that gallant chieftain Isa Boletin. He had fought on the side of the Serb till he saw what Serb victory would mean. The three pleaded their cause in the capitals of Europe. Europe meanwhile seethed with intrigue.

Russia's plans were overset by the premature outbreak of the Balkan war. But she was bent on getting all she could out of it for her side, and dragged France along with her. At the beginning of the Italy-Tripoli war, Izvolsky had written: "We must even now not only concern ourselves with the best means of preserving peace and order in the Balkans, but also with the matter of extracting the greatest possible advantage to ourselves from coming events."

The Powers called a Conference of Ambassadors in London to try to arrange a Balkan settlement. The Russian Ambassador in London reports, February 25, 1913, that England wishes peace and a compromise. Of France he states that M. Cambon "has directed himself in reality entirely to me. . . . When I recall his conversations and . . . add the attitude of Poincare, the thought comes to me that of all the Powers, France is the only one which, not to say that it wishes war, yet would look on it with least regret. . . . The disposition of France offers us on the one hand a guarantee, but on the other it must not happen that the war breaks out on account of interests more French than Russian, and in any case not under circumstances more favourable to France than to Russia."

The Conference inevitably became a struggle by Russia to obtain all possible lands for her proteges regardless of the wishes of the inhabitants. Possession of land for a short time in the Middle Ages was given as reason for handing it over now.

"We might as justly claim Calais," I said to a Podgoritza schoolmaster, "for it was ours at the same time!"

"Why don't you," said he. "You have a navy?"

Sir Edward Grey, in the interests of justice, stood out against Slav rapacity, but Russia insisted on having either Scutari or Djakovo for the Slavs; though Djakovo, a town of between two and three thousand houses, contained but one hundred Serb families. Nor was there a single Serb village near it. All were Albanian Moslems or Catholics, but they were offered up as a living sacrifice on the altar of Russia's ambitions.

Montenegro meanwhile was very bitter. Yanko had failed to take Prizren. The population railed against the Government. The King had never recovered popularity since the bomb affair. Some of the condemned were still in prison.

Had Prizren been taken, things would have been very different. All Montenegro had been trained from childhood to sing: "Onward, onward, let me see Prizren!" and though the town consisted of nearly four thousand Albanian houses and but 950 Serb ones, Prizren had become a sort of insanity with them. Not only Prizren was not taken by Montenegro, but Scutari was not either. The population now turned with savage desire on Scutari, about which previously little had been said.

It had been believed that Constantinople would soon fall, and that the four Crown princes would enter it in state. Though how they could have been so simple as to think Russia would permit this, it is hard to understand.

The cry rose: "Russia helped us in 1877, why does she not come forward now?" Whatever the heads of the land knew, the rank and file had confidently expected Russian intervention.

Only by dragging in Austria could Russia's hand be forced. The Serbs endeavoured to goad Austria into action. News reached us that they had imprisoned and maltreated Prochaska, the Austrian Consul in Prizren, and Montenegro's delight and expectation were immense. His nose, said the Montenegrins, should be cut off just as though he were a Turk. Prochaska was, in fact, a brother Slav, a Czech, a capable man, whom I had met in 1908. Austria, it was confidently asserted at the inn dinner table, would be forced to fight—or for ever hide disgraced. Yanko Vukotitch's secretary, who had been up at Prizren, described to me with the greatest gusto what happened: "Oh, if you could but have seen what the officers did to Prochasko! They rolled him on the ground, spat in his face, tore the Austrian flag, did all that you can imagine that is most dirty upon him! Austria will never dare tell the world what we did to her consul. All Europe would laugh at her, and she would have to declare war."

"But why was this done?" I asked.

"Because he asked some dirty Albanians to his consulate."

"But a consul has the right to ask whom he pleases to his consulate. It was his duty also to protect the Catholics."

"Very well. This is to teach Austria we have no need of her consuls. Austria is finished!" He, as all the Montenegrins, was furious at any attempt to save the Albanians from extirpation. All those who would not be Slavized were to be killed.

Austria would have been fully justified in making war on Serbia. And as Russia was not ready, and the Serbs engaged with the Turks, then was the moment to do it. But Germany was strong for peace. "Berlin had applied itself, above all, to calm the exasperation and desire for intervention at the Ballplatz," says Baron Beyens, Belgian Minister in Berlin. "The Archduke Ferdinand stated at Berlin that Austria had come to the end of the concessions it could make to its neighbour. The Emperor and his councillors showered upon him, none the less, counsels of moderation, which William II when conducting his guest to the railway station summarized in these expressive words: "Above all, no folly (pas de betises). . . . But to lead Austria to show itself more tractable, as it is believed here the Imperial Government has succeeded in doing, is not enough to pacify the conflict. It yet remains to bend the obstinate resistance of Serbia, and to effect a diminution of her demands. There was a rumour last week in the European Chancelleries that M. Sasonov had ceased to struggle against the Court party, which wishes to drag Russia into war, though the soil of the Empire is undermined with revolution and military preparations are yet insufficient."

Prochaska, after some weeks of imprisonment, was released. Austria humbled her pride and accepted an apology. Prochaska was compensated and bound to secrecy. As my informant had foretold, Austria dared not tell her humiliation.

In Montenegro this produced a howl of contempt. Austria was finished; you could do what you pleased with her with impunity; the next war would be with Austria. Montenegro, on her side, thought well to insult her. Perhaps one more stab would make her fight, and then hurrah for Russia and Constantinople!

From the conquered districts came piteous reports of the hideous cruelties which Serb and Montenegrin alike were committing on the Albanian populations. Far from concealing their deeds, the conquerors boasted of them. A Serb officer nearly choked with laughter over his beer, as he told how his men had bayoneted the women and children of Ljuma. And one of the Petrovitches boasted to me that in two years no one in the conquered lands would dare speak "that dirty language" (Albanian). Moslem men were given the choice of baptism or death, and shot down. The women were unveiled, and they and the children driven to church and baptized. "In one generation we shall thus Serbize the lot!" they said. And later evidence proved that these reports were true. No Turk ever treated Armenian worse than did the two Serb peoples treat the Albanians in the name of the Holy Orthodox Church. Stanko Markovitch, Governor of Podgoritza, forbade the giving of any food to the starving people of the burnt villages, and told me flatly that they were doomed to die. Podgoritza exclaimed he was a fool to tell me this: "Now she will denounce us in England and America, too!" But they did not deny it. News came from Djakovo that Father Palitch, a plucky Franciscan, whom I had met there in 1908, had been bayoneted to death for refusing to make the sign of the cross in Orthodox fashion. The account of his death, given by Moslems and Catholics alike, was denied by the Montenegrin Government. Austria rightly insisted on an examination, for, as a Catholic, he was under her protection. This was made by a commission under Mgr. Miedia, Bishop of Prizren. Father Palitch's body was exhumed. It was proved that he was killed by bayonets, and the tale of the Montenegrins that he had been shot when trying to escape was devoid of foundation, there being no gunshot wounds in the body. The case was gone into fully. Austria a second time accepted apology and certain compensations, and failed to respond to provocation. No

Russian intervention could now be expected. But the Slavs continued to cry: "Death to Albania," and it was the clear duty of Austria, and should have been also of Italy, to save it. The organ of the Serb Black Hand, Piemont, advocated the slaughter of all the inhabitants of Scutari, to punish them for having dared to resist. War, as is always the case, had aroused the worst passions of this—at best—semi-civilized race. But the Powers realized that Russia's unbridled greed on behalf of her Serb proteges must be checked.

Scutari was a town of 35,000 Albanian inhabitants. Montenegro was ordered by the Powers to withdraw from Scutari, and Serbia from Scutari and Durazzo. The Powers sent a naval demonstration, and prepared a collective Note. The Tsar ordered King Nikola to yield. But while he spoke publicly, the representatives of France and Russia did all they could to impede the delivery of the Note till too late, in order to give the Montenegrins time to acquire by fraud what they could not take by force. King Nikola and many of his subjects went about swearing aloud that if they did not get all they wanted they would set the whole of Europe on fire, and the combined Serb and Montenegrin armies would take Vienna.

The plans for the taking of Scutari by fraud had probably been long laid. In February came news that the gallant commander of Scutari, Hussein Riza Bey, had been murdered-and his place taken by the notorious Essad Pasha. Essad had been servant of the Old Turk, and then member of the Committee of Union and Progress. He aimed solely at power for himself, and now became servant of the Slav. Hussein Riza, seeing no help could be expected from the Turks, and determined not to yield the town to the Slavs, decided to hand it over to the Albanians. On his mother's side he was of Albanian blood. His plan was to communicate with all the tribesmen, and to arrange that they should fall on the besieging army in the rear while he and his army made a simultaneous sortie. He hoped thus to cut up the Montenegrin army and save the town. One of the Franciscan fathers and another man were to steal through the lines at night and arrange that the tribesmen should attack when Hussein Riza hoisted the Albanian flag on the citadel. That night after Hussein Riza had supped with Essad, he was shot dead a few yards away from the house by two men disguised as women. Osman Bali and Mehmed Kavaja, both servants of Essad, boasted afterwards they had done the deed. The town crier proclaimed that nothing was to be said about the murder and Essad, who was second, now took command,

and soon entered into communication with the Montenegrins. As he knew only Turkish and Albanian, the letters went through the hands of the dragoman of the Italian consulate.

Italy played an oddly double game. She was bound by Treaty to assist Austria to preserve the integrity of Albania. But she did not object to King Nikola—father of the Queen of Italy—taking the town if he could. Italy was striving for influence in Montenegro, out of hatred of Austria, and failed to see that the South Slav, not the German-Austrian, was her real danger.

While France and Russia delayed matters, Petar Plamenatz drew up terms with Essad. Provided he evacuated the town in time for Montenegro to occupy it before the Powers could stop it, he was to leave with all honours, and a large supply of arms and food. He was also to aid the Serbs to reach Durazzo later, and as a reward was to be recognized as ruler in his own district of Tirana. A vile enough plot.

In order to deceive Europe, the Montenegrin Government telegraphed everywhere an account of a huge fight, in which Scutari had been taken, and thousands of Montenegrins wounded. But it was such a lie that they dared not give it either to The Times' correspondent or to me.

Essad withdrew. The Montenegrins entered without firing a shot. Thus was Scutari betrayed to her enemy. That the plot was known to the Italian Legation is clear, for the Italian war correspondents had the information from the Legation and hurried to the spot the day before.

King Nikola having obtained the town, tried to effect a bargain with Austria by offering the Lovtchen in exchange for it. But I fancy the Powers burked this.

The war was over. All through I used to say to myself: "War is so obscene, so degrading, so devoid of one redeeming spark, that it is quite impossible there can ever be a war in West Europe." This was the one thing that consoled me in the whole bestial experience. War brings out all that is foulest in the human race, and the most disgusting animal ferocity poses as a virtue. As for the Balkan Slav and his vaunted Christianity, it seemed to me all civilization should rise and restrain him from further brutality.

Of the saving of Scutari by the arrival of International forces under Admiral Sir Cecil Burney I have told elsewhere, and of the months of relief work in the villages burnt by Serb and Montenegrin, who had destroyed nearly every olive and fruit tree, and devastated the land.

But even when their army of saviours arrived the luckless Scutarenes were ordered to make no demonstration, and had to lay aside the flowers and flags they were joyfully preparing. In return for their obedience, their enemies reported in the papers that the "naval force was received without interest or enthusiasm."

The Montenegrins left, after having burnt and pillaged nearly a third of the bazar as vengeance.

At Podgoritza, where I went to fetch my store of relief stuff, I was set on by a number of officials at the parcel office. Furious at losing Scutari, they swore they would retake it and take Bosnia, too. I told them not to talk so foolishly. They cried: "We—the Serb people—have beaten the Turk. We are now a danger to Europe. We shall take what we please. The Serbs will go to Vienna. We shall go to Serajevo. We have the whole of the Russian army with us. If you do not believe it—you will see. We shall begin in Bosnia!" This was in May 1913. Yougourieff, by the way, was delighted at the capture of Scutari, and told me that the fait accompli could not be upset. "Except by accomplishing another," I said. The French and Italian legations, too, were indecently elated.

The Great Serbia party explained its plans freely. King Ferdinand was to be assassinated, and Bulgaria be suzerain to Serbia. There was to be war with Austria. Any one in Great Serbia's path was to be "removed." A friend, who was doing relief work at Uskub, told me that there the Serb officers talked incessantly of their next war with Austria, and were savagely extirpating the Bulgarian and Albanian populations from the newly annexed districts.

As for M. Krajewsky, the French Consul, he now "outjuggered" the Jugoslavs. "Never," he declared, "would France allow independent Albania to exist." The Russian Consul Miller, on the contrary, said he had written the strongest possible report against Montenegro to his Government, saying "that the Montenegrins by their disgraceful conduct in war had forfeited all right to it." His report did much to save the town.

The Dalmatian doctor, who had cured me of my long illness in 1910, was also most emphatically anti-Serb and Montenegrin, though a Slav himself, declaring them to be a set of savages who should not be allowed to take Albanian lands. This was the more noteworthy, as he had previously been by no means pro-Albanian.

On June 12th Mr. Nevinson arrived with Mr. Erickson, an American\ missionary who had done much work in Albania, and on the 15th we started to ride through the country to learn the state of things. As little has been written of Albania at this period I give a rsume of my diary.

June 15th.—Rode to Alessio, past the villages burnt by the Serbs. Found the Albanian flag flying on the bridge of Alessio, and Albanian guards. Town dead, inn ruined. District patrolled by Ded Soko's men. Perfect order. Heard tales of Serb brutality to prisoners.

Tuesday, 17th.—Provisional government of Kruja welcomed us in grand old house. The government, with old Kadi at its head, hoped anxiously for appointment of a Prince. Full of fear of Essad. Told sad tale of suffering. When war began they determined not to help the Turks, and declared independence in November, hoping thus to escape complications and take no part in the war. When the vanguard of the Serb army arrived they believed that, as there were no Serbs in the district, there was no danger. It is pathetic to note that the luckless Albanians at first believed that the Serbs and Montenegrins spoke truth when they said the war was in order to liberate their brethren. That whole districts of solid Albanian population would be seized, did not occur to them. They sat up all night and made bread for the Serb army, and treated them as guests. Later, they found their mistake. The Serbs treated them as conquered. . . . People were arrested by the wayside and hanged without trial. Three women were brought from villages to Kruja and hanged there. In all fifty quite innocent people suffered. The two Serb officers responsible for these atrocities were Dragoslav Voinovitch (artillery) and Dragoljub Petrovitch (infantry). . . . Left Kruja. Stopped at wattled shed for coffee. Han burnt by Serbs. Folk gathered and told how Serbs had swooped on village, robbed and arrested innocent people, taken them to Kruja and hanged them. All said they had expected the Serbs to be allies and not foes.

At Tirana (18th) we visited Essad Pasha, and were struck with the number of troops in the town. Essad explained they would leave by a Turkish transport. He spoke with contempt of Ismail Kemal and the provisional governmental Liter, at the house of Avdi bey, a number of refugees from Dibra arrived and told of the sufferings in the villages annexed by the Serbs. They asserted five hundred burnt-out destitute persons had been prevented by the Serbs from receiving help from the agent of the Macedonian Relief Committee. We arranged to send maize.

At Durazzo folk were very nervous about Essad Pasha, who alone had an armed force and was said to be in constant communication with the Greek Bishop at Duiazzo, a notorious intriguer.

The Italian consul reported: "Perfect order prevails, but the delay of the Powers must make for unsettlement." This, alas, was what certain Powers intended. At the time the journey had the glory of a plunge into a freed land rejoicing in liberty won after centuries of anguish.

At Kavaia and Pekinj we heard of the massacre of prisoners by the Serbs and the relief of the people that the invaders had gone, they hoped, for ever.

At Elbasan admirable order was being kept by Akif Pasha. Here we heard how the Serbs had imprisoned Albanian patriots. All hoped a Prince would soon come and suppress Essad, who was feared as a possible danger. The Americans were buying land and planning a big college, to which the people looked forward as a means for national regeneration. Parents were already refusing to send children to the Greek school, in spite of the fulminations of the Greek priest.

A young man arrived from Starovo and told how he and two others had been taken prisoners by the Serbs and offered their lives for a heavy ransom. Only he had enough to pay. Both the others were killed. A rumour came that the Serbs and Bulgars had begun to fight for the possession of Monastir. It had been allotted by agreement to Bulgaria, but the Serbs were in possession and refused to yield it. We decided to push on to Ochrida to learn what was happening.

Arrived at Stiuga we found Serb officers in possession. We had left free Albania and were in a conquered land under military rule. They at once started "propaganda," and had the impudence to say that the dialect of Struga was as pure Serb as that of Belgrade. But an officer bent on annexation will say anything. Poor old Jovan Golubovitch, the innkeeper at Podgoritza, was a native of Struga, and was known always as Jovan Bulgar.

We visited the uniquely interesting fishtraps on the Drin, built like a prehistoric lake-village. These, said our Serb escort, would be a source of great wealth when modernized. "But," we objected, "perhaps this will not be yours. The question has to be arbitrated." They retorted they would accept no arbitration, and cared nothing for agreements. What Serbia had taken, Serbia would keep. The Bulgars should never recover one kilometre.

Friday, 27th.—At Ochrida—after ten years. Town most melancholy. A tablet on the big plane tree commemorates the "liberation" of the town. But there are no signs of joy. Even in 1904, after the Bulgar revolution and under Turkish military rule, the town was not so dead and hopeless as now under the Serb. All seems crushed beneath an iron heel. Then the Bulgar population hoped for union with Bulgaria. Now the Serb was dominant. The Bulgar school was closed, and soldiers were at the door. The Bulgar churches were shut, and their priests had disappeared. So had the bishop. Some people recognized me. An old woman rushed up and told me things were worse than under the Turk, but we dared make few enquiries lest our informants should suffer. Only the great lake was the same as before in its marvellous beauty. I felt like a ghost among the shadows of all we had striven for ten years ago.

The bazar, once full of Moslems, was half deserted. The intransigence of the Serb officers was here as blatant as at Struga. They were eagerly waiting the declaration of war on Bulgaria. And would accept no form of arbitration that did not give all to themselves. We spoke strongly of the wickedness of fighting their allies. They said they cared for no treaty, and meant to fight—the sooner the better. All they had taken they would soon Serbize. They —the military—had the power, and would do what they chose.

That the policy was a deliberate one we now know from published documents.

On February 4, 1913, the Serb Minister at Petersburg telegraphed: "the Minister for Foreign Affairs told me Serbia was the only state in the Balkans in which Russia had confidence, and that Russia would do everything for Serbia." Serbia felt quite safe in tearing up her Bulgarian "scrap of paper." The Serb officers were, in fact, most explicit, and told us they had all their plans laid and expected soon to be back in Durazzo, and to keep it.

So set were they on fighting Bulgaria that had the Bulgars waited but a few hours the Serbs would probably have saved them the trouble of firing the first shot. The whole guilt rests with Serbia, for it was she who broke her pledged word and threw down the glove.

Kosovo Day was a melancholy spectacle. Nothing is more dolorous than a people forced "to rejoice" by an army of occupation. All shops are shut, and the population summoned to church to celebrate the "freeing" of the land. Once how pleased I should have been. Now I have seen and know too much! The people of Ochrida had to officially rejoice that their nationality was destroyed, though it had survived some six centuries of the Turk.

At Pogradech we again found the Serbs. Here the whole population is Albanian. There was no doubt of their sentiments. They asked anxiously as to the fate of their town, and dreaded lest the Serb occupation should be permanent. Wanted news of free Albania, and asked when the Prince would arrive. At the han, when paying for my horse, I asked for Turkish money as change, for we were leaving the Serb zone. The hanjee and those in the inn burst into sudden joy: "Ah, she too does not want anything Serb!" I was alarmed lest a prowling Serb should overhear and make them pay dearly for patriotism.

We arrived at Koritza on June 30th and found it "in a state of great tension." "Persons afraid of arrest. A sort of silent terror in the air. Great Greek propaganda going on, and Greek troops everywhere. People called on us and said many wished to come, but dared not. They prayed us to save Koritza. Called on the Commandant, Colonel Condoulis, to whom Mr. Nevinson had an introduction." I learnt what a mistake the Americans had made in 1903, when they put the mission under Austrian instead of English protection. The Greeks now, in consequence, pretended that the Albanian school was an Austrian school, and declared there was no Albanian movement. The Albanian Nationalists, on the other hand, were in bitter trouble, for, through the years of Turkish rule, they had with danger and toil kept this school "the beacon light," open. They now found the Greek more oppressive than the Turk. The American missionaries had been expelled from the town at twenty-four hours' notice. The school was closed. The Turkish troops had behaved well in the town, and never entered a private house. The Greeks had shown themselves as conquerors bent on pillage, and behaved with cruelty and violence.

Colonel Condoulis did not even pretend to be out for anything but wholesale annexation. He showed on a map frontiers which should include even Tepeleni. I exclaimed, horrified: "But that is half Albania!" Condoulis did not deny it. He merely said: "There is a French proverb which says—appetite comes with eating. We have eaten; now we must eat more and more." I replied: "Monsieur, those that eat too much get bellyache." Which annoyed him.

I have met few things more repulsive than a military man bent on conquest, for lust of conquest brings a man lower than the beasts. The beasts eat for hunger. Condoulis wished to eat for sheer greed. May the day come when such men will be looked On as mad dogs to be destroyed painlessly before they have time to inflict misery upon peoples.

What with the Serbs at Ochrida and tijle Greeks at Kctitza, I began to regret that I had ever wished to send the Turk from Europe. While he was there, there was yet hope. These "Christian" conquerors were a hundredfold worse.

They showed their devilry by arranging a meeting that should cause Mr. Nevinson to write to his paper that Koritza wished to be Greek. The arrival of a well-known journalist was a chance to be exploited.

Unluckily for Condoulis, we were not in the Balkans for the first time. The visit arranged for us at the Bishop's therefore missed fire. We found his Grace seated at a table, at which there were some fourteen local shopkeepers, who, when told to do so by the Bishop, stated to us that they wanted to be Greek. It would, indeed, have needed some courage to say in the presence of Greek officials that they did not want to be Greek! "You see," said our guide, "the Christians of Koritza want to be Greek!"

We were trotted off to the house of an old Moslem, who also replied obediently. What else could the poor man do?

An unarmed population faced with a big army is helpless. Many an English village would declare itself Choctaw if five thousand armed men bade it do so—or be extirpated.

We lunched with Condoulis, and learnt that the Greeks were as anxious to fight the Bulgars as were the Serbs. "Death to Bulgaria" was their cry. Not a metre of land to be ceded to those "cochons de Bulgares." "We went," they said, "willingly to fight the Turk. We go with ten times more joy to fight the Bulgars; they are our worst enemies." And they would listen to no remonstrance. So strong were they on this that I could only think Greece and Serbia had a secret understanding on the subject, and that Greece, like Serbia, knew that Russia had no use for a Big Bulgaria. And so indeed it was.

The Greeks next invited us to a mass meeting, which was to be held to ascertain the wishes of the population. We accepted, and on returning to our quarters learnt that Greek soldiers and priests were going from house to house ordering every one to attend the meeting and close their shops. It was intended to make use of us, for the women were told to come and hear what an Englishwoman had to say to them. The Greek authorities, aware that we knew no Greek, would have been able to interpret bogus messages from us.

We decided, therefore, to arrive so late as not to be put on the platform and made use of, and went for a walk lest an officer be sent to fetch us. One was—but we had already left. We arrived late at the meeting. Surrounded by Greek military, the populace had had to consent to the sending of a telegram to the Ambassadors' Conference in London, stating that Koritza voted unanimously for Greece.

So soon as it was dark, people came to visit us. Sixty Moslems outside the town sent an emissary to know if they could speak with us. We dared do nothing that would subject them to arrest. We had heard too much of the fate of prisoners. We were prayed to send a counter telegram to London, but there was no nearer telegraph station than Berat. The wire controlled by the Greeks was, of course, useless. The crisis was acute, and the prayers of the Koritzans pressing. We gave up our plan of travelling further South, and started for Berat so soon as mules and guide could be prepared.

The Greek authorities prepared a strange pantomime at Moskopol, our first halting-place. They sent up overnight a number of people who danced out to meet us like stage peasants, crying: "Welcome to a Greek town!" Moskopol is, in fact, inhabited by Vlachs and Albanians. The imported gang went everywhere with us to try to prevent our discovering this fact. It was clear they were imported, for they seemed to be in the town for the first time. One spoke Albanian to a woman as we passed. I asked how he had learnt it. He replied: "From my mother."

"Then you are half Albanian," I said.

"No," he answered, much vexed. "My mother is Greek, but there were no Greek schools when she was young, poor woman, so she never learnt to speak [i.e. she only knew Albanian] properly!" This is a fair sample of Greek propaganda. We reached Berat, and were received with great enthusiasm. The telegram was sent, and, we hope, helped to save Koritza. At Valona, where our journey ended, we met a number of refugees from Chameria, splendid mountain men, who had been till now under local autonomy with their own old Albanian law. They were threatened with Greek annexation, and prayed us piteously to save their Fatherland.

We visited the Albanian provisional government. A small assembly in a poor house. But it represented the hopes of a little nation. Its members were earnest and anxious. War had broken out between Serbo-Greek against Bulgar. They feared that Bulgaria could not stand against the combined forces, and the victory of Greek and Serb would spell ruin for Albania.

I returned to Scutari and resumed relief work. Things were going badly. The Powers who wished to ruin Albania had arranged that the international control should not have jurisdiction beyond ten kilometres from the town, and gave no signs of appointing any form of government for the country, nor recognizing a native one.

The two gallant tribes of Hoti and Gruda begged hard not to be included in Montenegro.

In Montenegro I learnt there was disgust at having been dragged into the second Balkan war Montenegro could not refuse to take part as, then, if the Serbs won, she would lose all her war-spoils. I noted in my diary: "The Powers are making a damned mess of everything by their shilly-shally. . . . What rot it is for five Powers to be spending the Lord knows what on these warships, admirals, soldiers, etc. hanging about Scutari while the people up-country are dying of hunger." The suffering in the burnt villages was terrible. People were cooking grass for their starving children, and the death-rate from diarrhoea was high. Anything the Belgians suffered in 1914 was child's play in comparison. Meanwhile Roumania entered into the second Balkan war and stabbed Bulgaria in the back. History records few dirtier actions, nor need we waste pity on Roumania for the punishment which has since fallen upon her.

That the destruction of Bulgaria was early planned by Greek and Serb seems likely, for, as early as April, the Serb Minister at Bucarest proposed a Serbo-Roumanian alliance against Bulgaria, and the Serbian General staff began fortifying Ovtchepolje. Bulgaria fell, and the Treaty of Bucarest was signed on August 10, 1913. Albania was deadly anxious. The victorious Serbs and Greeks were drunk with blood, and thirsted for hers, too. And still the Powers made no move to send a Prince.

At the end of August I went up to the Shala mountains, where refugees from the Gusinje district seized by Montenegro, came in misery; survivors of the massacres which, in the name of Christianity, were going on. I examined witnesses. Four battalions of Montenegrins were carrying on a reign of terror. Moslems were given choice of baptism or death. Praying in Moslem form was forbidden. Men were slaughtered, and their wives unveiled and baptised, and in some cases violated as well. I was prayed to ask the King of England, who has many Moslem subjects, to save these hapless Moslems from extinction.

To Scutari came similar news of the hideous cruelty, by means of which Great Serbia was being created. An Ipek man, well educated and of high standing, told of what happened there: "Every day the telal cried in the streets 'To-day the Government will shoot ten (or more) men!' No one knew which men they would be, or why they were shot. They were stood in a trench, which was to be their grave. Twelve soldiers fired, and as the victims fell the earth was shovelled over them, whether living or dead. Baptisms were forced by torture. Men were plunged into the ice-cold river, and then half roasted till they cried for mercy. And conversion to Christianity was the price." Many, terrorized into baptism, came to me. One man with tears in his eyes assured me he had consented only to save his wife and children, but that he felt now that he was defiled and wished he were dead.

The International forces did nothing. They had no jurisdiction outside Scutari.

Unfortunately, also, the British staff knew no language but English, and the most reliable dragomans knew only French, Italian, or German. England was thus more heavily handicapped than the representatives of the other Powers, and the Albanians asked with wonder: "Are there, then, no schools in England?" And, in general, Scutari's high idea of European civilization shrivelled and shrank.

By the end of September the conduct of the Serbs in the Dibra district was so bad that the maddened populace, profiting by a moment when the garrison was reduced, revolted, drove out the Serbs and retook Ochrida, where they were welcomed by both Bulgars and Albanians. As I wrote at the time: "It is criminal of the Powers to delay the frontier commissions. Both Serb and Montenegrin are working to clear off the Albanians from the debatable districts so as to show a Slav majority to the Commission." The ill-timed revolt gave them a chance of doing this. The Serbs fell on the Gostivar district, burning the villages with petroleum, and throwing such people as could not escape, back into the flames with their bayonets. An urgent appeal for bandages and medicaments came from Elbasan, into which refugees were pouring. Our naval force was not allowed to supply any, but I begged two cases of stores from the Italian consulate and started across country to Elbasan to the horror of the International control, who had the idea that travelling in Albania was dangerous. As I soon got beyond their zone they could not interfere. At Tirana and at Elbasan I found thousands of destitute creatures pouring in, footsore and exhausted. Their accounts of Serb brutality up-country was amply confirmed by a letter of a Serb in the Radnitchke Novina (see Carnegie Report): "My dear friend," writes a Serb soldier, "appalling things are going on. I am terrified of them. . . . I dare not tell you morer but I may say Ljuma (an Albanian tribe) no longer exists. There is nothing but corpses and ashes." A Franciscan, who went there, told me of the bodies of the poor little bayoneted babies. "There are villages of 100, 150, 200 houses where there is literally not a single man. We collect them in parties of forty to fifty and bayonet them to the last one," The paper says it cannot publish the details, "they are too heart-rending."

Nothing could make the luckless refugees believe that the Powers had really given them to the Serbs. They asked piteously when the Prince was coming to drive the Serbs out. And still the Powers did nothing. Some Bulgars among the refugees told that life under the Serbs was impossible. The only time they had been free from persecution was when the Serb army was busy fighting the Bulgar army.

It was feared the Serbs would descend on Elbasan, and I carried away a whole mule-load of valuables to save them from being pillaged, and rode with it across country without an escort or weapon. I learnt from the refugees that twenty-six villages had been wholly or partially burnt and pillaged by the Serbs. Few of the refugees had any weapons. I reported all this in vain in Scutari. Not a Power would move. The Serbs, grown impudent, then entered strictly Albanian territory in defiance of the International forces, and camped in Mirdita while the Montenegrins devastated the Gashi and Krasnichi tribes.

At last the Commission for delimiting the northern frontier started. The Russian, troubled doubtless by a guilty conscience, had feared to start without a strong military escort, and lack of forage made this impossible. Hence much delay. Our military attache from Rome represented England, but it was reported that France and

Russia were out to grab all they could for the Serbs, regardless of the nationality of the population, and were furious whenever he protested, for, as England belonged to the Entente, they considered it his duty to support them on every point, regardless of fact and justice.

More attacks of the Serbs on the Albanians in the annexed lands brought more misery. "October 21st.—Thousands of refugees arriving from Djakovo and neighbourhood. Victims of Montenegro." My position was indescribably painful, for I had no funds left, and women came to me crying: "If you will not feed my child, throw it in the river. I cannot see it starve."

I decided to return to England after three and a half years' absence, to try and rouse help and action there.

And I said goodbye with sorrow to Scutari, beautiful and sorrowing, which had been my most kind home for so long.

On arriving in London I packed up the Gold Medal given me by King Nikola and returned it to him, stating that I had often expressed surprise at persons who accepted decorations from Abdul Hamid, and that now I knew that he and his subjects were even more cruel than the Turk I would not keep his blood-stained medal any longer. I communicated this to the English and Austrian Press. The order of St. Sava given me by King Petar of Serbia, I decided to keep a little longer till some peculiarly flagrant case should occur, and this I expected soon.

So apparently did Austria, who, exasperated by the repeated outrages of the Serbs, and aware of the activity of Hartwig at Belgrade, realized she was marked down as Russia's next victim on the proscribed list, and that the hour was arriving when she must kill or be killed.

Austria's position was now perilous. Russia had come to an agreement with Japan, and had her hands free for the Near East. Hartwig was pre-eminent in Belgrade. Roumania had been roped in, and had dealt the stab in the back to Bulgaria, which had assured the Serbo-Greek victory. Bulgaria was "put in the corner." France, the financier of the Near East, refused her a loan. Italy it is true, took Tripoli with the consent of the Powers, and France, tied as she was to Russia, could not object. But she viewed with great jealousy any increase of Italian power on the Mediterranean, and began therefore to build up Greece as a naval counterpoise.

When Bulgaria approached Paris for a loan, Greece protested: "Do not finance our most hated rivals." France refused the loan. Bulgaria turned to England, who looked very favourably on the plan, recognizing Bulgaria's industry and capability. Those who are in a position to know, state that almost the whole sum had been arranged for when France heard of the transaction and requested that England, as a member of the Entente, would not finance a loan that France had thought fit to refuse. England drew back, and Bulgaria had to go to Germany for the necessary money. Russia had no use for Bulgaria. Therefore France had none. And England, or the section of it bitted and bridled by The Times, went the way it was driven. Or, perhaps, like a certain animal, was induced that way by dangled carrots. The Times' supplements, full of praise of Tsardom, must have cost some one a pretty penny. Meanwhile Russia was assuring the Serbs that the Balkan war was but a first step, and that Bosnia and the Herzegovina would soon be theirs. Ristitch, Serb Minister at Bucarest, states on November 13, 1912: "The Ministers of France and Russia advise, as friends of Serbia, that we should not 'go the limit' as regards the question of an outlet on the Adriatic. ... It would be better that Serbia . . . should strengthen herself and await with as great a degree of preparation as possible the important events which must soon make their appearance among the Great Powers."

December 27, 1912.—The Serb Minister in Petersburg telegraphs: "The Minister for Foreign Affairs replied that in view of our successes he had confidence in our strength, and believed we could give a shock to Austria. For that reason we should feel satisfied with what we were to receive and consider it as a temporary halting-place. . . . The future remained to us. . . . Bulgaria, meantime, would bring her ethnic mission to a close." Small wonder that in May 1913 the Montenegrins boasted to me: "We, the Serb nation, are a danger to Europe. We have all the Russian army with us, and shall take what we choose." Small wonder, too, that Austria, realizing she must soon fight for her very existence against a very strong combine, approached Italy in September 1913 and asked what would be her attitude in case of an Austrian war with Serbia. Italy, who was already dabbling with the Entente, though nominally a member of the Triple Alliance, replied: "Such a war would be a most dangerous adventure." Austria knew then that Italy could not be reckoned on.

We now slide into 1914, and Yougourieff's date, for "our great war" approaches. Russian preparations went on apace, and France, under Russian pressure, extended her term of military service to three years.

CHAPTER TWENTY
1914

DURING the winter of 1913-14 I gathered funds for Albania, and the American missionaries worked hard at feeding the refugees of Gostivar and Dibra. General Phillips, in command at Scutari, did all his funds would allow for the refugees there, but reported that the Serbs' victims were dying of hunger in the Gashi mountains at the rate of twenty a day. But the Mansion House refused to start a fund. Mr. Willard Howard took cinema photographs of the starving people in their burnt ruins, hoping to rouse public feeling against the Serbs and stop their further war plans.

At the Foreign Office I begged protection for the Balkan Moslems, who were being barbarously exterminated, and stated that until it was seen that the Balkan conquerors were capable of just rule, the Capitulations should remain in force. Those with whom I spoke admitted that the consular reports from Uskub and Monastir were very bad, but that it was not advisable to publish them. In truth, we were hopelessly tied to Russia and could say nothing about her pet lambs, even though the truth of the accusations had been proved up to the hilt by the Carnegie Report. The laws signed by King Petar in October 1913 for the purpose of crushing the annexed regions are alone enough in their barbarity to condemn Serbia. They are published in the Carnegie Report, which should be read by all interested in forming a just and lasting Balkan peace.

It was also made clear by the Carnegie Commission that the accusation that the atrocities were planned and carried out by the Serb "Black Hand" society were true. Damian Popovitch, the leader of the regicides, led the massacres of Kosovo. All was part of a prearranged Great Serbian plan. "The Serbs," I overheard two Montenegrins say in the inn at Rijeka, "are right. They put these gentry (non-Serb population) to the sword as they go, and clean the land." As the Black Hand was a "government within a government," and unofficial, Belgrade could always pretend to be ignorant of its doings. Both the Tsrna Ruka (Black Hand) and Iarodna Odbrana (National Defence) societies had a free hand. The Carnegie Report tells: "The population at Uskub called their station the Black House, from the name of the League itself, The Black Hand. The worst crimes were committed by this organization, known to all the world, and under powerful protection. It was of distinct advantage to the regular government to have under its hand an irresponsible power like this, which soon became all powerful, and could be disowned if necessary. . . . Our records are full of depositions which throw light on the activities of these legalized brigands. Each town had its captain. . . . Where complaints were made to the regular authorities they pretended to know nothing, or, if the person were obscure, punished him. If he were a personage, as for example the Archbishop of Veles, the bands were sent from the town down to the villages, only to be replaced immediately by bands from Uskub."

In February 1914 I received a letter from Monastir, from my former dragoman of 1904. Since then he had worked for years for a well-known Greek firm in India, and returned invalided home to Monastir just before the first Balkan war broke out From him I had heard of the first joy of the populace when the Turkish army fled before the invading Serb, and then of the speedy revulsion of feeling when they found that the Serb came not as a liberator, but as a conqueror. In January 1914 he wrote: "Hardly a year has elapsed since Monastir fell into Servian hands, and this very short period has been enough to turn it into a desert city." And he detailed the reasons.

In February, 1914, he wrote: "I write from Monastir, or I should say Bitoli, for there is no city of the name of Monastir in the vast Serbian Empire whose Emperor, Peter Karageorgevitch is daily wheting (sic) his sword sharp in order to be able to inflict a death-blow on the old Austrian Emperor. The conquest of Bosnia and Herzegovina and the creation of a vast and powerful Serbian Empire, even mightier than that of Dushan, is occupying the minds of all army men. . . . Travelling from Salonika to Monastir one is struck with the fewness of the passengers . . . where have all these people gone? The average number does not exceed ten, against hundreds in Turkish times. It is roughly estimated twenty thousand persons have emigrated from Monastir. . . . Taxes are tremendous; this city must pay a war tax of 1,000,000 francs. We see we have only exchanged a bad rule for a worse rule. This amount will go to the War Office, for in Serbia the army has twofold duties—to rule and to fight. There is hardly any other country in the world where military men have concentrated such a great power in their hands. The King and the civil authorities, needs must comply with the wishes of the officers. The Serbian officer has no respect for any one, and Albanian subjects, natives of Elbasan and Koritza, are enlisted by force in the army. And when Mr. ——- interfered on behalf of a man from Koritza, saying that they compelled people to complain to the foreign consuls, the recruiting officer replied: 'We shall imprison every blessed man who steps over the threshold of a consulate. You mean to say you will go to that big idiot the British consul. That fool of a consul must think himself very lucky for England is a friendly power, otherwise we would have killed him!'" He had, in fact, reported their conduct, and they seem to have been aware of this. The letter continues: "You cannot but pity us who are ruled by such men. . . . The only thing they are interested in is to collect taxes and to send gendarmes from house to house telling people that if they do not send their children to Serbian schools they will be punished. Of vino and beer they drink abundance. 'Bozhe, Bozhe, bez vino ne se mozhe!' . . . Corruption in all branches of the administration Is the essence of Serbian rule."

This picture, corroborating as it does the Carnegie Report of the "government within a government," is the more valuable, as it is evident that early in 1914 the writer had heard the plans for a "death-blow to the Austrian Emperor" discussed. Possibly his death and not that of his heir was first intended. The Serbs seem to have been so sure of Entente support that even the adverse reports of a consul had no terrors for them.

It was the last letter I had from the writer. He is dead, the bright and honest boy who used to discuss endlessly to me the happy land that Macedonia would be if once "freed from the Turk." From Montenegro news was no better. I learnt of the boycott of the Albanian population of Podgoritza—the people who, in fact, carried on most of the trade of Montenegro, and heard: "As to the Moslems there is a regular exodus of them from the 'liberated' country. Four thousand have gone, four thousand five hundred are in process of going, and two to three thousand more are to go as soon as possible." The unfortunate tribes of Hoti and Gruda been handed over to Montenegro and devastated.

It was reported that Prince Mirko was out of his mind, and Princess Natalie had definitely left him and claimed the children —Montenegro's only heirs.

Meanwhile the Powers could not longer delay the election of a Prince for Albania.

The combined efforts of France and Russia had whittled down Albania to nearly half her size, and had made a very cruel frontier, whereby all the populations of a wide mountain tract were cut off from their market town, Djakovo. The Dibra refugees were still camped in Albania, and the Prince hoped for as a Messiah still did not come. Prince Arthur of Connaught was the desire of the Albanians. "Give us even your King's youngest son," they said, "and we shall be safe. No one will dare attack us."

Essad now insisted on being a member of the provisional government. All feared him. None wanted him. He started a government of his own at Durazzo. In February the British and German Commissioners went there. Sir Harry Lamb worked hard on Albania's behalf, and did all he could to establish her safely. "The Albanians," he once said to me, "are the only Balkan race which ever tells the truth." He and the German tried to persuade Essad to resign, but he refused, and as he had an armed force at his command, the Commission' thought it risky to press him. He undertook to meet the Commission later at Valona. Ismail Kemal asked the Commission to take over the government till a Prince should arrive, and resigned. Essad then was induced to resign by being promised he should be president of the delegation which was to meet the newly-elected Prince, of Wied. After months of squabbling the Powers in their united wisdom had chosen this man. Why, it is hard to see. The feelings of the Albanians were not considered. Even Sir Edward Grey said: "The primary thing was to preserve agreement between the Powers themselves." The infant state of Albania was to be flung to the wolves to save its elders.

It was decided that Albania should be governed by a Prince elected by the Powers; that it should enjoy perpetual neutrality under the collective guarantee of the Powers, and that these six Powers should be represented in Albania by an International Commission, with one Albanian on it. Dutch officers were to train the gendarmerie. On paper it looked well. But France raised Albania's worst enemy, Krajevsky, from Vice-consul to International Commissioner. France was represented thus by a Levantine Slav. Italy, too, selected a Levantine, Aliotti, to carry out her schemes at Durazzo. Only England and Germany were acting honestly.

Essad Pasha began to move soon. He demanded that the provisional government should be removed to Durazzo, where it would be in his power, and where he had two partners, the Montenegrin Gjurashkovitch and the Greek bishop. The International Commission chose Valona as its seat.

Meanwhile Scutari was ruled by the International force separately. The Powers had thus given two international governments to Albania. One with plenty of force and very limited jurisdiction, and the other with wide jurisdiction and no force. And there was also the little provisional Albanian government. The Prince was an officer with a limited military mind, and without experience of the Near East. His one qualification for the post was that he was "the nephew of his aunt," Carmen Sylva of Roumania, and she pressed his candidature. The true reason for his unanimous selection was probably that the Powers who had planned Albania's destruction knew him to be a man of little ability, and therefore the more easily to be got rid of. France and Russia were combined to overthrow him, even while agreeing to his election.

When Greece and Bulgaria were respectively liberated and put under a foreign Prince, he was given in each case sufficient military force to maintain order till a native army should be organized. In the case of Albania it was arranged that he should be provided with no armed force—otherwise he would be difficult to evict. The International forces in Scutari were to squat there and look on. Essad Pasha was the agent of the Italians, Serbs, and French, and intrigued, so soon as the Prince was appointed, to obtain power over him. He bargained to be one of those who went to invite the Prince to Albania, and, accompanied by a party of Albanians, many of them better men than himself, he went to Neu Wied. How he contrived to worm himself into the Prince's confidence is a mystery. But he did, and in a luckless moment for the Prince, induced him to make Durazzo his capital. There he would be completely in the hands of Essad. He was welcomed at Durazzo by rejoicing Albanians, who knew nothing of the sinister plots of the Powers. But his fate was already sealed. The tale of William of Wied is among the most sordid that the Powers have woven.

Only an extremely able man could have forced his way through the mesh of intrigue which surrounded him. Already, in February, he had been warned in Austria to have no dealings with Essad. The "end soon began."

A Prince having been appointed, the Powers notified the Greeks they must evacuate South Albania within the limits drawn by the Frontier Commission. Members of this Commission told of the amazing series of tricks by which Greek agents had tried to hoodwink them. Wherever the Greeks had a school they dragged out a cartload of little children bidden to sing or shout in Greek. They tried to steer the Commission away from places which knew no Greek, and in one place actually shut up the women in a house for they could speak nothing but Albanian. Greek soldiers, while pretending to tell people not to make a noise, threatened them with punishment if they did not shout for Greece. They even imported Greeks, and dumped them on the path of the Commission. And ordered people, under threat of flogging, to paint their houses blue and white—the Greek colours. But they overacted the part so badly that in many cases they succeeded only in disgusting the Commissioners. At Borova a number of school children were sent to play in front of the house where the Commission was, and ordered to speak Greek only. Signor Labia, the Italian commissioner, threw out a handful of coppers. In their rush to pick up the money the poor children forgot their orders, and disputed aloud in their mother tongue—Albanian, to the amusement of the Commission, which, disgusted by these tricks, drew a frontier which gave the Albanians less than they had hoped for, but very much more than the Greeks had intended. These hastened to make another grab at the land, and sent Zographos, formerly Greek Minister for Foreign Affairs, and a gang of Greek officials to South Albania to claim it as Greek, and appoint themselves as the "Provisional Government of Epirus." A Greek colonel was made War Minister to this so-called government, and a Greek member of Parliament, Karapanos, was its Minister for Foreign Affairs. An American called Duncan, who had a Greek wife and went about dressed mainly in bath towels, collected much money, incited the people to resist Wied, armed them, and urged them to a fratricidal war. The Greek Government denied all connection with this "provisional government," just as the Serb Government has always denied responsibility for and knowledge of the deeds of the Black Hand.

At the command of the Powers the Greek regular army was obliged to evacuate the occupied districts. It departed from Koritza, but left a so-called hospital of wounded "not fit to be moved," and joined it to the Greek frontier by a telephone. Much of the army, however, remained in out-of-the-way spots, removing and concealing their insignia, so that the Greek Government might be able to deny that they were soldiers.

Formally the Greeks handed over Koritza to the Dutch gendarmerie officers under the International Control, on March 1, 1914. Had the Powers meant honestly by Albania they would have sent a force to clear the land of the lurking Greek bands of soldiery. But in spite of several questions asked in the House of Commons, Cretan and Greek komitadjis continued to land at Santa Quaranta, the Greek Government persistently denying all knowledge. "There are none so blind as those that won't see."

Such was the state of things when Prince zu Wied landed at Durazzo on March 7th. Had he at once made a journey throughout his domain, gone to Koritza via Berat and Elbasan, and claimed it as his, he might have triumphed. But it was Essad's business, as agent of Albania's enemies, to keep the Prince in Durazzo till the plans for his eviction were matured.

The International Control Commissioners handed over their authority to the Prince, and he, to the general dismay of the Albanians, appointed Essad War Minister, thus putting the armaments into his hands.

All this news seemed to me very bad. I was detained in London. My book on the war, The Struggle for Scutari, was finished, but my publisher was bent on keeping it for the autumn publishing season. I stood out for immediate publication in May. He said: "You know nothing about publishing." I said: "You do not know the state of the Near East. Anything may happen by October."

I offered to risk having no payment at all for it. It came out in May, and the thing that happened before October (Yougourieff's date) was bigger than even the shouts of the Montenegrins in 1913 had led me to expect.

Meanwhile the Greek "wounded" at Koritza telephoned for medical comforts, and the Greek Bishop sprang his plot. The "medicine" arrived in the form of armed bands and weapons. The Greek "wounded," the Bishop's servants, and a band of Grecophile students made an attack within the town on the night of April 11th, and the bands of lurking Greek soldiers attacked from without. Koritza was taken by surprise, was not well armed, and had but fifty newly trained gendarmes, commanded by the Dutch officers. Nevertheless the town put up a gallant resistance. Reinforcements arrived, and the Albanians "rushed" the house of the Bishop and carried him off a prisoner to Elbasan, along with a number of Greek soldiers, who readily gave their names and regiments, and told of the orders they had received. They had long been kept in readiness on the frontier. The Greek Government, as usual, declared the men must all be deserters, over which it had no control, which, at best, was a poor compliment to the Greek army, and did not explain how the "deserters" became possessed of artillery and ammunition.

The Greeks, furious at being beaten out of Koritza, avenged themselves on their retreat by committing outrages and burning villages. The Albanians drove back the Greeks to Argyrokastro, and would have chased them over the border had not the Greek General Papoulias come to the aid of his compatriots with large reinforcements and artillery. The Greek Government still "knew nothing" about the actions of its officers.

It is to be hoped that a future League of Nations will be in readiness to investigate at once similar occurrences, and that "ignorance" on the part of a government shall not be accepted as innocence without full inquiry. In this case the Albanians had no tribunal before which to present their case. The invading Greeks burnt and sacked numbers of villages, and destroyed the town of Leskoviki, committing at the same time terrible atrocities.

The International Commissioners went to Corfu to meet the Greeks and arrange peace. The Greeks were told to evacuate the district delimited by the Frontier Commission, and certain privileges were accorded to the very few Greeks it contained.

I learnt from Dr. Totirtoulis and others the following facts about the so-called "Epirote" government of Zographos. The plan was made in Paris, for, as Krajevsky had declaimed, France did not mean Albania to exist. The Greeks brought some Greeks from America and presented them to Cambon, and, it is believed, to Sir Edward Grey also, saying that they were "Epirotes." The Greek society in Paris was a strong one, and pushed them. Cambon, in November, advised them to form an independent government, which was done, as we have shown. Mr. Lamb (now Sir Harry) told me that at Corfu he told Zographos to his face that most of his "Epirotes" were Cretans, and that the mere fact that a Greek ex-minister of Foreign Affairs was running this "independent government" and trying to dictate terms, was enough in itself to "give the whole show away," but for the fact that certain Powers were determined not to see.

The Albanians in the defence of their land had been much hampered by shortage of ammunition, though quantities had been sent from Durazzo. It never reached Koritza, for Essad, who was Minister of War, diverted if for his own purposes. He was in league with the Serbo-Greek combine, and did not mean the Albanians of the South to win. He was hated by all the South for his conduct when commanding gendarmerie in Janina, and also for betraying Scutari. He knew that a victory for the South meant ruin for him.

A rumour rose soon that the ammunition had gone up to Essad's town, Tirana, and that there was unrest at Shiak, a village on the road leading there. Mr. Lamb and the German commissioner hastened to Durazzo. The foul play over the munitions convinced the Nationalist Albanians that Essad was brewing mischief. Unless he was preparing a coup against the Prince, he could have no need of a private munition store. Information was given to the Prince, who had him arrested by the Dutch gendarmes and a band of Nationalists on the night of May 18th. A few shots were fired amid shouts of "Down with the tyrant." He was arrested by the Dutch officer in command, and taken first to the palace, and then to the Austrian battleship Szigetvar. Essad was, as most folk knew, the agent of the combine against Austria and Germany. Italy was ready to partition Albania between the Greeks and Serbs, rather than let Austria gain power there. Now she has realized that the Slav is her enemy, but then, in May 1914, she was furious at Essad's arrest, and demanded his release. The correct course was to try and, if guilty, execute him. But trial would have meant conviction, and Italy would not hear of it. The Italian and Austrian battleships cleared for action, though the Powers had neutralized the Albanian coast. For twenty-four hours the position was precarious, but Austria once more swallowed her pride and yielded—this time to Italy. The Prince surrendered Essad to the Italians on condition that he did not return to Albania. With amazing effrontery the Italians took him to Rome and feted him in such a way as to make it clear they were rewarding him for his action.

Italy's conduct as a member of the Triple Alliance was in the highest degree insulting to her allies, and can be explained only by supposing that for the sake of the Adriatic she was ready to stab them on the first opportunity.

It was soon plain that the report of a prepared rising was true. Armed men were concentrating at Shiak on the road to Tirana.

The ignorant Moslem inhabitants had been told that the Prince meant to abolish Islam and promote incestuous marriages, and bidden to demand his immediate withdrawal. There were also the mass of refugees from Dibra and Gostivar. They had passed the winter wretchedly enough, and were told that if they would combine and drive out Wied the Serbs would restore to them their lost lands. In vain the American missionaries warned them not to believe this. Dibra was their one hope and desire.

A party of armed men, led by one of the Dutch officers, went to parley with the insurgents, and took a machine gun. Unluckily, Captain Saar was ignorant of local customs. He and his party were unduly nervous, for when an Albanian has given his "besa" (peace oath) he keeps it. Alarmed unnecessarily, he ordered his men to fire at a group of three armed men. One escaped, fled to Shiak, and spread the alarm that the Prince had begun to massacre Moslems. A number of people rushed to aid the Shiak men, and a fight took place. How much foreign influence was behind it all it is hard to say. That Italy was not unconcerned in it seems proved by the fact that the Italian representative at Durazzo at once hurried to convince the Prince that he was in imminent danger, and persuaded him to go on board an Italian battleship. The Italians may have believed that the plot, engineered by Essad, was sure of success. Other members of the International Control persuaded the Prince to return to land. But by his flight he had hopelessly compromised his position.

That Italy was mixed in the affair appeared a little later. Red signal lights were seen flashing to the insurgents from a house in Durazzo by many persons, among them the British Vice-Consul. Lieutenant Fabius, of the Dutch gendai'merie, entered the house and caught an Italian officer, Colonel Muricchio, red-lamp-handed. Again no trial was allowed. It was pleaded that the Capitulations had not been abrogated! And the officer was released. We may blame Wied for incompetency, but only a man of unusual force of character and intimate knowledge of the land could have made headway against the Powers combined against him.

All this I learnt from members of the International Control, from the Dutch officers, from the Albanians, from the American Missionaries, and from some private individuals.

That the rising was planned and the ammunition embezzled by Essad and his gang hardly admits of doubt.

On June 8, 1914, I reached Trieste. Here our vice-consul, M. Salvari, himself an Albanian, was very anxious about the situation. I had intended going to Scutari, but he begged me to go to Durazzo, where I arrived on June 11th. On board the boat I met Mr John Corbett, who had lately been in South Albania, and said it was nonsense of the Greeks to pretend no Greek troops had remained there as he had seen parties of them in many places, and had seen money being collected in Corfu to aid Zographos's enterprise. Durazzo was crammed with people of all races. Fighting had ceased, but a large force of armed men was some miles outside the town and negotiations were going on. Dr. Dillon, the well-known correspondent, was there, and his strong Russian proclivities caused much anxiety, more especially as he and his young wife had been staying with Essad shortly before his arrest. The Russian agents were suspected of taking active part in the anti-Wied intrigues, and the correspondent of the Birzhevije Viedomosti was in Durazzo and on friendly terms with Dr. Dillon. The Russian, Olghinsky, I had met in Andrijevitza in 1912, when the Montenegrins were making ready for the Balkan war. He then complained to me freely of the apathy of the Russians, and said he and his paper were doing all they could to rouse the country to war. His paper (Birzhevije Viedomosti) had already, in March 1914, blown the war trumpet loudly:

"Until now the Russian plan of military operations had a defensive character; to-day it is known that the Russian army will, on the other hand, play an active part. . . . Our artillery possesses guns which are in no respect inferior to foreign models. Our coast and fortification guns are even superior to those of other states. Our artillery will no longer have to complain of want of ammunition. The teachings of the past have fallen on fruitful soil. Military automobile service has reached a high degree of perfection . . . all our military units have telephonic appliances."

More details are given, and the writer says: "It is important that Russian public opinion be conscious that the country is prepared for all possibilities." Yougourieff had given October as the date when "we should be ready for our great war." The Birzhevije Viedomosti said all was ready in March. To find Dr. Dillon, an avowed partisan of Russia, in company with a correspondent of Birzhevije Viedomosti, supporting Essad in Durazzo, was a sinister omen. He protested Essad's innocence to me, but had no proof to offer save that Essad was in bed when arrested, and that no documentary evidence was found. The first proved only that the rising was not timed for that night. The second was valueless in a land where few could write and messages go from mouth to mouth. Subsequent events have proved that Essad, as we suspected, was a Serb agent.

During the following days very bad news came from the South. Eye-witnesses gave evidence of the Greeks' atrocities. It was generally believed that as Italy was determined to keep the Greek islands, she was conniving at the Greeks finding compensation at Albania's expense.

At the house of Dom Nikola Kaciorri, a plucky little Catholic priest, I found an Orthodox Albanian priest from Meljani, near Leskoviki, who told how the Greeks had burnt his village and ordered all those who belonged to the Orthodox Church to come along with them, using force to make them, and falling on those who refused. They had driven a number along before them, including his wife and children, whom he could not rescue. He told how the Greeks had given the inhabitants of Odrichan permission to return to it, and had then fallen on them and slaughtered them. Mr. Lamb ascertained that this man's wife and children were alive, but the Greeks refused to give them up.

Almost as soon as I arrived I was invited to have an audience with the Princess of Wied. She was very friendly, and much distressed by the web of intrigue in which she found herself tied. I regretted that she and the Prince had fallen into the wrong hands, and begged her to go to Valona or Scutari, and at once start a tour through the land. I offered to go with her, and assured her safe conduct, saying all misunderstanding would have been avoided had she and the Prince made such a journey on arrival. She said she had wished to, but that Essad always advised against it. I spoke to her of the Russo-Serbo-French-Italian combine, and said the Albanians wanted none of it, and that she could yet have the whole country on her side But she continually quoted the advice of. Carmen Sylva, Queen of Roumania, till I had to say: "Yes, ma'am. But Albania is not Roumania. Here you will do much better by appealing direct to the people." I left promising to support her to the best of my ability. She struck me as honest, intelligent, and very well-meaning. She would have made a good Queen for the country had she been given a chance, and might have done as much for it as did Carmen Sylva for Roumania.

That same day Mr. Lamb told me that the inhabitants of three Moslem villages, Nenati, Mercati, and Konispoli, recently burnt by the Greeks, had sent to beg help, and asked me if I would go and investigate.

That night, June 12th, came a fresh development. The Dutch gendarmerie arrested Gjurashkovitch, the Montenegrin, who had still been allowed to function as Mayor of the town, to which he had been appointed in Turkish times. Again Albania's enemies stood up for him. His brother was dragoman to the Russian commissioner; Russia claimed him as under her protection, and raised the old cry of "Capitulations." He, too, was released. The thing was becoming a farce. The Prince was unable to try any suspect. The Italian papers raised choruses of blame against the Dutch gendarmerie, which at that time was very honestly trying to do its duty. The Prince, who was like a large, good-natured St. Bernard dog, yapped and snapped at all round, completely confused by the din, yielded each time, and so soon alienated the sympathy of the Dutch officers, who, as more than one of them complained to me, got into trouble on his behalf and then received no support.

News arrived that Osman Bali, one of the two men reported to have assassinated Hussein Riza in Scutari, had been seen among the insurgents, and was probably this time also acting for Essad. The Italians put in a demand that Lieutenant Fabius, who had arrested the Italian Colonel Muricchio, should apologize. This Fabius very properly refused to do, and many of us supported him. I had known him during the Balkan war, and found him a very honest boy. Italy then demanded his dismissal. But this time the Prince stood firm.

Fachinetti, the Italian correspondent, whom I had known well during the war of 1912-13, was also in Durazzo. In the Balkan war he had warmly taken the part of the Albanians, and had worked with me. Now he knew I should not approve his doings, and he kept out of my way, dodging whenever he saw me coming. Crajevsky, too, was not pleased to see me. He was now more pro-Slav even than the Russians, and as he had been more Turk than the Turks only two years before, he must have known that his volte face was, to me, rather comical. And he is the kind of man that does not like being thought funny.

Colonel Thompson, who was commanding the Dutch gendarmes, met me and told me that he was going to =give an ultimatum to the insurgents in the next few days, and asked me to call at eleven next morning and talk the matter over with him. I never did. That night things seemed shaky. I overheard Fachinetti, whose room was next mine, tell the landlord to knock him up if anything happened. So I did very little undressing, thinking he was probably behind some plot. I put my boots handy, and laid down as I was, for a bit of sleep, and jumped up to the sound of rifle fire as the landlord banged on Fachinetti's door. Sharp firing sounded close. I dashed out so soon as I could lace my boots, and went down to the entrance of the town where Fabius was in great haste serving out ammunition from the depot there. He begged me not to go out towards the scene of the fight, as he suspected the Italians, and wanted to give an order that no foreigner should leave the town. Up rushed the Italians, greatly excited, and were headed back by Fabius. I told them I, too, was forbidden to go, and we sent them back. We got the artillery ammunition on donkeys and sent it up the hill. Dutch and Austrian officers were to serve the guns. A wounded Albanian, crying feebly "Rrnoft Mbreti" (Long live the King), was carried by on a stretcher, and one of the bearers whispered to Fabius: "Thompson is hit. I fear he is dead." To lose the commander in the first hour of the fight was a terrible blow. Fabius begged me to tell no one. Later, Arthur Moore, The Times correspondent, came and told how poor Thompson had been struck down and died almost immediately in his arms in a hut by the wayside.

Too many battle books have been written of late, so I will not describe the fighting In the afternoon. I was under cover behind a bank on the top of the hill with Mr. Corbett when the Prince came up on horseback with a small suite. He dismounted and climbed the bank, a tall, lean man, worn and anxious, with a yellow-white face as from a touch of fever. We called to him he had better take cover as the bullets came over pretty often. He looked dazed and stupefied. I said: "A bullet has just cut down that plant, Sir!" pointing to one close by. He roused himself, mounted, and rode away. Our side soon got the upper hand, and all danger of the town being rushed seemed over.

Meanwhile, within the town, the Italians did all they could to create a panic. They built rubbishy barricades, and annoyed me by making one across the street near the hotel door. I pulled it down so as to be able to get in and out easily. The officer was very angry. I explained that the town was not his to barricade, and if it were it was no good to build a barricade there, as men behind it could only fire into the house opposite. Which made him the more angry, because it was true, and the thing a mere dummy to scare people. So sure were the Italians that they were 'going to get the town taken this time that the correspondents wrote gory accounts of its capture and the slaughter of the inhabitants, and sent them to Italy, where they were published. I do not now believe in Italian correspondents every time.

The Russians were as bad as the Italians. They, too, hoped for the fall of the town.

The Russian secretary was a typical ultra-neurotic Slav. Could not exist, he told me, without operas, ballets, and "stir tout des Emotions." Was horribly vexed that the Albanian Nationalist party proved so strong, and that Albania had not yet been overthrown. In order to keep himself alive meanwhile in this miserable hole he tried to get people to play bridge with him for as high stakes as possible. And this did not suffice him. He told me that having run through all the sensations of life he thought of committing suicide.

"Why don't you, then, Monsieur?" I asked enthusiastically. "No one will regret you. Suicide yourself, I beg you, quickly!" Which so infuriated him that I dare say he is alive still. It roused him to an attack on the English, who, he said, were ruining civilization by the way they treated the Jews. I retorted by hoping that the terrible accounts we had had of Jewish pogroms were exaggerated. "Exaggerated!" cried he. "You may believe everything you have heard. Nothing is bad enough or too bad for those brutes."

"You have no right," said I, "to speak so of any human beings."

"Human beings!" cried he. "What you English must learn is that they are not human beings. They are bugs, and must be cr-r-rushed."

This is a mere detail. But what sort of peace can be expected when men such as this are in the diplomatic service helping to pull the strings?

At night the heat was terrible. The motionless air was shrill with mosquitoes from the fever swamps. The Italian forces were camped just under my window and he stench of unwashed men and sweaty uniforms penetrated the miserable garret I slept in with suffocating acridity. I lay awake for hours thinking of the fate of thousands of human beings dependent on such men as Petar Karageorgevitch, with his blood-stained hands; his hoary father-in-law, Nikola, weaving spider webs; the decadent Russian, fanatical and cruel; the Levantine Slav, agent of France; the

Italians like a pack in full cry with the victim in sight; the Greek Varatassi mainly playing bridge, but plotting behind the scenes with the Greek bishop, and probably with Essad too. All bent on war, and meaning to have it in some form.

Only Mr. Lamb and the German commissioner were playing straight. On 16th H.M.S. Defence and Admiral Troubridge arrived. Fighting went on, on and off, for the next few days. The Russian correspondent chuckled indecently over the Albanian wounded. On the 20th a deputation of townsfolk went to try and make terms with the insurgents. From the messages they brought it was clear that the luckless Albanians without the town were being used as cat's paw by more than one Power. A truce was called, and the insurgents asked to give up their arms and leaders. They replied they would yield their arms, but not their leaders. Who the leaders were remained a mystery.

While the armistice lasted at Durazzo the insurgents began to march to other places. No other town was armed. The people in vain asked what it was all about, and what the Powers wanted them to do. The Russian Vice-consul at Valona sent messages about to say that the Powers would be very angry if they fought on the side of Wied, The Albanians did not want to fight each other. Towns at once surrendered to the insurgents. The police changed their badges and business went on as usual. The populace did not want civil war, and continued to believe that the Powers would keep their promises. News then came that the Greeks were massing on the frontier ready to again fall on Koritza.

The insurgents now sent a message into Durazzo that they wanted to parley with an Englishman. They believed in England. General Phillips came from Scutari and went to meet them. He reported that the leaders were certainly not Albanians, and that they had refused to give their names. One was a Greek priest.

The game of the Greeks, then, was to incite the Moslems to ask for a Moslem ruler. With this in view they blackened Wied as an "anti-Moslem," hoping thus to split Albania and more easily destroy it.

One of the chief spokesmen said to General Phillips: "In England there is a Liberal Government. Many of you do not like it, but you must accept it because it is the will of the majority. We are the majority here, and we will have a Moslem Prince." This man the General "believed to be a Young Turk leader disguised." He asked why they objected to Wied, and they replied: "Because he is against our religion!" which was entirely untrue. And they added that they could easily take Durazzo because they knew that the international battleships off the coast had orders not to fire. In the end General Phillips made a strong appeal to them to cease this foolish warfare and accept Wied as the choice of Europe.

The Albanian crowd, he reported, appeared to agree and to be anxious to come to terms. But the five foreign leaders stuck out. And the ignorant crowd which believed that by following these leaders they would regain Dibra and other districts finally refused to come to terms.

Mr. Lamb also made a vain attempt to obtain the names of these leaders, and they obstinately refused to come into Durazzo to discuss terms with the Commissioners and the Prince. Nor would they permit any delegates to come. The Mirdite and Maltsor reinforcements who arrived were all reluctant to fight. "We are not in blood with these people," they said, "Why should we fight them?" We had a number of the enemy wounded in our hospitals along with our own men. They were most grateful for the care bestowed upon "them, and bore no ill-will at all. It was sadly true that these poor people were being killed and wounded, offered as human sacrifices at the altar of the rival ambitions of the Entente and the Central Powers.

The Breslau, since notorious, and a Russian warship now arrived. There were many Germans, both military and civilian, in the town, and the Germans and English worked together in the hospital. The surgeon, from the Russian warship, claimed the right to work in the English hospital as a member of the Entente. But as he proposed to give an anaesthetic to a man whose arm we had promised not to amputate, and then to take it off, we got rid of him in spite of his protests that a promise to "an animal like that" did not count.

I took my meals very often with the Germans, and we discussed often the danger caused to Europe by the Anglo-Russian Alliance. I said that though I believed Russia was heading for war I was sure we should not support her, and we drank to a speedy Anglo-German alliance. They were disgusted with Wied's folly, and said the Kaiser had been reluctant to appoint him, but had been over-persuaded by Carmen Sylva. They took me on board the Breslau, where I was received with great cordiality, and the captain, who took me on to the bridge, said his ship for her size was one of the fastest.

On Sunday, June 28th, I was having tea with Mr. and Mrs. Lamb, when we saw

Admiral Troubridge climbing the hill towards us. He came into the house very hot, and said almost at once: "I have come to tell you our wireless has picked up a bit of a message. The Archduke Franz Ferdinand has been murdered at Serajevo. Just that!"

My first idea was: "They have done what they said they would last year. They have begun in Bosnia."

I said to Mr. Lamb: "This means war, doesn't it?"

He replied: "Not necessarily." And seemed surprised. His manner reassured me. But unless very strong pressure were brought to bear, I could not see how war between the Slavs and Austria could be avoided, for "we the Russian army with us" was part of the programme.

No official confirmation of the news came till next day.

That the Serbo-Greek combine expected to have more than the Russian army to support it seemed shown by a remarkable letter the insurgent leaders wrote to Berat, advising the town to surrender, because "we are supported by the Triple Entente." Berat, however, refused to surrender.

The insurgents sent a message to Durazzo that they were willing to be ruled by the International Commissioners if Wied were dismissed.

Terrible rumours came as to what was happening at Koritza. A force of Albanians went to its defence, led by Dutch officers. Greeks were pouring in over the border. At the same time it was said that Essad was returning to Tirana via Serbia, and meant to proclaim himself as Prince. No one wanted him.

On July 11th came a telegram from Berat. "With heart full of grief I send the bad news that Koritza, after two days' fight, has fallen into the hands of the enemy. More than fifty thousand people are coming away. Take measures for these unfortunates. The Greek army is spreading on all sides, killing, and burning, and turning into ashes every Albanian place it enters."

The Albanians were aghast. The Nationalists had all trusted Wied and the Powers. Without artillery and short of ammunition, with no trained army and no officers save the Dutchmen, they had done their best. The "insurrection" had been engineered by Albania's enemies for the express purpose, among others, of giving a door by which the Greeks could enter. Not until the Greeks began the wholesale destruction of Moslems and their villages, accompanied by every kind of atrocity, did the luckless Moslems of Tirana realize how they had been tricked.

On July 13th I went at Mr. Lamb's request to Valona to examine into the number and condition of the refugees. I have no space to describe the horrors of the next few weeks. The Dutch officers, who had flung away their uniforms and bolted down to Valona in civilian dress before the Greek onrush, gave terrible accounts of the mass of struggling refugees in their flight across the mountains; the dead and dying children en route; the aged falling by the wayside; the jam of desperate creatures in a pass; the hideous cruelties of the advancing Greeks. It had been impossible, said the Dutch officers, to hold Koritza with irregular troops against an army with artillery. The Greeks burned as they advanced, and burnt Tepelcni and all the villages near it.

The refugees crawled into Valona in the last stages of exhaustion, thousands and thousands of them, and lay about under the trees in all the surrounding country. Food and shelter there was none. The heat was overwhelming. I look back on it as a nightmare of agony. In a century of repentance the Greeks cannot expiate the abominable crime of those weeks.

Mr. Lamb telegraphed to appoint me as English representative on an international relief committee, which consisted of the Italian and Austrian Consuls, the Russian Vice-Consul, and some of the Albanian headmen.

I proposed at our first meeting that we should report to our respective Governments that an international naval demonstration off Athens should be at once made to stop this scandalous state of things, and save the miserable victims of the Greeks.

The Russian was indignant; the other two consuls looked at their boots, and said they would get into trouble if they did so; the Albanians were delighted. The Austrian, an old friend of mine, told me in private I was right, and only international intervention would have any effect.

All Valona was Nationalist. Even the little children shouted: "Rrnoft Mbreti!" (Note.—The spelling Mpret was invented by The Times for reasons of its own.) The luckless refugees hoped that the Prince, as a sort of supernatural power, would arrive with an army, drive out the Greeks, and restore them to their homes. Numbers of Bektashi dervishes were among them, reverend white-robed men, who prayed me to send a special petition from them to King George, who has so many Moslem subjects. Their rich monasteries especially had been set on and pillaged by the andartis, and Greek fanaticism would, they said, wipe out Bektashism from the land.

The place was a hell of misery. We dealt out maize flour and bread in tiny rations. It was all we could do. There were by now at least seventy thousand in and around Valona, 'more between Berat and Valona, and more always crawling in.

One ray of hope came. On July 27th it was rumoured that Austria had declared war on Serbia. A sort of gasp =of relief ran through the starving, miserable refugees. A great Power, they hoped, was now coming to their Rescue. All were aware that they owed their misery to the Greco-Serb combine. All knew of the martyrs of Fostivar and of Kosovo. I shall never forget the inspired enthusiasm with which one of the headmen of Valona cried, as he raised his hands to heaven: "God is about to avenge the innocent! The Serbs will be punished for their crimes!" He was an Ipek man, and knew too well what those crimes were.

A letter came to me from England from a man versed in military matters, suggesting a line of attack, and urging the Albanians to hasten at once to Kosovo and take the Serbs in the rear, should Austria attack in the front. No official news of any kind or sort came through. The Italian consul had no news, the Austrian none since the news that the Serajevo murderers had confessed that they and their bombs had come from Belgrade, and the latter had been supplied by a Serbian officer, and that the Belgrade papers approved the crime. To me it appeared that the affair was similar to the attempt on King Nikola in 1907. I said: "I suppose Russia is mixed up in this?" The Consul said: "Probably. We shall insist on a very complete investigation as to all the guilty parties."

Meanwhile, it was daily clearer that the refugees could not remain in the terrible heat and fever-laden atmosphere of the Valona plains. They were doomed to die in that case. Small-pox as well as malaria had broken out. It was barely possible to feed the poor creatures, let alone give them quinine. One lump of bread per head per day was all we could manage. I laughed bitterly later on when I was called on to sympathize with Belgians who, after a short though uncomfortable journey, had arrived in England and were living like fighting cocks.

At the last meeting of the Relief Committee we decided we must try and move them to higher land. The question was, where was the Greek army? Could any of the refugees return in safety to their burnt villages, or, at least, cut the corn that must now be ripe? The three consuls said it was impossible for them to spy the Greek position as, if caught, they would get into political trouble. Nor could Albanians be sent, for fear of starting fighting and bringing the Greeks down on Valona.

I therefore volunteered to go myself, if provided with a guide to take me up to the limit held by the Albanians. Ernst Gorlitz, a very friendly youth, of whom I had seen a good deal, and who was acting as correspondent to the Deutsches Tages Zefamg, came at the last minute and asked if he might accompany me, and I gladly consented, as he would be another witness. We started early on July 31st. Neither of us had the least idea of what was going on outside. It was a terrible ride. All along the track were camps of miserable beings, who hailed us as angels come to save them. Poor young Gorlitz, who had never done refugee work, was almost broken down by it. He cried at intervals: "It is the work of Huns—Huns. We must expose the Greeks to all Europe." At Skozi we found an almost desperate Kaimmakam trying to cope with 7,000 refugees in most miserable condition. He warned us to be careful, as the Greeks were not far off, and were still burning villages. We promised to make a united appeal in Berlin and in London, and do all we could to rouse European indignation. Gfirlitz was so upset he could not sleep, and looked bad when we started at dawn next day. We reached the last Albanian outpost beyond Thembla, and there left our horses. Gorlitz and I then scrambled along the mountain till on the opposite side of a deep valley we could see clearly with his field-glasses the camp of the Greek outposts, their tents and the men in khaki uniforms. It was a regular camp with military tents, and completely refuted the Greek lie that "Epirote insurgents" and not Greek regulars were concerned.

We had attained our object. All the mountain side was covered with black patches. The fields of the standing corn we had hoped to reap, the Greeks had burnt to ensure the starvation of the population. It was growing late. To advance further would mean we could not get back that night. We might also be arrested and detained too long to be able to act efficiently. We decided to return to Thembla, and next day make a forced ride to Valona. Starting about 5 a.m. we arrived tired and dirty at Balona rather after 8 p.m., and dismounted at my inn. Gorlitz said he would sup with me. Returning to the dining-room after a "wash and brush up," I found him collapsed with his head in his arms on the table. "What is the matter? Are you ill?" I asked anxiously. He looked up with horror on his face, and half-stunned.

"Russia has mobilized, and we have mobilized, too. They have all gone!" he said. I was thunderstruck. All the Germans had left Valona. Possibly the steamboat service would cease. Gorlitz was in despair, as if he could not get away he might be reckoned a deserter.

"And I shall never see my father again," he said. "He is on the Russian frontier. They will have killed him before I can get back." We went to the post office the first thing next morning, but as the boats from Trieste had stopped running, his remittance from his paper had not arrived, and never would arrive. The Austrian consul could advance no money, having barely enough for his own subjects.

A Thessalian liner was due that night, and might be the last boat up. There was no time to lose, so I paid Gorlitz's fare and gave him enough to see him through. Neither of us having an idea of what was happening, I saw him off at the port, with best wishes for Germany's rapid victory over Russia and an Anglo-German alliance. "As for us," I assured him, "you may be certain we shall side with the assassins." He left. Mr. Moore, of The Times, passing Valona on his way to Salonika, dropped at the quay a hasty scribbled note for me. "Nothing but a miracle can now stop the biggest war in history. Clear out while you can, or you will be cut off, money and food. Please take this seriously." I took it to the Austrian consulate. The Italian was there. Neither had any news. If I left, I wanted to go to Austria. But unless a gunboat came for the consul that was not now possible. Neither of them had any idea England would be dragged in, and assured me I should be all right anywhere. I asked the Italian point-blank: "Are you going to war as Austria's ally?" He replied: "The Triple Alliance is a secret one. I do not know its terms. But I have my own ideas about them. My opinion is that we are not obliged to fight, and in that case we certainly shall not." A letter arrived from Mr. Lamb at Durazzo, asking me to find the kavas of the British Embassy at Constantinople, who, with his family, was among the refugees burnt out by the Greeks, and send them on to Constantinople! by the first possible boat. No mention of war or warning.

Valona was in huge enthusiasm over the news that Belgrade was attacked. "Now the Serbs and Russians and Austrians will have their own affairs to attend to, and will leave us in peace!" they cried.

August 4th, the fatal day, I spent hunting up the family of the kavas, and doing relief work.

August 5th I went to the bank and found a sort of panic. Orders had come to close in two days. That meant no more cash for relief work or anything. I asked for all the gold he had, and the manager let me draw almost all the balance of my relief fund, which I distributed, and 30 pounds for myself. More he could not give. The Italian consul said an Italian coasting-boat would touch that night, and that as it was impossible for me to go to Austria I had better take the kavas' family to Brindisi and there tranship them, see the British consul, and learn what was happening. If things were all right, I could return and make fresh arrangements for the relief work. Without money it was useless to stay, as the whole of the mass of wretched sufferers would come to me for help, which I could not give. And at 10 p.m. I left for Brindisi. Shortly before the boat started an American came on board and shouted: "They've got news at the consulates that your people are in it, too." But I did not take it at all seriously.

Only next day at the British consulate, after I had transhipped my proteges and been examined for small-pox by the doctor—for I was from an infected area—did I learn to my amazement that not only had Great Britain declared war, but to my shame and disgust had done so on the side of the Slav. After that I really did not care what happened. The cup of my humiliation was full.

No more help could be got for the refugees. It was no use to go back. The difficulty was indeed to go anywhere. I wondered which flag would fly in Valona next time I saw it—the Austrian or the Italian.

Had I had enough money I should have gone to the Pacific islands, or anywhere out of the dirty squabbles of Europe. As it was, the only thing to do was to clear out of Italy lest she should be drawn in by the Triple Alliance. A White Star liner chartered to take off British tourists, who were swarming down from the Tyrol and South Germany, took about a thousand of us from Genoa on August 13th.

It was years since I had been with a large crowd of English. They seemed to me a strange race. To me the boat was the acme of comfort, and coolness, and cleanliness. But the bulk of my compatriots thought they were roughing it. I thought of the seventy thousand houseless creatures under the sun and the rain, starving on a daily bread dole—and these people wanted two or three courses for breakfast. None of them had seen war. None knew what a burnt village or a rotting corpse, or a living man with his abdomen shot through was like. None had the faintest idea of the thing that had happened. Many would have liked, I believe, to throw me overboard when I said that the war would last two years for certain, and how many more I did not know. When I told them that Russia would crumple like wet brown paper, they said I ought to be ashamed of myself. Nor when I added that I expected to live to see England fighting the Russians would they believe me.

And I saw the steamer as typical of England. Masses and masses of blind people, wilfully blind, who had never even troubled to try and find out whither they were going, but filled with an overwhelming conceit. Some even genuinely believed the war would be nearly over by the time we reached Liverpool. I could not help hoping we should meet my friend the Breslau, just to bring them up against facts. "If these are the English" I used to say to myself, "what an hell of a mess there will be before this is finished." And the war lasted more than two years, and we have already fought the Russians.

CHAPTER TWENTY-ONE
THE YEARS OF THE WAR

THE first thing I did in London was to send back to King Petav the Order of St Sava he had bestowed upon me, with a letter telling him I had heard the attack upon Austria freely discussed the previous year, and that I considered him and his people guilty of the greatest crime in history.

I will add here only a few notes on some of the events of the next few years which concerned the lands we have been considering. First, I ascertained that in Cetinje the Archduke's murder was accepted unhesitatingly as Serb work. None even suggested that any one else had been responsible, and it was thought rather a good way of showing patriotism. Montenegro desiring, like many greater Powers, to obtain territory, declared war and occupied the strip of land between the bay of Trieste and Antivari, which the Austrians evacuated almost at once. Prince Petar led the Montenegrin force, and to the pain and surprise of the Great Serbian party they found that such was the reputation of the Montenegrin army that a very large part of the Serb population fled along with the Austrians without waiting to be "liberated." Even the Orthodox priest of Spizza fled, and the lot of those who remained was not too happy. Being liberated by Montenegrins is a painful process. Montenegrin troops also crossed the Bosnian frontier, but did not get far, and failed to carry out their boast that they were going to Serajevo.

When the great Russian retreat was taking place Montenegro began to waver. Without Russia it was believed that the war must collapse. Petar Plamenatz, though he had every belief in the British navy, had none in the army. Peace was expected to ensue shortly. Montenegro came to some arrangement with Austria, which enabled her to shift her troops and occupy Scutari in the summer of 1915. A detachment of the "Wounded Allies" society, which hastened to Montenegro, found "neither wounded nor allies," so some of its members reported.

The mountain Albanians strongly resisted the Montenegrin advance, but Scutari had been disarmed by the International Control, and was easily taken.

The Serbs also anticipated peace, and concentrated forces in such a position as also to be able to enter and occupy Albanian territory.

In April 1915, as we learnt later, the Powers who had guaranteed Albania's independence, bought Italy's intervention by promising her Albania's best port, Valona, and by the same secret Treaty bound her over not to object should "France, Russia, and Great Britain desire to distribute among Montenegro, Serbia, and Greece the northern and southern portions of Albania." The Powers who rushed to war over the violation of the Belgian Treaty, thus themselves tore up their Treaty with Albania. Secrets usually leak out. Serbia got wind of the Treaty in a garbled form two months later, and believed that the whole coast down to and including Durazzo was promised to Italy. Therefore, when it was yet possible to win Bulgaria's support by giving her her "Alsace-Lorraine", Macedonia, the Serbs refused. "If," said Prince Alexander to my informant, "I am to lose land in the west, I will yield none in the east."

Another evil result was, that as we had planned the destruction of North Albania, we could not call upon its help. In the autumn of 1915 I received a telegram from Sir Edward Grey suggesting that I and some others who knew the land should go to North Albania and recruit the tribesmen on our side. The frontier could thus have been held, and the Serbian debacle prevented in all probability. But to do this it was necessary to guarantee to the Albanians the independence of their land, and to this Russia and France, it would appear, refused consent. And the plan was dropped. The Serbs fled over the mountains, where the Albanians, who had suffered much at their hands two years previously, could have destroyed them, but trusting to the honour of England and the Allies they let them pass and even fed them.

In Montenegro the news of Serbia's defeat caused no undue grief. One man's misfortune is another's luck. Montenegro might now become top-dog.

I Was in Egypt when a Reuter telegram announced that the Austrians had taken the Lovtchen, occupied Cetinje, and appointed as Mayor "the Bulgarian Vuletitch." I guessed at once this was my old friend Vulco of the Grand Hotel. His son-in-law, Rizoff, who had had to leave Rome, where he was working a pro-

German propaganda, was now Bulgarian Minister at Berlin. There was something truly Balkanic in the surrender of Cetinje, arranged by the Grand Hotel and his son-in law, which appealed to my sense of humour. I soon learnt my guess was true. The Fates willed that I should meet a Montenegrin official. Last time we met during the Balkan war I had vituperated him about the cutting off of noses. Now in a strange land we were old friends.

"Tell me," said I, "what happened? The Austrians cannot really have taken the Lovtchen. One does not march troops up two thousand feet of rocks under guns, when one can walk in by the back door." Cheerfully he replied:

"Gospodjitza, you have been up the Lovtchen yourself. It is not worth while lying to you. Frankly, we welcomed the Austrians, even with enthusiasm. A small detachment on the road had not been warned, and fired. Otherwise nothing occurred. Yes, Vuko is Mayor! All your old friends remain, Yanko Vukotitch, and all! Only the King and suite left. Mirko, as you know, remains." Here he burst out laughing. "He is tuberculous, you know, and will go to Vienna to consult a doctor! The King told Petar to remain, too, but it bored him, and he came away afterwards. Mon Dieu, but the King was angry with him. You know our Montenegrins. They are funny dogs. When those at Antivari heard that the Austrians had arrived in Cetinje, they pillaged the palace of Prince Danilo. But before the house of the Austrian consul they put a guard. A good fellow this consul, is he not? For me this war is the struggle of the Slav and the Teuton for the only unexploited lands in Europe. We always knew it would come. But in the past we have never reckoned that England will range herself with Russia and permit her to take Constantinople. That would mean the end of Roumania, of Bulgaria, of Serbia, of us, and of you, too, Gospodjitza, if you are not careful. Therefore we ranged ourselves with Austria. Those who have travelled in Austria know that the Slavs there are richer, better educated, and better off in every way than we poor devils of Serbia and Montenegro. In return for the taxes they pay they get roads, schools—what you will. Our taxes all run out of the breeches pockets of those Two Families (Petrovitch and Karageorgevitch). The war is not ended, but I can tell you those Two Families will go and never return. Our King is in France. If the French want a king, they may keep him!"

"And who is responsible for killing the Archduke?"

"Who knows? It was done certainly by some of those mad students of Belgrade.

You remember how they tried to kill King Nikola? Well! The Serbs wanted war. Now they have got it let us hope they are content. Politics, as you know, are all cochonnerie. As for me, I have had enough, and I wash my hands of them."

His account squares with others. The Greek Minister in Cetinje, who, as a neutral remained there, related that not long after King Nikola left Montenegro a telegram from Vienna arrived inviting him to stay. Prince Danilo was already abroad when the crisis arose. Serbia as well as Montenegro made an attempt to come to terms with Austria in 1915, it would appear, from an unsigned convention, a copy of which has been lately reported to have been found in the archives at Vienna. It would account for the fact that in spite of the advice of more than one English authority, they persisted in making no preparation for the further defence of their country, and disposed their troops only for an advance into Albania.

Thus tragically ended poor King Nikola's life's ambition and his golden dream. Mirko, whom he would fain have seen on the throne of Serbia, died in Austria in 1918. The records of Danilo and Petar are such that they are not likely to succeed their father. Prince Danilo in vain refused the spiritual headship of the land. No Petrovitch seems destined to be followed by his son, though their dynasty is the older, and their hands are not so stained with murder as those of the rival dynasty.

Nikola is not wholly blameworthy. Powers stronger and more crafty than he, planned Great Serbia and ruthlessly ruled him out of it. No reinforcements came to him; no troops to help him hold the Lovtchen. Russia was once his god—and she forsook him.

The Montenegrin opinion of the Serajevo murders is corroborated by several facts. The Serb students refuged in London had post cards printed of the murderer Princip, on which he was described as a national hero! One said to me: "Yes, it is a pity so many people were killed. But you see the plan quite succeeded, and Great Serbia has been made." He seemed to think it the object of the war. Another told a friend of mine that bombthrowing had been taught at Shabatz, and a Serbian officer boasted to Lady Boyle, when she was doing Serbian relief work, that he was one of the men who taught the murderers to shoot. He took their photographs from his pocket, and called on her to admire how well he had taught them.

The bombs used, like those prepared for King Nikola, came from Kraguyevatz. The assassins told in great detail at their trial that they had been supplied with weapons, and taught to use them, by a Serbian railway employe, Ciganovitch, and by Major Tankositch the komitadji trainer He was a well-known komitadji himself, and a member of the Narodna Odbrana and of the Black Hand. And he was in constant touch with the Belgrade students at the Zelenom Vjencu eating-house. A Serb student, who himself had frequented this place, told me that Princip was chosen because he was so far advanced in tuberculosis he could not live long in any case. He saw him just before he left for Serajevo, looking very ill indeed. He described that when the news of the murders arrived three hundred Bosnian students rushed through Belgrade shouting and singing, and led by a Montenegrin playing the gusle.

"But did not the police stop them?" I asked.

"No, why should they?"

"And were no arrests then made?"

"Oh, no." This corroborates the official letter of Chevalier von Storck of the Austrian Legation in Belgrade, who wrote (see the Austrian Red Book) on June 30th to Vienna:

"I have addressed to M. Gruitch, secretary to the Minister of Foreign Affairs, the question appropriate to the moment, to enquire what measures the police have already taken, or intend to take, to follow up the traces of the crime which are notoriously spread through Serbia. He replies that up till now the police have not occupied themselves with the affair."

The consummate impudence of which remark needs no comment. The planners of the crime had indeed Intended to bury their traces, as they supplied the wretched boys each with a tube of cyanide of potassium, which he was to take immediately after doing the deed. An Instruction they did not follow.

The attitude of the Serb Government was precisely the same as that it adopted in 1907 with regard to the Cetinje affair. It "knew nothing," and made no inquiry. Nor, during the whole three weeks that elapsed before the ultimatum, did the Serb Government do anything to clear up the matter and mitigate Austria's just anger. One can only deduce that war was expected and intended.

The military party was in the ascendant, and did as it chose. There was great tension between it and the Government, and already before the murders Prince Alexander had been selected to replace his father as Regent.

"In order," according to Bogitchevitch, "to postpone the inevitable conflict (between the two parties) and that responsibility for present events should be evaded, and in order perhaps that he might not have to assume responsibility for future events, King Petar retired from government and entrusted the Regency to the Crown Prince." He adds: "Can any one who knows Serb conditions, even partially, believe that the Government knew nothing of the conspiratory activities of certain circles of officers and komitadjis in Bosnia, and that it knew nothing of the preparatory measures in Serbia for the attentat on the Austrian royal couple?"

The Government, he adds, carried its nonchalance to "such an extent that Pashitch did not remain in Belgrade, and the Austrian ultimatum had to be handed to the Minister of Finance, who temporarily replaced him."

Documents obtained by Mr. Bottomley from the Serbian legation in London show that its members were aware of the plot. Time, the revealer of all secrets, will one day unveil the whole of this one. Meanwhile, I am glad that the Order of St. Sava is not in my house.

Time will show, too, whether the Serb is to be top-dog in Jugoslavia, or whether, after all these oceans of blood that have been spilt and the untold misery, we shall arrive at an arrangement which could have been obtained by patience and Trialism.

The Teuton for the time is broken, and the Slav is loosed. Whether for better or worse time again will show.

It remains to consider Albania. When I left it in 1914 folk said: "Now that the Powers are busy fighting each other they will leave us free to manage our own affairs." The International forces left almost at once. The Defence left Durazzo before war was declared. The Prince of Wied left on September 3rd. And the former insurgents wrote and begged him to return.

Essad Pasha then arrived at Durazzo, and was publicly embraced by Alliotti the Italian. Most of the International Commission left. Krajevsky remained, and with the aid of French money tried to establish Essad as Prince in vain. Essad, however, levied custom dues, and with that and the French money was wealthy, and withdrew to Salonika, where he tried to pose as an exiled monarch, but failed to raise an Albanian army. He never dared return to Albania but lived in luxury in Paris on his ill-gotten wealth till he was assassinated on June 15th by an Albanian student.

On December 25th the Italians landed suddenly at Valona under pretence of protecting it from the Greeks.

All now made ready to tear Albania to pieces, in spite of the International guarantee. The Montenegrins seized Scutari in 1915. The Serbs hurried to take Durazzo. But then came the Austrian attack. Caught in a bad position, the Serbs had had to fly to Scutari with the Austrians after them. In consequence the Allies evacuated Scutari, and left the Albanians to their fate. Had the Allies resolutely forbidden the Montenegrins to seize Scutari in 1915, and enlisted the Albanian tribesmen, guaranteeing their independence and the restoration of at least a portion of their lost land, the Serbian debacle might have been saved, and the results been very different. Such a plan was proposed by the Foreign Office, and I and some others asked to enlist the men. But Russia and, I believe, France vetoed it. Consequently the Bulgars and Austrians took and held most of north and central Albania till the armistice.

In the south King Constantine's troops seized Albania and used it as a line of communication with the Austrian army till the Italians pressed down from Valeria to evict them, and the French advanced from Salonika to Koritza, which they found guarded by armed Albanians. These gladly admitted the French on condition the whole district was recognized as Albanian. The French Government agreed, and on December 11, 1916, Colonel Descouins proclaimed the Koritza district an Albani Republic, and hoisted the Albanian flag amid great popular rejoicing. A government was speedily organized, and a great number of Albanian schools opened, and filled, throughout the new Republic, which included two hundred thousand souls, and flourished till Greece joined the Allies. Trouble then began, as the Greeks demanded Koritza as part of their price for "coming in." And to placate Greece, Greek schools, which had been closed, were re-opened. The dismay of Albania, who had trusted in the promises of the French, was great.

But hope rose strongly when President Wilson proclaimed to the world his gospel of self-determination and the rights of small nations. Seldom has a politician inspired greater hope and belief. All secret treaties, it was believed, would be laid aside, and a Peace of the peoples would result.

Nor was it till the eve of the Peace Conference, when France showed her enmity by trying to prevent the representation of Albania in Paris, that the Albanians took alarm. An Albanian delegation was at last accepted, only to be told that the Secret Treaty of 1915 held good, and the Powers that prated of justice and the inviolability of Treaties now desired to partition Albania among her worst foes.

Against this Albania appealed, and is appealing, and her fate is yet in the balance. French, Italian, and Serb troops have occupied the land ever since the Armistice. Every possible obstacle has been thrown in Albania's way by those who wish her destruction. The Albanians have elected, last January, a Government of their own, and the Powers have refused to recognize it. The British Government, in order to stifle Albania's cries, have withdrawn both the British representatives from Albania, General Phillips and Mr. Morton Eden. Both are friends of Albania's independence, and General Phillips reported that the Albanian Government was working remarkably well. Albania now has no means of communicating with the outer world, save through those who wish her destruction—Greece, Italy and Jugoslavia. All three are working to overthrow the Albanian Government. At the moment of going to press the Serbs have made a wanton attack on North Albania from three points. But they will not kill the spirit of the Albanian people, who have resisted denationalization for a thousand years, and who beg only for the right to take their place in the Balkans and live in freedom and harmony with their neighbours, and who now at the time of going to press are fighting bravely for Liberty.

I will not write Finis, for the tale of the Balkan tangle does not end here.

INDEX

Abdul Hamid; abdicates
Aehrenthal (Baron von)
Albania
Albanians
Albanian language
Alexander (King of Serbia); murder of
Alexander (Crown Prince)
Ambassadors' Conference
America
Andriyevitza
Anglo-Russian agreement
Antivari
Austria; in Bosnia; in Albania; Austrian attache.

Balkan Alliance
Balkan war
Balkan railways
Beaconsfield (Lord)
Belgrade
Berlin (Treaty of)
Black Hand
Bocche di Cattaro
Bogitchevitch
Bogumils
Bosnia; annexation of
Bulgaria.

Carnegie report
Catholics
Cetinje
Constantinople
Constantinovitch
Constitution (in Montenegro); (in Turkey)
Croatia.

Dalmatia
Danilo (Vladika)
Danilo I (of Montenegro)
Danilo (Crown Prince)
Djakovo
Draga (Queen); murder of
Dulcigno
Durazzo
Dushan Gregovitch
Dutch officers.

Earl's Court
Edward VII
Egypt
Elbasan
England
Essad Pasha.

Ferdinand (of Bulgaria)
Fimilian (Bishop)
Fitzmaurice (Lord)
France
Franz Ferdinand (Archduke); murder of
Franz Josef (Kaiser).

George (Prince of Serbia)
Germany
Ghilca (Albert)
Gjurashkovitch
Gladstone
Goluchowski
Great Serbian Idea
Greece
Greeks; in Albania
Grey (Sir Edward)
Gusinje.

Hartwig
Herzegovina.

International Commission
Ipek
Ismail Kemal
Italy
Izvolsky.

Jannisariea
Japan.

Karageorge
Karageorgevitch
Koritza
Kosovo
Kragujevatz
Krajevsky
Kruyff (Baron de).

Ljuma
Lobatcheff.

Macedonia
Manicheism
Marusitch
Milosh (Ofrenovitch)
Miouschlcovitch (Lazar)
Mirdites
Mirko (Grand Voyvoda)
Mirko (Prince)
Montenegro; tribes of; eighteenth century; history of
Moslems; in Bosnia
Mrasteg.

Nastitch
Nikola (King of Montenegro); accession of; reign; made King.

Obrenovitch
Ochrida
Orthodox Church; in Bosnia; atrocities of.

Pashitch (Nikola)
Petar I (of Montenegro)
Petar II (of Montenegro)
Petar Karageorgevitch (King); accession
Petar (Prince of Montenegro)
Peter (The Great)
Petrovitches
Plamenatz (Petar)
Plamenatz (Vladika)
Plot (against King Nikola)

Prenk, Bib Doda
Prizren
Prochashka.

Radonitch (Gubernator)
Radovitch
Ragusa
Rizoff
Romans
Russia
Russian Consuls.

Salonika
Sanjalc (of Novibazar)
Scutari
Serajevo
Serbia
Serbs
Skenderbeg
Slavs (invasions); conversion of; v. Teutons
Slovenski Jug
Sofia
Sofia Petrovna
Stefan Dushan
Stefan Mali.

Tomanovitch
Triple Alliance
Tripoli
Tuberculosis
Turks.

Uskub
Uvatz.

Valona
Venice
Vesnitcli
Vienna
Vlachs
Vladan Georgevitch
Vladikas (of Montenegro)
Vuchidol
Vuletitch (Voko).

Wied (Prince of).

Yanko Vukotitch
Yougourieff
Young Turks.

Zographos
Zorka (Princess).

THE END

www.bookjungle.com *email: sales@bookjungle.com fax: 630-214-0564 mail: Book Jungle PO Box 2226 Champaign, IL 61825*

The Codes Of Hammurabi And Moses
W. W. Davies

QTY

The discovery of the Hammurabi Code is one of the greatest achievements of archaeology, and is of paramount interest, not only to the student of the Bible, but also to all those interested in ancient history...

Religion ISBN: *1-59462-338-4* Pages:132 *MSRP $12.95*

The Theory of Moral Sentiments
Adam Smith

QTY

This work from 1749. contains original theories of conscience amd moral judgment and it is the foundation for systemof morals.

Philosophy ISBN: *1-59462-777-0* Pages:536 *MSRP $19.95*

Jessica's First Prayer
Hesba Stretton

QTY

In a screened and secluded corner of one of the many railway-bridges which span the streets of London there could be seen a few years ago, from five o'clock every morning until half past eight, a tidily set-out coffee-stall, consisting of a trestle and board, upon which stood two large tin cans, with a small fire of charcoal burning under each so as to keep the coffee boiling during the early hours of the morning when the work-people were thronging into the city on their way to their daily toil...

Childrens ISBN: *1-59462-373-2* Pages:84 *MSRP $9.95*

My Life and Work
Henry Ford

QTY

Henry Ford revolutionized the world with his implementation of mass production for the Model T automobile. Gain valuable business insight into his life and work with his own auto-biography... "We have only started on our development of our country we have not as yet, with all our talk of wonderful progress, done more than scratch the surface. The progress has been wonderful enough but..."

Biographies/ ISBN: *1-59462-198-5* Pages:300 *MSRP $21.95*

www.bookjungle.com *email: sales@bookjungle.com fax: 630-214-0564 mail: Book Jungle PO Box 2226 Champaign, IL 61825*

The Art of Cross-Examination
Francis Wellman

QTY

I presume it is the experience of every author, after his first book is published upon an important subject, to be almost overwhelmed with a wealth of ideas and illustrations which could readily have been included in his book, and which to his own mind, at least, seem to make a second edition inevitable. Such certainly was the case with me; and when the first edition had reached its sixth impression in five months, I rejoiced to learn that it seemed to my publishers that the book had met with a sufficiently favorable reception to justify a second and considerably enlarged edition. ..

Reference   ISBN: *1-59462-647-2*   Pages:412   MSRP $19.95

On the Duty of Civil Disobedience
Henry David Thoreau

QTY

Thoreau wrote his famous essay, On the Duty of Civil Disobedience, as a protest against an unjust but popular war and the immoral but popular institution of slave-owning. He did more than write—he declined to pay his taxes, and was hauled off to gaol in consequence. Who can say how much this refusal of his hastened the end of the war and of slavery ?

Law   ISBN: *1-59462-747-9*   Pages:48   MSRP $7.45

Dream Psychology Psychoanalysis for Beginners
Sigmund Freud

QTY

Sigmund Freud, born Sigismund Schlomo Freud (May 6, 1856 - September 23, 1939), was a Jewish-Austrian neurologist and psychiatrist who co-founded the psychoanalytic school of psychology. Freud is best known for his theories of the unconscious mind, especially involving the mechanism of repression; his redefinition of sexual desire as mobile and directed towards a wide variety of objects; and his therapeutic techniques, especially his understanding of transference in the therapeutic relationship and the presumed value of dreams as sources of insight into unconscious desires.

Psychology   ISBN: *1-59462-905-6*   Pages:196   MSRP $15.45

The Miracle of Right Thought
Orison Swett Marden

QTY

Believe with all of your heart that you will do what you were made to do. When the mind has once formed the habit of holding cheerful, happy, prosperous pictures, it will not be easy to form the opposite habit. It does not matter how improbable or how far away this realization may see, or how dark the prospects may be, if we visualize them as best we can, as vividly as possible, hold tenaciously to them and vigorously struggle to attain them, they will gradually become actualized, realized in the life. But a desire, a longing without endeavor, a yearning abandoned or held indifferently will vanish without realization.

Self Help   ISBN: *1-59462-644-8*   Pages:360   MSRP $25.45

www.bookjungle.com email: sales@bookjungle.com fax: 630-214-0564 mail: Book Jungle PO Box 2226 Champaign, IL 61825
QTY

	Title	ISBN	Price
☐	**The Rosicrucian Cosmo-Conception Mystic Christianity** by *Max Heindel*	ISBN: 1-59462-188-8	$38.95
	The Rosicrucian Cosmo-conception is not dogmatic, neither does it appeal to any other authority than the reason of the student. It is: not controversial, but is: sent forth in the, hope that it may help to clear...	New Age/Religion Pages 646	
☐	**Abandonment To Divine Providence** by *Jean-Pierre de Caussade*	ISBN: 1-59462-228-0	$25.95
	"The Rev. Jean Pierre de Caussade was one of the most remarkable spiritual writers of the Society of Jesus in France in the 18th Century. His death took place at Toulouse in 1751. His works have gone through many editions and have been republished...	Inspirational/Religion Pages 400	
☐	**Mental Chemistry** by *Charles Haanel*	ISBN: 1-59462-192-6	$23.95
	Mental Chemistry allows the change of material conditions by combining and appropriately utilizing the power of the mind. Much like applied chemistry creates something new and unique out of careful combinations of chemicals the mastery of mental chemistry...	New Age Pages 354	
☐	**The Letters of Robert Browning and Elizabeth Barret Barrett 1845-1846 vol II** by *Robert Browning* and *Elizabeth Barrett*	ISBN: 1-59462-193-4	$35.95
		Biographies Pages 596	
☐	**Gleanings In Genesis (volume I)** by *Arthur W. Pink*	ISBN: 1-59462-130-6	$27.45
	Appropriately has Genesis been termed "the seed plot of the Bible" for in it we have, in germ form, almost all of the great doctrines which are afterwards fully developed in the books of Scripture which follow...	Religion/Inspirational Pages 420	
☐	**The Master Key** by *L. W. de Laurence*	ISBN: 1-59462-001-6	$30.95
	In no branch of human knowledge has there been a more lively increase of the spirit of research during the past few years than in the study of Psychology, Concentration and Mental Discipline. The requests for authentic lessons in Thought Control, Mental Discipline and...	New Age/Business Pages 422	
☐	**The Lesser Key Of Solomon Goetia** by *L. W. de Laurence*	ISBN: 1-59462-092-X	$9.95
	This translation of the first book of the "Lernegton" which is now for the first time made accessible to students of Talismanic Magic was done, after careful collation and edition, from numerous Ancient Manuscripts in Hebrew, Latin, and French...	New Age/Occult Pages 92	
☐	**Rubaiyat Of Omar Khayyam** by *Edward Fitzgerald*	ISBN: 1-59462-332-5	$13.95
	Edward Fitzgerald, whom the world has already learned, in spite of his own efforts to remain within the shadow of anonymity, to look upon as one of the rarest poets of the century, was born at Bredfield, in Suffolk, on the 31st of March, 1809. He was the third son of John Purcell...	Music Pages 172	
☐	**Ancient Law** by *Henry Maine*	ISBN: 1-59462-128-4	$29.95
	The chief object of the following pages is to indicate some of the earliest ideas of mankind, as they are reflected in Ancient Law, and to point out the relation of those ideas to modern thought.	Religion/History Pages 452	
☐	**Far-Away Stories** by *William J. Locke*	ISBN: 1-59462-129-2	$19.45
	"Good wine needs no bush, but a collection of mixed vintages does. And this book is just such a collection. Some of the stories I do not want to remain buried for ever in the museum files of dead magazine-numbers an author's not unpardonable vanity..."	Fiction Pages 272	
☐	**Life of David Crockett** by *David Crockett*	ISBN: 1-59462-250-7	$27.45
	"Colonel David Crockett was one of the most remarkable men of the times in which he lived. Born in humble life, but gifted with a strong will, an indomitable courage, and unremitting perseverance...	Biographies/New Age Pages 424	
☐	**Lip-Reading** by *Edward Nitchie*	ISBN: 1-59462-206-X	$25.95
	Edward B. Nitchie, founder of the New York School for the Hard of Hearing, now the Nitchie School of Lip-Reading, Inc, wrote "LIP-READING Principles and Practice". The development and perfecting of this meritorious work on lip-reading was an undertaking...	How-to Pages 400	
☐	**A Handbook of Suggestive Therapeutics, Applied Hypnotism, Psychic Science** by *Henry Munro*	ISBN: 1-59462-214-0	$24.95
		Health/New Age/Health/Self-help Pages 376	
☐	**A Doll's House: and Two Other Plays** by *Henrik Ibsen*	ISBN: 1-59462-112-8	$19.95
	Henrik Ibsen created this classic when in revolutionary 1848 Rome. Introducing some striking concepts in playwriting for the realist genre, this play has been studied the world over.	Fiction/Classics/Plays 308	
☐	**The Light of Asia** by *sir Edwin Arnold*	ISBN: 1-59462-204-3	$13.95
	In this poetic masterpiece, Edwin Arnold describes the life and teachings of Buddha. The man who was to become known as Buddha to the world was born as Prince Gautama of India but he rejected the worldly riches and abandoned the reigns of power when...	Religion/History/Biographies 170	
☐	**The Complete Works of Guy de Maupassant** by *Guy de Maupassant*	ISBN: 1-59462-157-8	$16.95
	"For days and days, nights and nights, I had dreamed of that first kiss which was to consecrate our engagement, and I knew not on what spot I should put my lips..."	Fiction/Classics Pages 240	
☐	**The Art of Cross-Examination** by *Francis L. Wellman*	ISBN: 1-59462-309-0	$26.95
	Written by a renowned trial lawyer, Wellman imparts his experience and uses case studies to explain how to use psychology to extract desired information through questioning.	How-to/Science/Reference Pages 408	
☐	**Answered or Unanswered?** by *Louisa Vaughan*	ISBN: 1-59462-248-5	$10.95
	Miracles of Faith in China	Religion Pages 112	
☐	**The Edinburgh Lectures on Mental Science (1909)** by *Thomas*	ISBN: 1-59462-008-3	$11.95
	This book contains the substance of a course of lectures recently given by the writer in the Queen Street Hall, Edinburgh. Its purpose is to indicate the Natural Principles governing the relation between Mental Action and Material Conditions...	New Age/Psychology Pages 148	
☐	**Ayesha** by *H. Rider Haggard*	ISBN: 1-59462-301-5	$24.95
	Verily and indeed it is the unexpected that happens! Probably if there was one person upon the earth from whom the Editor of this, and of a certain previous history, did not expect to hear again...	Classics Pages 380	
☐	**Ayala's Angel** by *Anthony Trollope*	ISBN: 1-59462-352-X	$29.95
	The two girls were both pretty, but Lucy who was twenty-one who supposed to be simple and comparatively unattractive, whereas Ayala was credited, as her Bombwhat romantic name might show, with poetic charm and a taste for romance. Ayala when her father died was nineteen...	Fiction Pages 484	
☐	**The American Commonwealth** by *James Bryce*	ISBN: 1-59462-286-8	$34.45
	An interpretation of American democratic political theory. It examines political mechanics and society from the perspective of Scotsman James Bryce	Politics Pages 572	
☐	**Stories of the Pilgrims** by *Margaret P. Pumphrey*	ISBN: 1-59462-116-0	$17.95
	This book explores pilgrims religious oppression in England as well as their escape to Holland and eventual crossing to America on the Mayflower, and their early days in New England...	History Pages 268	

www.bookjungle.com *email: sales@bookjungle.com fax:* 630-214-0564 *mail:* Book Jungle PO Box 2226 Champaign, IL 61825

QTY

The Fasting Cure by **Sinclair Upton** ISBN: *1-59462-222-1* **$13.95**
In the Cosmopolitan Magazine for May, 1910, and in the Contemporary Review (London) for April, 1910, I published an article dealing with my experiences in fasting. I have written a great many magazine articles, but never one which attracted so much attention... *New Age/Self Help/Health Pages 164*

Hebrew Astrology by **Sepharial** ISBN: *1-59462-308-2* **$13.45**
In these days of advanced thinking it is a matter of common observation that we have left many of the old landmarks behind and that we are now pressing forward to greater heights and to a wider horizon than that which represented the mind-content of our progenitors... *Astrology Pages 144*

Thought Vibration or The Law of Attraction in the Thought World ISBN: *1-59462-127-6* **$12.95**
by *William Walker Atkinson* *Psychology/Religion Pages 144*

Optimism by **Helen Keller** ISBN: *1-59462-108-X* **$15.95**
Helen Keller was blind, deaf, and mute since 19 months old, yet famously learned how to overcome these handicaps, communicate with the world, and spread her lectures promoting optimism. An inspiring read for everyone... *Biographies/Inspirational Pages 84*

Sara Crewe by **Frances Burnett** ISBN: *1-59462-360-0* **$9.45**
In the first place, Miss Minchin lived in London. Her home was a large, dull, tall one, in a large, dull square, where all the houses were alike, and all the sparrows were alike, and where all the door-knockers made the same heavy sound... *Childrens/Classic Pages 88*

The Autobiography of Benjamin Franklin by **Benjamin Franklin** ISBN: *1-59462-135-7* **$24.95**
The Autobiography of Benjamin Franklin has probably been more extensively read than any other American historical work, and no other book of its kind has had such ups and downs of fortune. Franklin lived for many years in England, where he was agent... *Biographies/History Pages 332*

Name	
Email	
Telephone	
Address	
City, State ZIP	

☐ **Credit Card**   ☐ **Check / Money Order**

Credit Card Number	
Expiration Date	
Signature	

Please Mail to: Book Jungle
PO Box 2226
Champaign, IL 61825
or Fax to: 630-214-0564

ORDERING INFORMATION

web: *www.bookjungle.com*
email: *sales@bookjungle.com*
fax: *630-214-0564*
mail: *Book Jungle PO Box 2226 Champaign, IL 61825*
or PayPal *to sales@bookjungle.com*

Please contact us for bulk discounts

DIRECT-ORDER TERMS

**20% Discount if You Order
Two or More Books**
Free Domestic Shipping!
Accepted: Master Card, Visa,
Discover, American Express

www.ingramcontent.com/pod-product-compliance
Lightning Source LLC
Chambersburg PA
CBHW080241170426
43192CB00014BA/2524